FIGMENTS OF THE ARCHITECTURAL IMAGINATION

FIGMENTS OF THE ARCHITECTURAL IMAGINATION

and Other Essays

Todd Gannon

Introduction by Joe Day

a r + d

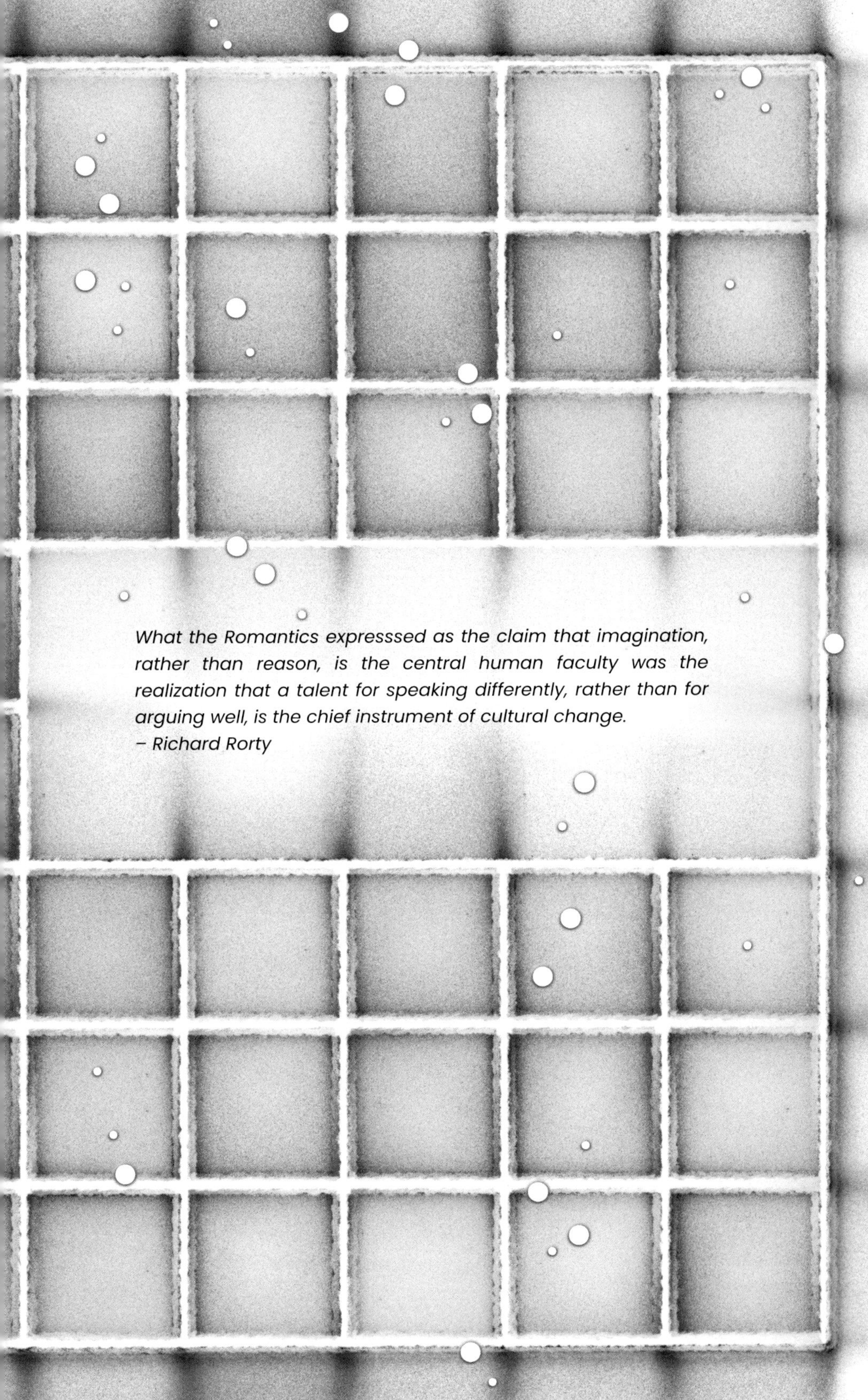

What the Romantics expresssed as the claim that imagination, rather than reason, is the central human faculty was the realization that a talent for speaking differently, rather than for arguing well, is the chief instrument of cultural change.
– Richard Rorty

Contents

Preface

In 2004, to celebrate the release of Peter Eisenman's long-awaited book on Giuseppe Terragni, Jeff Kipnis convened *The Shape of Things to Come* at the Wexner Center for the Arts at The Ohio State University. It was an illuminating conference, but what sticks in my mind now—and created a sustained buzz then—is Jeff's fantastic poster, which presents the conference participants as bodybuilders and the event as a get-fit-fast program for wannabe heavyweights in the arena of complex architectural form [**Fig. 4.1**].

Cynthia Davidson loved that poster and was looking for a reason to include it in the new journal she had launched the previous fall. On Bob Somol's recommendation, she reached out to me for a review of the conference. (Bob thought I'd be a good fit because he knew of my affection for *McSweeney's*, the literary quarterly which Cynthia had taken as a rough model for her endeavor.) A few months later my review ran in *Log* 2, with a page and a half devoted to Jeff's poster and a blow-up of its cheeky transformational pitch.

Thus began my long affiliation with *Log* where, fifty issues later, I remain a semi-regular contributor and protagonist. A dozen years after that first essay, Cynthia invited me to contribute a short piece to *Log* 37, the "cata*Log*" for *The Architectural Imagination*, which she co-curated with Monica Ponce de León for the American Pavilion at the 2016 Venice Biennale. Though I didn't set out to do so (I thought I was just riffing on the curators' topic), with "Figments of the Architectural Imagination" I wound up encapsulating many of the themes that have structured my writing and thinking about architecture for the past twenty-five years—the twin responsibilities of the profession and the discipline, the necessary illusions that shape our field's rhetoric of form and space, and, above all, the unique pleasures of paying sustained, informed attention to an interesting object.

Beyond these themes, readers will find here no overarching theoretical argument or ideological position that binds these essays together. (They will find a certain methodological consistency, which I'll explain in a moment.) Most of these essays were written for specific occasions and often on the invitation of colleagues; none of them were conceived as coordinated parts of a broader narrative whole. Rather, they were written one-off, usually in a hurry, and primarily as attempts to make sense of what was going on around me and to figure out where my colleagues and I might be headed.

As I outline in "The Shape of Things to Come," for example, each of Eisenman's protégés at Kipnis's conference—Scott Cohen, Wes Jones, Thomas Leeser, Greg Lynn, and Lindy Roy—seemed to be grappling with the question of how to achieve escape velocity from Eisenman's influential orbit. In a way, so was I. As a graduate student at Ohio State in the mid-1990s, I had been steeped in a formalist rhetoric that drew heavily on Eisenman (and Colin Rowe) but also had been filtered through brilliant teachers like Kipnis and Doug Graf, whose diagram-driven approach set the tone for much of the school's pedagogy [**Figs. 20.11**, **20.12**, and **20.14**]. I remember being confused and appalled when I first encountered the term *formalist* used as a slur—none of my teachers had bothered to clue me in to formalism's many detractors. It was only later that I learned that a bias toward form was seen by some as a dilettantish conceit or as ideological dogma. At Ohio State, where I began teaching soon after graduation, the language of form was simply How Things Were. It was accepted without question as a kind of universal grammar, as obvious and infallible as arithmetic.

The aim of our brand of formalism was to provide a disciplined way of looking at things, a lens through which salient relationships—between the elements of an object or environment with each other and with an attentive observer—come vividly into focus. Though now I tend to exchange the formal diagrams of my training for a style of detailed description more common to literary studies, my tendency to begin any analysis by unpacking compositional particulars is evident in just about every essay in this collection.

Even so, toward the end of graduate school I had already begun to sense formalism's limitations. *The Light Construction Reader*, a collection I began as a student and finally published in 2002, was conceived primarily to find a way to talk about the surface-driven work I found so attractive in Terry Riley's 1995 exhibition, *Light Construction*, work that operated well outside Eisenman's (and Rowe's) sphere of influence and seemed impervious to elucidation by my (or their) formalist vocabulary. My work on the Source Books in Architecture series, from which the essays here on Bernard Tschumi and UN Studio emerged, brought me into contact with an array of practitioners whose work further impelled me to find ways to operate beyond the formalist ken in which I had been educated.

These endeavors, like most of the essays in this volume, each ask the same question: "Where to from here?" In the *Reader*, I find an answer in the materiality of architectural surfaces. In "The Shape of Things to Come," seduced as I was by Somol's projective swerve away from Eisenman, I arrive at a much simpler answer, "Follow Bob," which I did that fall, to the PhD program at UCLA. Bob left a year later (for Ohio State!), and Sylvia Lavin took over as my dissertation advisor. She guided me as I undertook archival studies of the *Archigram* pamphlets and later, Reyner Banham, and encouraged me to pursue my collaborations with the literary critic N. Katherine Hayles, whose work on the materiality of literary texts dovetailed nicely with my prior work on *Light Construction* and more recent interest in the material specificity of the *Archigrams.*

Before long, I was spending increasing amounts of time at SCI-Arc, first as a guest juror and later as a member of the faculty, and another question began to emerge: "Where am I?" To find out, I began to investigate Los Angeles's still inadequately documented recent history, which led to the 2013 exhibition, *A Confederacy of Heretics,* co-curated with Ewan Branda and Andrew Zago to examine the formative years of a group of architects, including Frank Gehry, Craig Hodgetts, Coy Howard, Thom Mayne, and Eric Owen Moss, who would become known (problematically) as the L.A. School. The controversy that erupted over *A New Sculpturalism,* a parallel exhibition at the Los Angeles Museum of Contemporary Art, prompted a review in which I attempt to seize the opportunity MOCA had missed by extending our *Heretics* investigation into the present.

In the scrum of SCI-Arc studio juries, I learned to better fit my formalist training to contemporary concerns. And I learned the hard way! It seems all I did for the first few years there was argue—mostly with Florencia Pita, but also with Hernán Díaz Alonso, Marcelyn Gow, Elena Manferdini, Marcelo Spina, and Tom Wiscombe, all of whom I now count among my closest friends and colleagues. At first, I found the experimental, often intuitive ideas that drove their students' designs to be maddeningly free of clear organizational principles, and they thought my attempts to read such principles into the work were either anachronistic, ill-conceived, or just plain bizarre. In any case, I kept coming back, and eventually I seem to have convinced them that I had something to offer, just as I became convinced that their approaches had merits I had failed, initially, to understand. The essays here on the work of Oyler Wu Collaborative, Jason Payne, and PATTERNS document these developments in my thinking and represent some of the earliest sustained treatments of these architects. It was a great privilege—and great fun—to spend some time trying to figure out my friends, and I look forward to returning to each of these practices in future writing, as they assume their roles as the heirs apparent to the architectural legacy of Los Angeles.

From these monographic essays, this collection opens onto larger themes and more overtly socio-political issues: the spatial politics of hotels, the environmental politics of the desert, and the aesthetic politics of US federal buildings. In these occasional pieces, as in most of the essays gathered here, I bolster my arguments with some "theory" (read the scare quotes as you choose), but most of the time I take on overtly theoretical issues in the company of friends—materiality and virtuality with Kate Hayles; object-oriented ontology with Graham Harman, David Ruy, and Tom Wiscombe; the legacy and possible futures of abstraction with Andrew Zago. Why this is the case is difficult to say. I guess I've always seen theory more as a tool than a topic. In any case, I believe it is important to understand the essays in this volume—whether written alone or collaboratively and however theoretically freighted they may be—as products of ongoing conversations with my colleagues. It is equally important to understand them in the context of teaching at Ohio State, UCLA, Otis College, and SCI-Arc, which occasionally prompts musings on pedagogy such as those in "On Prophets and Professionals," a response to a friend's misgivings about architectural education; "Five Points for Thesis," a summation of my approach to graduate thesis at SCI-Arc; and "Mind the Gaps," a stocktaking of my first few years as head of the architecture program at Ohio State.

So, where to from here? Twenty-plus years of typing has not revealed a clear answer, though I believe it has provided a few hints. I hope these are enough to justify the present collection and, more importantly, to fuel further conversation among architects at work charting a course for the future of our field.

Columbus, August 2021

All In / All Out: Todd Gannon's Circuits and Banquets

Joe Day

In July 2021, Todd Gannon visited Los Angeles for a week to complete research and interviews for a forthcoming book on Frank Israel, a brilliant contemporary of Thom Mayne and Eric Owen Moss, whose life and meteoric career were cut short in 1996, at the age of fifty, by AIDS-related pneumonia. I tagged along with Gannon on his last meeting of the trip, to see Israel's 1993 Woo Pavilion and meet its client, former L.A. City Councilman Michael Woo. I wanted to see the building—I had worked with Israel in the years in which that small but pivotal project was gestating—but also really wanted to hear how Gannon would conduct the conversation, how he would set Woo's story to unspool and then capture it.

Interviews are not a lost art, certainly, but teasing the significant from the anecdotal requires discipline, in a few senses of the term. And to be valuable for a book well underway, they demand an odd balance of premeditation and open-mindedness. As has often been the case and the pattern of our friendship, I simply wanted to learn from Todd how it was done. He obliged. With a recorder at the ready, an easy rapport with his newly met subject, and just a few orienting queries, he elicited a previously untold story, a client's first-hand account of events almost thirty years ago, with a cadence and clarity of structure already embedded in the telling. History, small *h*, in the making.

Gannon is a model scholar, and by that I don't mean precisely an academic. He finishes every book he starts—both those he writes, shaming the rest of us, and those he reads, which only becomes impressive, almost perversely so, when you learn which tomes he prefers.[1] In a field often characterized by dithering and dabbling—however fruitful those distractions often prove—Todd is a closer.

He is also a social and intellectual amalgamator. On that particular trip to Los Angeles, over dinners and drinks and otherwise, Gannon brought together more of the city's vanguard architects, spanning multiple generations, than had likely seen one another in the whole of COVID-19 quarantine and its lifting that summer.[2] The "All In" of my title alludes to this, to Gannon's radical inclusivity, both as a person and as a writer. Whether it be for an event or an essay, Gannon does not like to leave out people or their work, and—not unlike his literary heroes—he will risk some plot convolution to bring all of a given data set into frame. However, he will also pare away extraneous criteria, so that a multitude of firms or projects take distinct shape within their milieu. As I believe Strunk and White would have it, he is generous with nouns and verbs, more parsimonious with modifiers.

An avid historian far beyond his PhD mastery of Reyner Banham and his milieus,[3] Gannon once surprised me with an aside that he had visited and analyzed most of the temple sites in Vincent Scully's *The Earth, The Temple, and The Gods* (1962). This is an ambitious pilgrimage, made more so by the very specific and often distant station points that Scully claims governed the orientation and scalar development of Greek antiquity. Gannon not only visited the temples but orbited them until he found Scully's loci.

This is in fact the template for much of Todd's writing—an actual, not metaphorical visitation, followed by an exploration of a work's context, constraints, and ambitions. Todd reestablishes his credibility as an author and critic early in most texts with savvy but patient observation and beautifully crafted description. He always provides a shared object of inquiry to his reader, and whether you agree with his verdicts or not, the gift of that object in the mind's eye sparkles clearly. When I fretted about framing Gannon too narrowly as a defender of formalism—as it is form he describes so well—this was his response: "Well, it's like an English-speaker defending English, or a fish defending water." He is in any case a formalist with legwork: maybe a bit Platonic in his tastes, but decidedly Aristotelian in his methods, and, afterward, remarkably Socratic in how he shares his findings. Or, put in another way and in a less classical timeframe, Gannon's engagement with the real echoes Banham's, but his judgments often run closer to those of Banham's arch-formalist rival Colin Rowe.

Figments includes twenty essays, the majority ganged comfortably under "Architecture," and the remainder under "Collaborations" and "Education." A pair of opening pieces, "The Shape of Things to Come," of 2004, and the title essay from 2016, together deliver a précis for the whole. In the former, Gannon surveys the formalist establishment circa 2000, led by Peter Eisenman, Jeff Kipnis, and their most formidable digital protégés, and looks for some breathing room. In "Figments of the Architectural Imagination," a call-to-arms for the Venice Biennale of that year, Gannon identifies themes and issues that stalk almost all of his writing: the gestation and resonance of great design; the brokerage between abstract and concrete; architecture as a both discipline and profession; but most of all a leap of imagination. Architecture, Gannon often insists, cannot be reduced to buildings. Rather, it exists only when the array of artifacts produced by our field—buildings, drawings, writings, and more—come to life in the mind of an attentive observer.

Most of the essays within the section "Architecture" profile other architects and do so with generosity and panache. A few of these locate Gannon's canon, as it were, as an extrapolation of a European techno-visionary tradition. In his 2008 essay "Return of Living Dead," Gannon offers a wicked, almost Hegelian summary of the parameters of post-'68 contemporary architecture in which Archigram (thesis) opposes Peter Eisenman (antithesis), yielding Rem Koolhaas (synthesis). He also teases out the way the Archigram pamphlets complemented a zombie invasion of B movies like George Romero's *Night of the Living Dead* in which technology breeds an unlikely, deracialized utopia from dystopia.

For those reading *Figments* for a better sense of contemporary architecture in Los Angeles, there is a nice diptych in Gannon's 2013 introduction to *A Confederacy of Heretics,* a catalog he co-edited with Ewan Branda, and his review of another exhibition from the Getty's Pacific Standard Time Presents series that year, *A New Sculpturalism.* In the former, Gannon follows his lodestar Banham west to assess the so-called Los Angeles School as well as the less sung but often more professionally astute "Silver" architects. The L.A. scene of the 1970s and '80s is thus diversified to include not just the atelier vanguard practices, but also those more corporate firms that shaped (and made so reflective) the city's skyline. The latter reads like an "outro" to the scope and period of *Heretics.* Both a sweeping outline of L.A.'s recent past since *Heretics* and a minutely attentive response to a problematic exhibition, Gannon's review of *A New Sculpturalism* is a model of critical integrity, finding its way to actual works in the exhibition, and the architects behind them, against the considerable odds of the show's poor organization, installation, and lighting. And if, in these essays, he broadens the scope of that era, he does so again for the digital generation. His essays addressing the work of Oyler Wu Collaborative, Jason Payne, and PATTERNS (led by Marcelo Spina and Georgina Huljich) are acute readings of work by younger architects who have likely never been so closely studied by a peer.

Gannon's pieces in "Collaborations" and "Education" go on to explore the limits, adjacencies, and transmission of the discipline further. As he was working toward his dissertation on Banham at UCLA, Gannon was the only student to minor in literature (most of his peers added sub-specializations in urban design or art history). Such was his passion for contemporary fiction that colleagues sometimes wondered whether he was pursuing a graduate degree in literature, while moonlighting in architecture. Though he developed a fruitful habit of collaboration with authors and literary theorists, Gannon's allegiances were never seriously in doubt.

He does not flee a fight, or back down from outbursts of design(er) hubris. In such a fit of pique, a colleague of ours, Peter Zellner, delivered a 2016 manifesto denouncing the state of architectural education and proposing a Free/New school model not too far removed from John Baldessari's mooted restructuring of CalArts, circa 1970. (To his credit, Zellner would in fact test this proposition with the Free School of Architecture, including twenty to thirty students over three years.) Gannon's response is instructive on a few levels. First, he underscores his common cause with Zellner—both want architectural education to better serve students, the discipline, and the profession, perhaps in that order—then he sharpens his terms of engagement, and his own polemic that architectural education must strive to bring shape to the lives of architects, not merely to buildings or firms.

As befits an author who was first a practitioner, Gannon does not hesitate to employ "I" and even "We" with regard to architects. While many outside the field, especially some rarified producers and critics of texts in the more traditional, word-based sense, appreciate Gannon's clarity and infectious enthusiasm for explaining buildings and their representations, Todd writes to his own—our own—tribe. Though his precise, generous prose does not require specialization, Todd writes to architects: before they are so, as they are becoming so, and especially as they navigate the field for themselves. His comingling of internal and exogenous expertise, an especially wide expanse of contemporary criticism in architecture, literature, and fine art, is curated for their benefit. He even writes for architects and architectural historians in absentia. I so wish Banham and Israel could read Todd's analyses of their works, as they'd likely see new patterns in play. They would also be impressed by the grand, long-frame analogies he draws to make the contemporary heroic, as in this passage, which opens his unpacking of Oyler Wu's Pendulum Plane:

> Past architecture routinely directed our attention upward. Think of the intricate tracery of a Gothic cathedral, the dazzling *trompes l'oeil* of Baroque Rome, or the shimmering vaults of the Crystal Palace. In the past, the impact of architecture could be attributed in large part to a work's capacity to compel us to look up.

Almost all of Gannon's essays ruminate at some point on fundamentals: In what way does a firm call into question a basic premise of the discipline? What assumptions does a groundbreaking work throw into relief, or into doubt? Often Todd asks these questions at an almost existential level: What exactly makes architecture *architecture*, or architects *architects*? His answers to these two are interestingly divergent, and evolve through *Figments*, but might be summarized thus: Architecture is so because of its effects; architects because of how they work.

Todd's entry into the discipline corresponded with the MoMA show *Light Construction*, and a broader inquiry, circa 2000, into the nature of walls—their assembly, performance, opacity or translucency, etc.—as much as their limits—the inner and outer bounding surfaces and commensurate volumes—in the more traditional domains of formalist debate. Much of Gannon's criticism strives to reconcile this bifurcation in the nature and limits of architectural expression, especially his two collaborations with N. Katherine Hayles, "Mood Swings: The Aesthetics of Ambient Emergence," of 2007, and "Virtual Architecture, Actual Media," of 2011. In these, he and Hayles consider American cultural production after both postmodernism and Jacques Derrida's influence in the '80s and '90s and amid the millennial dominance of Gilles Deleuze, a point that Gannon will reemphasize in the group discussion "The Object Turn." The conclusions he and Hayles draw in "Virtual Architecture, Actual Media" circle back to some of Gannon's first assertions on Archigram and their *Archigrams*: if buildings are indeed texts, it is worth considering how they are woven, as much as how they may be read.

After visiting the Woo Pavilion, I had a chance to "interview" Todd over coffee, an opportunity I squandered for lack of preparation and recording technology.[4] I did however confirm a couple of biographical details. I was aware Gannon came early in a big Irish-American clan, but he is in fact the first of twelve siblings, born over a twenty-year period between 1971 and 1991. His generation of siblings, combined with their partners and offspring, now numbers near fifty. Gannon was also an avid bicycle motocross competitor in his teens and a bicycle messenger while in college in Philadelphia.[5]

I'm inclined to tether the essays in *Figments* to either of these biographical anomalies. Gannon's many profiles read with the intensity and pyrotechnics of a well-executed race, run through a course set by a given practice's accomplishments. These "circuit" pieces bring out the competitive cyclist in Todd, his tactical savvy and fitness, and the more diverse the terrain—the more sophisticated and varied an architect's work—the more his speed builds and the more radical his aerial maneuvers. Inclusiveness in this register requires that he not miss a feature, make the most of the whole course, and ride it end-to-end fast and clean. In his assessments of his peers, especially, Gannon seeks a winning line—his first passes at theorizing our generation set a high bar, or perhaps more aptly, a wicked pace—and miss no turns in their work to date. Criticism here tilts all-out, a race in which history builds in momentum and urgency to an event horizon of the present.

The other pieces in *Figments*—especially the collaborative essays—operate differently. These are my "banquets," and each has its own rationale, guest list, and shape. In these less bounded formats, Gannon allows ideas and voices to proliferate and spread in unlikely directions, as I imagine his vast family gatherings must capitalize on every available space in the Gannons' family home in Cleveland. I harbor a theory that Gannon's inclusivity builds on this dynamic, and especially on the complex accommodations required to host all of his parents, sisters, and brothers at once—the plethora of repurposed seating and long tables built to suit and extending through living and dining rooms, out onto decks and beyond. Todd's is necessarily always a movable—or, as Banham might have it, clip-on or plug-in—feast.

The discussion that Todd hosted on object-oriented ontology, including that movement's chief protagonist Graham Harman, Tom Wiscombe, and David Ruy, is perhaps the most "banquet" of these texts, a most curious object among many, and an exchange to compete with Francis Ford Coppola's 1974 *The Conversation.* As in that film, the best passages in *Figments* read more like an almost private *tête-à-tête* with an unlikely but brilliant dinner companion, here stolen at a big family gathering.

I will borrow again from Todd to conclude, as he closes my favorite of the pieces in this collection, "Strange Loops." Nominally a book review, the essay becomes instead a transdisciplinary green manifesto joining Timothy Morton's *Dark Ecology* to two of Gannon's most persistent protagonists, Reyner Banham and Graham Harman. It's an unlikely hat trick, as Gannon knows that neither Banham nor Harman are often taken for eco-warriors, but he finds an ingenious kinship among all three:

> Pleasure and Responsibility. In place of the stark choice between (apparently extraneous) form and (supposedly productive) function with which we began, a last strange loop, this one between an end effect of beauty and a root cause of justice.

> Linked through language in shared affinities to the word "fair," the two concepts are analogous; beauty motivates the slackening of self-interest from which justice springs.

By these standards, Todd Gannon's *Figments* elevate the pleasures and responsibilities of our field to levels both scrupulously and delectably fair.

NOTES

1. Gannon's library is a litany of PoMo monsters, beginning with Thomas Pynchon's *Gravity's Rainbow* (1973) and David Foster Wallace's *Infinite Jest* (1996), both read end-to-end many times. He was so impressed by the recursive, cult-inducing *House of Leaves* (2000), by Mark Z. Danielewski, that he sought out and befriended the author.
2. His trip list included twenty-three architects in all, and six clients (or their relatives) of Frank Israel.
3. See Gannon's "Theory and Design in the Last Machine Age" (PhD Diss., UCLA, 2011), which would evolve into his sweeping treatment, *Reyner Banham and the Paradoxes of High Tech* (Los Angeles: Getty, 2017).
4. The site visit had left its mark on me as well—the stained ocher walls and clever cuboid facets of the pavilion left me feeling more bereft of Israel than I had in years, but eager to reconnect with its very influential project architects, Annie Chu and Barbara Callas.
5. This came to light just days before Alexis Sablone, who holds a degree in architecture from MIT, narrowly missed the bronze medal in Street Skateboarding at the Tokyo Olympic Games. I look forward to the cohort she will inspire into the field!

ON ARCHITECTURE

Figments of the Architectural Imagination

2016

Fig. 1.1 Canaletto (Giovanni Antonio Canal), *Piazza San Marco* (late 1720s).

> *In the past decade and a half, at architecture schools in Los Angeles, "city talk" has gone deeply—and fruitfully—out of fashion. In advanced architecture studios at SCI-Arc, for instance...faculty often wonder aloud whether urban analyses or arguments about city context can usefully inform the creation of new architecture. By now the question is largely rhetorical and the answer a rarely qualified "No."*
> *– Joe Day* [1]

It should come as no surprise that so many architects who cut their disciplinary teeth in the heady 1990s have little patience for "city talk" today. For those whose first forays into city design involved weaving intricate spatial patterns into the warp and weft of an already unruly urban fabric, who honed their skills conjuring complex form from the dynamic forces of metropolitan life, topics that now dominate the conversation—bike lanes, walkable streets, workable public transit, and the quotidiana of the urban milieu—are understandably tiresome. It's not that these architects necessarily have anything against biking, walking, or any of the other activities pursued with docile consistency by the translucent figures that populate every rendering of every new urban proposal for every city in the world. It's just that so much city design today can seem, well, unimaginative.

With *The Architectural Imagination*, curators Cynthia Davidson and Monica Ponce de León have cleverly reversed the question quoted above. Rather than rehearse the unproductive assertion that city talk can no longer usefully inform the creation of new architecture, they ask whether architectural speculation, specifically, might be of use in imagining new cities. Their answer, reinforced by the twelve proposals for Detroit on display this summer in the American Pavilion at the Venice Biennale, is an unrhetorical and unqualified "Yes."

This reversal offers not only a more promising way to frame an urban agenda, but also a way out of a debilitating impasse that has emerged in recent decades between many of today's advanced architects and innovative city designers. On one side, as the widely accepted caricatures go, egotistical architects (backed by private fortunes) pursue irresponsible formal complexity with blissful lack of regard for the supposed "realities" of the cities in which they work. On the other, earnest grassroots organizations eke out modest gains in the interstices of the urban fabric unconcerned by the negligible impact of their efforts in a broader cultural context. Neither side seems to have much actual knowledge of or interest in the activities of the other, and all involved tend toward a deep insularity. The crux of the impasse, however, has less to do with the difference between making cities and making buildings than with a widespread misunderstanding of both the professional and the disciplinary responsibilities of the people who make them. Andrew Zago and I took on this issue in a recent essay.[2] The *profession* of architecture, we argue, undertakes building- and city-making as a service to society, and therefore attends primarily to issues of accommodation, efficiency, sustainability, and cost-effectiveness. The *discipline*, on the other hand, pursues building- and city-making as an art form, and thus works primarily to advance the public imagination, a term we use in the strict sense of forming images in the mind. While the professional responsibilities of architects require close attention to the physical matter of buildings and cities, their disciplinary responsibilities are by definition abstract and take place in the virtual space of the imagination.

Architects, like painters and novelists, deal primarily with images, with semblances of things rather than with things themselves. It is easy to forget that the field's central concepts, form and space, refer not to physical entities but rather to specific disciplinary illusions. Architectural form is irreducible to tangible matter, just as architectural space is irreducible to volumes of air. Rather, architectural form and space are abstractions, virtual doppelgängers of physical entities, figments of the architectural imagination. As abstractions, architectural form and space are suffused with a vitality and dynamism unthinkable, except metaphorically, in the physical masses and volumes they represent. In the design studio, for example, architects routinely stretch, bend, twist, extrude, and otherwise manipulate forms in ways that even the most pliable construction materials could not withstand. Spaces, too, are made to flow, expand, penetrate, and intersect in ways impossible in the physical world. When describing the built environment, professional critics and lay observers alike reflexively speak of buildings that soar, elements in tension with one another, spaces suffused with psychological qualities like serenity, agitation, and frenzy. As the philosopher Susanne Langer observed, this sort of talk quite simply makes no sense with respect to everyday or scientific understandings of space.[3] Yet it is perfectly appropriate to *architectural* space. This is because architecture, in the specific disciplinary sense outlined above, does not take place in the physical world we inhabit. Rather, it is in the virtual domain of the architectural imagination that human environments, be they rooms, gardens, buildings, or cities, eclipse their origins in vulgar utility and obtain to the level of art. Langer offers a succinct encapsulation:

> The work of art...if it is successful, detaches itself from the rest of the world.
>
> Every real work of art has a tendency to appear thus dissociated from its mundane environment. The most immediate impression it creates is one of "otherness" from reality—the impression of an illusion enfolding the thing, action, statement, or flow of sound that constitutes the work. Even where the element of representation is absent, where nothing is imitated or feigned—in a lovely textile, a pot, a building, a sonata—this air of illusion, of being a sheer image, exists as forcibly as in the most deceptive picture or the most plausible narrative.[4]

For Langer, an image is what an artist creates when she is being creative. In her view, an object "becomes an image when it presents itself purely to our vision, i.e., as a sheer visual form instead of a locally and practically related object."[5]

This brand of transcendentalism can be hard to swallow today. It is particularly difficult to square with the gritty realities of buildings and cities. How, one might ask, given the pressing and acutely real challenges facing contemporary cities, can an architect offer abstract images, virtual forms detached from the physical places she was tasked to improve, as a solution?

A better question might be to ask, How could she not? Even a cursory survey of the canonical literature on the design of cities demonstrates the centrality of abstract images to the endeavor. Consider, for example, Le Corbusier, in *The City of To-morrow and Its Planning*: "A town is a mighty image which stirs our minds."[6] Or Aldo Rossi, in *The Architecture of the City*: "The urban image, its architecture...invests all of man's inhabited and constructed realms with value."[7]

To stir our minds, to invest our constructed realms with value, these are the activities for which the discipline of architecture takes responsibility. Of course, such concerns in no way absolve architects of their professional obligations. To speak of both a profession and a discipline of architecture is not to parse the field into distinct populations of service providers and artists. Rather, these terms denote two sets of contrasting but ultimately complementary cultural concerns. For all her insights into the fundamentally abstract nature of architecture, Langer was mistaken in her dismissal of architecture's primary professional motivation, utility, as an "affliction."[8] Reyner Banham, who in response to Langer suggested that a corresponding disciplinary concern for "symbolic expression...was the affliction of architecture," also got it wrong.[9] Simply put, anyone worthy of the title architect must address the full gamut of the field's professional and disciplinary obligations.

Tipping the balance too far in one direction is detrimental to both ambitions. Shirking professional responsibilities quite simply cannot be tolerated, but inattentiveness to the disciplinary project of advancing the public imagination is the more serious concern. For while substandard professionalism can result in the rampant inefficiencies, patent absurdities, and, occasionally, real dangers that plague our cities, these issues are more easily remedied than the cultural impoverishment that results from sidelining disciplinary concerns. In the best cases, the functional, structural, mechanical, economic, and other obligations administered by the profession attend to our immediate needs so efficiently that our consciousness of those features of the built environment can fall away. This hard-won freedom from quotidian concerns affords our minds the opportunity to slip into the realm of abstract images for which the discipline takes responsibility. For proof, just return to a favorite place in the city—the concourse at Grand Central Station, the bluffs overlooking the Santa Monica pier, the broad expanse of the Piazza San Marco. Notice, in spite of the obvious functional services provided, the "air of illusion" with which such spaces are suffused, their tendency to "detach themselves from the rest of the world" and present themselves as "sheer images." Notice, too, the tendency to lose oneself, to become, as the critic A. O. Scott memorably put it, "an instrument of pure perception."[10] These are effects for which we routinely invest the products of other art forms—painting, sculpture, literature, music—with value. Architecture too is an art, and its value accrues, to paraphrase Ruskin's famous aphorism, not only in service of the human frame, but also in its effect on the human mind. If architects are to remain agents of cultural production as well as organizers of everyday existence, we must remain committed not only to the coarse realities of utility, but also to crafting, out of the raw stuff with which we make buildings and cities, abstract images that fire both the public and the architectural imagination.

NOTES

1. Joe Day, "The iUrbanisms of Los Angeles," *Places Journal* (July 2015). https://placesjournal.org/article/the-iurbanisms-of-los-angeles/
2. Andrew Zago and Todd Gannon, "Tabloid Transparency," 226–45 in this volume.
3. Susanne Langer, *Feeling and Form* (New York: Scribner's, 1953): 94.
4. Ibid., 45.
5. Ibid., 47.
6. Le Corbusier, *The City of To-morrow and Its Planning* (New York: Dover, [1929] 1987): xxi.
7. Aldo Rossi, *The Architecture of the City* (Cambridge: MIT Press, [1966] 1982): 27.
8. Langer, *Feeling and Form*, xi.
9. Reyner Banham, "Convenient Benches and Handy Hooks: Functional Considerations in the Criticism of the Art of Architecture," in *The History, Theory, and Criticism of Architecture*, ed. Marcus Whiffen (Cambridge: MIT Press, 1965): 105.
10. A. O. Scott, *Better Living through Criticism: How to Think About Art, Pleasure, Beauty, and Truth* (New York: Penguin Press, 2016): 118.

Tschumi's Roadside Attraction

2003

Fig. 2.1 Bernard Tschumi Architects, Zénith de Rouen (2003).

Big, undifferentiated buildings, built cheap and fast and surrounded by a sea of asphalt, are the stuff of the contemporary roadside. Whether they are outside Indianapolis or Athens, they all look pretty much the same. Long ago we quit noticing this ubiquitous landscape of big boxes, parking lots, telephone poles, and power lines, preferring a single blurred continuum as we hurtle past at seventy miles per hour. But every once in a while, a defiant building refuses to fade quietly into the banal milieu. Through accident or intention, these renegade few demand closer scrutiny. On an unassuming stretch of highway in northern France lies one such building: Bernard Tschumi's Zénith de Rouen.

A cursory survey of massing and materials reveals nothing out of the ordinary. It is big (over a thousand feet long), blank, and for the most part unarticulated. It boasts precious few windows, off-the-shelf garage doors, and is clad in the same corrugated metal of countless suburban warehouses. In keeping with the roadside standard, acres of asphalt and the obligatory strip of lawn provide a buffer from traffic speeding past.

Affinities of scale and material are reaffirmed by the site plan, which discloses an unpretentious collection of warehouse buildings, two aligned with the adjacent roads, the others loosely defining a central courtyard. It all seems perfectly ordinary, except for the bulbous protrusion from the easternmost shed. Describing an aggressive curve in plan and section, its metal skin bulges precariously toward the roadway, as if the shed were gestating something terrible. Steel cables tied back to tall masts seem to keep everything intact, but a threatening gash of ribbon window suggests that it will not hold together for long.

Driving past, this strange object appears to rotate, as if pivoting about one if its rooftop spires. Turning back to gape after passing from the north reveals another surprise. This balloon-like volume is not a volume at all, but rather two thin planes, pinned at the ground and lashed at the top, their middles thrust forward by some unseen force.

What are we to make of this unearthly roadside attraction? At first pass, a critic might be tempted to associate the conspicuous steel masts, stay cables, and billowing facades with the maritime history of Rouen. From there, it would be an easy leap from the tectonics of sailing vessels to frames clad in fabric *à la* Gottfried Semper. A grimmer reading might suggest that the curved, feminine forms bound to vertical stakes recall the martyrdom of Joan of Arc, Rouen's patron saint. If not careful, a well-meaning critic might find himself spinning fantastical yarns that place Tschumi's concert hall in the unlikely company of religious monuments and the primitive hut!

Yet this Semperian observation may provide some insight. The building does call to mind frame-and-fabric structure, though not necessarily Semper's primal wellspring of architectural form. Rather, the Zènith de Rouen evokes a different building type, less venerated but more aligned with Tschumi's predilection for spectacle. Reviving an abandoned site on the outskirts of town, the concert hall is not so much sacred temple as circus tent.

Architecture, historians tell us, is about permanence and stability. Think pyramids, temples, and cathedrals—widely disparate archetypes that nonetheless share a privileged position in the canon and a reliance on the durability of masonry construction. The circus tent derives from a different lineage—one equally distinguished yet less likely to leave behind any evidence. From Bedouin oasis to Boy Scout camp, temporary structures throughout history engage us with all the intensity of their more lasting counterparts. If the most permanent buildings are masonry and therefore compressive, then the most ephemeral are surely tensile.

Tensile structures, like Tschumi himself, deal not with forms but with events. Their visceral tension derives not from material properties but from a latent impermanence. An affront to gravity itself, a structure in tension suspends more than physical mass. It suspends the certainty of its eventual collapse.

Thrown up overnight, the circus tent is one of these tensile wonders. Its enormous scale and bright colors mark the landscape as dramatically as any masonry pile of architectural history, but this monument does not last. As magically as it appeared, the whole thing is packed up, again under cover of night, and vanishes. The Zènith de Rouen, while decidedly more permanent, makes this imagery its own. The masts and stay cables appear to be pulling the curved walls into position, as if we had happened upon one of these clandestine nocturnal constructions. Or perhaps we are witnessing the reverse—a veil or curtain being cast off to reveal the spectacle within.

And when we consider the kinds of spectacles that grace the Zènith de Rouen, we find even more affinities with Tschumi's renegade tactics. For while most concert halls of architectural import defer to the acoustical needs of classical music, Rouen, with its amplified interior and absorptive acoustics, was made to rock.

Both Tschumi and rock music were born circa 1950 and matured in the political and social turmoil of the late '60s. Both share with their cousin the circus a taste for the spectacular, and all rely on precision, roughness, and shock in equal measure. Tschumi is at his best when working along these lines, which perhaps accounts for his uncomfortable intervention at Columbia University. Genuflecting to McKim, Mead, and White's austere beaux-arts campus, Lerner Hall resembles a mischievous child dressed up for the holidays, its irritation with its surroundings clear and its true impudence suppressed to the interior.

At Rouen, Tschumi revels in this youthful energy. The building is stripped down; like rock music it prefers to do a lot with a little. The restrained palette of materials—concrete, steel, and glass—recalls the power trio, rock's tried and true formula of drums, bass, and guitar. Interior concrete columns march in loose syncopation with the curved steel structure of the exterior skin, while stairs and ramps crescendo dramatically between. The asymmetrical arrangement denies the centripetal focus of traditional theaters and instead draws the eye to the periphery, where the three materials trade solos, weaving in and out of the spotlight of our attention. Thus, the building pays homage to the great halls of Jørn Utzon and Hans Scharoun, though here Tschumi distills the symphonic richness at Sydney and Berlin to deliver a more forceful wallop.

To achieve this no-frills effect in a building of this scale requires a particular diligence of the architect. The demands of mechanical distribution, fireproofing, lateral bracing, and other tectonic consideration—the interior corollaries of the roadside junk mentioned at the outset of this essay—all conspire to muddy such clarity of intention. Other architects might celebrate this cacophony of architectural tackle, but Tschumi suppresses it, staying true to the frankness of rock and roll. Double-walled seating construction conceals air distribution save for a single frieze-like duct that runs the length of the concourse. Light fixtures hide behind this ring of metal like roadies lurking backstage. Diagonal bracing was minimized, and an excessive number of exits were employed to allow the omission of interior fireproofing, maintaining the crispness of the structure. The effect is at once unabashedly visceral and highly abstract, the vastness of the space made palpable by its spare definition. During performances, dramatic lighting and frenetic crowds increase its efficacy, dematerializing the structure to near pure sensation.

By employing such stringent techniques, Tschumi avoids the pitfalls that subtly undermine the strength of some of his previous work. At Rouen, off-the-shelf components do not distract our attention, as do the fetishized details at Columbia and even at Le Fresnoy. Inside space and movement take center stage, making the Zènith de Rouen a tour de force of unbridled affect and Tschumi's most convincing rendition of event space to date.

Animate Urbanism: The Metabolic Infrastructures of UN Studio

2004

Fig. 3.1 UN Studio, Erasmus Bridge (Rotterdam, 1996).

Even the most inattentive observation of architects and Americans confirms Dutch architect Winy Maas's oft-quoted remark that architects use the word *landscape* as often as Americans use the word *fuck*. From Yokohama's new port terminal to Toronto's Tree City, landscape is all the rage today, and as far as Americans are concerned, well, fuck. But both groups possess slightly broader vocabularies, and further investigation reveals another popular pair of words: *infrastructure* and *shit*.

In the context of the present essay, this coupling is not accidental. For much of the twentieth century, and despite important work by practitioners and critics ranging from Rogers and Piano to Reyner Banham, architects have treated infrastructure with a level of disdain comparable to that usually reserved for its scatological counterpart. The profane accommodation of urban flows, whether traffic and sewage or power and data, has been the business of engineers. Only recently have infrastructural issues been admitted into polite architectural conversation, owing in large part to the work of UN Studio, the Amsterdam-based office of Ben van Berkel and Caroline Bos.

This newfound concern for infrastructure marks a profound shift after more than forty years of more abstract architectural thinking. In the 1960s and '70s, opportunities to build were rare for young practitioners and prominent members of that generation, Eisenman, Tschumi, Libeskind, and others, explored instead the isolated autonomy of theoretical writing and paper architecture. Major commissions such as the Wexner Center, Parc de la Villette, and the Jewish Museum came later, after world economies had rebounded and stellar reputations had been forged.

By contrast, UN Studio (originally known as Van Berkel and Bos Architectuurbureau) secured a number of commissions soon after its founding in 1988. Early projects include the typical fare of boutique practices—international competitions, gallery installations, and private residences—but it was the firm's embrace of utilitarian work, from low-profile power substations to the world-famous Erasmus Bridge, that launched UN Studio into the international spotlight. Van Berkel and Bos's continued pursuit of infrastructural work, combined with their frequent writing and teaching on the subject, has cemented their reputation within the discipline, making good on the ancient alchemical dream of turning shit into gold.[1]

Infrastructure usually operates below the level of attention. This vital equipment heats and cools our homes and illuminates our streets and offices. It transports fuels, waste, goods, and all of us and delivers unknowable amounts of data to any point on the globe. Yet we scarcely notice it, for infrastructure performs its tasks anonymously, plies its effects subliminally. Whether at the scale of a building or at the scale of a city, it is most often found in the poché within walls or below grade, as if its mysterious functions were best carried out in secret. The marionette strings of the contemporary metropolis, infrastructure gives life to inanimate matter. Its reward is near total effacement.

This performative silence is required because architecture, as codified and practiced over the last two centuries, has been concerned first and foremost with signification. As the discipline repositioned itself within the academy after centuries of close alignment with craft and building traditions, its attention shifted from problems of construction to problems of aesthetics and representation.[2] Fashionable architects busied themselves with increasingly arcane stylistic experimentation, delegating responsibility for newly developed mechanical and electrical systems to a growing number of technical specialists. Today, plumbers, engineers, and IT professionals continue to ensure that our buildings run smoothly, but for architects, efficient functionality has never been enough. Architecture, we have all been taught, has to mean something.

Meaning is best inscribed under controlled conditions. The contingencies of movement, temporality, and function tend to create unwanted feedback that clouds the legibility of form. Recall Colin Rowe and Robert

Slutzky's analysis of Le Corbusier's Villa Stein at Garches.[3] Here, the house is considered as abstract form, a collection of two-dimensional configurations represented in architectural drawings. Rowe and Slutzky uncovered a range of compositional readings at Villa Stein, but this legibility came at a price. As oblique views would alter the subtle effects they found, the critics had to sacrifice (or at least postpone) direct experience of much of the architecture to enjoy them, confining themselves in large part to a fixed point in the garden, well away from the house itself.[4] In truth, their astute readings were not devised at Garches at all. Proving that critical distance can be quite substantial, Rowe and Slutzky developed their analysis at the University of Texas, studying plans and elevations.

Design methods reliant on this combination of close attention and critical distance—the quotations of postmodernism, the destabilizations of deconstruction, the nostalgia of the New Urbanism—continue to hold sway over much of architectural theory and practice. But as pointed out by Stan Allen, "An architecture that works exclusively in the semiotic register and defines its role as critique, commentary, or even "interrogation" (laying bare the intricacies of architecture's complicity with power and politics) has, in some fundamental way, given up on the possibility of ever intervening on that reality. Under the dominance of the representational model, architecture has surrendered its capacity to imagine, to propose, or to construct alternative realities."[5]

Infrastructural projects offer the opportunity to reclaim that capacity. To deal in bridges, tunnels, and highways is to operate directly on the material life of the city. No mere representation, infrastructure choreographs the experience of the city, plying effects more potent than any single building could muster. History provides ample evidence. The Greeks elevated the arts as never before, but the Romans took over the world. Aqueducts and roads affect everyone. Erudition, however formidable, plays to a much smaller crowd.

On the surface, UN Studio's projects bear a striking resemblance to the work of semiotic practices, and many critics have explored their representational and expressive effects.[6] Even Van Berkel and Bos's own writings reveal a concern for signification. Regarding the Erasmus Bridge they write, "while deriving from a commission too complex to view entirely in this light, [the bridge] is generated by an intricate system of references to and deviations from typologies from the surroundings."[7] Demonstrating an uncommon ability to operate effectively in both discursive and performative modes, the firm does not abandon the semiotic register but rather deploys meaning as one of many effects in its arsenal. In recent projects, the manipulation of information remains a key component in their design process, though the legibility of that information in the final form is not a concern.[8] Instead, we see a persistent drive toward new possibilities of experience.

In his book, *Investigations*, theoretical biologist Stuart Kauffman builds on Charles Darwin's theory of evolution to explore the development of life in the universe. "The core issue," he explains, "arises with what Darwin calls 'preadaptation,' namely, causal consequences of parts of organisms that were not of adaptive significance in the normal environment of the organism, but might come to be of adaptive significance in some future environment and end up being selected for by natural selection. Thus arose hearing, lungs, flight—virtually all major and probably most or all minor adaptations."[9] New forms of life arise not through reactive adaptation to context, but rather through "emergence and persistent creativity," generating what Kauffman refers to as "new ways of making a living" in the world.[10]

In Kaufmann's view, life started out simply, the product of randomly occurring chemical reactions.[11] Over time, the complexity of these chemical combinations increases and the world (or body, or biosphere, or universe, or legal system, or economy) grows more diverse. This diversity gives rise to new forms of work (e.g., metabolism and photosynthesis) and new forms capable of doing that work (e.g., animals and plants). Further, the process of doing all this work affects the environment, creating additional "jobs" to be exploited.[12] In this model, an environment and its inhabitants co-construct one another, operating with equal impact on the infrastructural systems of bodies and biospheres as on the formal extravagances of fin, fur, and feather.

Applied to urbanism, Kauffman's insights accommodate the formal inventiveness of UN Studio's work as well as its affective potential on the city. Bridges, tunnels, and train stations, along with the proliferation of transportation, communication, and information networks, are the organs that generate metabolic processes that give life to the metropolis. The spectacular forms of the Erasmus Bridge, the Piet Hein Tunnel, or Arnhem Centraal, derived from the complex forces (political, representational, temporal, infrastructural) at play in the contemporary city, are not abstract representations of those forces but rather, like Kauffman's chemical reactions, the material manifestation of new forms of urban life. With them, Van Berkel and Bos chart a course away from the critical distance of semiotic practice toward an engaged, performative approach in which architecture once again operates directly on the ecology of the metropolis. These contorted forms and luxurious surfaces are the plumage of a new beast on the urban landscape. Their effects point to new possibilities for architects, allowing us to leave behind our role as commentators and to undertake the greater task of shaping new forms of life for the twenty-first century.

NOTES

1. See Dominique Laport, *History of Shit* (Cambridge: MIT Press, 1993); originally published as *Histoire de la merde: prologue* (Paris: Christan Bourgios, 1978).
2. Reyner Banham places the date of this rift between "the art of architecture and the practice of making and operating buildings" in the mid-eighteenth century. See Banham, *The Architecture of the Well-tempered Environment* 2nd ed. (Chicago: University of Chicago Press, 1984): 9.
3. Colin Rowe and Robert Slutzky, "Transparency: Literal and Phenomenal," *Perspecta* 8 (1963): 45–54.
4. As noted by Detlef Mertins in "Transparency: Autonomy and Relationality," *AA Files* 32 (1986): 3–11.
5. Stan Allen, "Infrastructural Urbanism," in *Points + Lines: Diagrams and Projects for the City* (New York: Princeton Architectural Press, 1999): 50.
6. See, for example, Bart Lootsma, "Ambidexterity and Transgression," and John Biln, "Lines of Encounter," both in *Ben van Berkel: Mobile Forces*, ed. Kristen Feireiss (Berlin: Ernst & Sohn, 1994). See also Greg Lynn, "Forms of Expression: The Proto-functional Potential of Diagrams in Architectural Design," in *El Croquis* 72 (1995), and Jeffrey Kipnis, "Hybridizations," in *A+U* 256 (1995).
7. Ben van Berkel and Caroline Bos, "Mobile Forces," in Feireiss, *Ben van Berkel*, 29.
8. For a specific discussion of legibility in UN Studio's work, see Jeffrey Kipnis, Steven Holl, Ben van Berkel, Caroline Bos, Jacques Herzog, and Rafael Moneo, "Discussion 3," in Cynthia Davidson, *Anything* (Cambridge: MIT Press, 2000): 124–29.
9. Stuart Kauffman, *Investigations* (London: Oxford University Press, 2000): x.
10. Ibid, 151.
11. A biosphere "construct[s] itself up from sunlight, water, and a small diversity of chemical compounds... over evolutionary time," (Kauffman, 82). For Kauffman, life evolves by organizing a complex interplay of matter, energy, and information. Entities measure displacements in equilibrium from which work can be extracted, as when a cat smells a mouse (measures displacement), pounces on it, and devours it (extracts work). In this sense, a living being, or "autonomous agent," is simply a self-replicating entity that manipulates the environment on its own behalf.
12. Think of the ecological complexity of the Pacific Northwest. As salmon swim upstream, elevation changes in rivers, caused by various geological occurrences, force the fish to jump from one level to the next. Salmon able to jump are more likely to get upstream to spawn than non-jumpers, thus jumping salmon are selected for. The jumping salmon catch the attention of hungry bears, and many of these fish wind up as lunch. Bears able to catch fish are better off than non-fishers, and the fishers, in turn, are selected for. Returning once more to scatological themes, bears shit in the woods. They also drag fish carcasses there. Nourished by these rich fertilizers, local trees soar to great heights, providing ideal nesting places for various birds. The shade beneath the trees provides optimal homes for other flora and fauna, and so on.

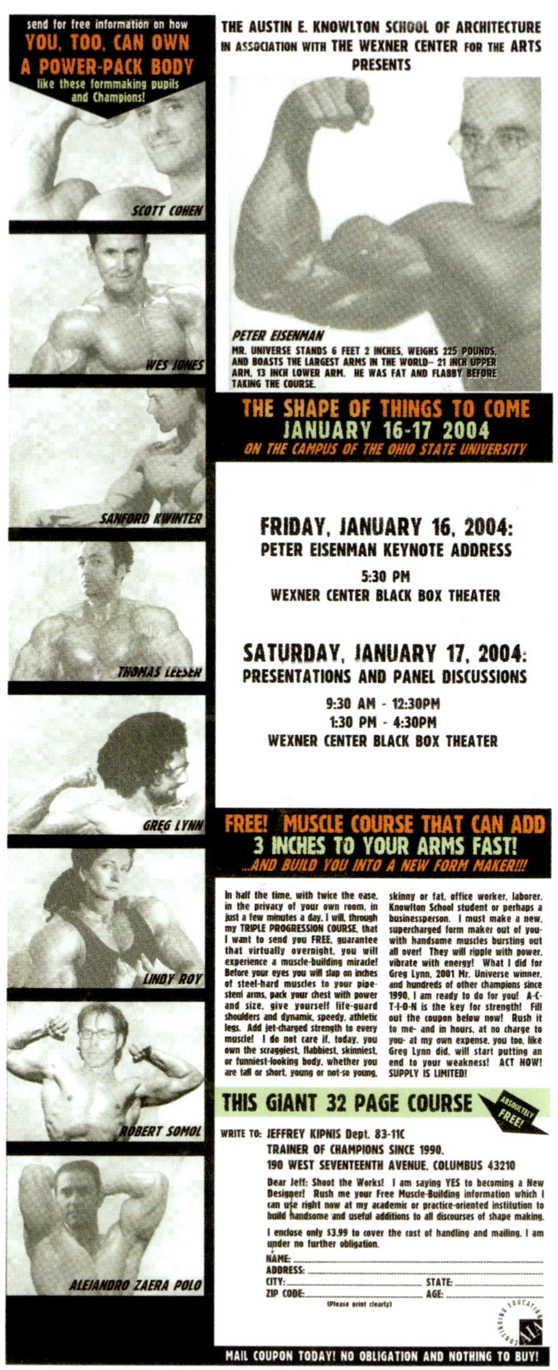

Fig. 4.1 Jeffrey Kipnis and Bart Overly, "The Shape of Things to Come," conference poster, 2004.

The Shape of Things to Come

2004

The Shape of Things to Come was presented at the Austin E. Knowlton School of Architecture at The Ohio State University, in association with the Wexner Center for the Arts, 16 and 17 January 2004.

When dealing with fortune tellers and soothsayers, one should always maintain a degree of suspicion. No matter how much we may want to believe what we're told, deep down we all know it's a scam. Indeed, the best fortune tellers don't predict anything at all—they simply tell us what we already know. Nonetheless we keep coming back, knowing full well that if we are not careful, we are certain to be ripped off.

Inviting Peter Eisenman, along with six younger practitioners and a distinguished panel of critics, to the black box theater in Eisenman's own Wexner Center for the Arts, Jeffrey Kipnis recently focused his crystal ball on "The Shape of Things to Come." Despite its prophetic title, the two-day conference offered little insight on possible futures. It did, however, elucidate the shape of contemporary discourse. Kipnis introduced the event as follows:

The "Shape of Things to Come" conference is convened to honor the long-deferred publication of Peter Eisenman's ground-break study, Giuseppe Terragni: Transformations, Decompositions, Critiques, *and his forty-year fixation on the intellectual possibilities of architectural form. In one way or the other, each of the conference participants began their career in Eisenman's sway, then each went on to develop original contributions to the problem of architectural form in his or her own right. Some advanced his research, others redirected it, while others still began to raise doubts about its basic premises. Given the dramatic upheavals in technology, material sciences, and intellectual/cultural discourse that distinguish our world fundamentally from the one in which the contemporary views of architectural form first emerged, the Knowlton School of Architecture convenes the conference to take stock of form, to assess its powers and limitations, and to speculate on its remaining relevance and possible futures, if any.*

Though Eisenman's Terragni book was barely mentioned (leading many in attendance to wonder how many of the participants had actually read it) its specter was present throughout.[1] The complex operational procedures that drove Eisenman's intricate analyses of the Italian modernist permeate his own work as well as that of each of the architects featured at the conference (Greg Lynn, Wes Jones, Lindy Roy, Thomas Leeser, and Preston Scott Cohen[2]), and the significance of those operations has been examined extensively by Kipnis as well as the two additional invited critics, Sanford Kwinter and R. E. Somol.[3]

Eisenman began with an extended monologue on "the future of the history of architecture" followed by the presentation of two projects, one he termed "analog," the other "digital"; the former his soon-to-be-completed Memorial to the Murdered Jews of Europe in Berlin and the latter an unrealized train station design for Naples, Italy. By categorizing the projects in these terms, Eisenman implied a technical divide between the by-hand techniques employed by his own generation and the computer-driven methodologies that currently dominate the discipline. Given the hegemony of digital techniques over all the conference participants (including Eisenman), such a partitioning would seem to offer little to the present debate. Nonetheless, differing attitudes toward these techniques reveal a telling shift in the conceptual and material ambitions of the younger generation from those of Eisenman's own.

Lacking the opportunities to pursue much built work in the economically depressed 1970s, many architects of Eisenman's generation turned their attention instead to theoretical projects and so-called "paper architecture." Much has been made of the conceptual significance of these works, but there has been surprisingly little mention of the objects themselves—the elegant drawings, models, and collages that these investigations produced.[4] Eisenman's cold, ink-on-mylar axonometrics that illustrate Terragni and his early houses, as well as the work of many of his contemporaries, exhibit a clinical, machinic rigor that belies the fact that each is an exquisitely hand-crafted object. For all their foregrounding of abstract intellection, latent in these works (and often absent from the few built projects of the period) is a highly sophisticated attention to craft and detail and their consequent tactile and material effects.

Today, all but a few retrograde practitioners have abandoned such painstaking analog processes for the relative immediacy of the digital. Some designers (including Eisenman) now employ the computational possibilities of the computer as a means of advancing this project of abstract formal investigation. For others the ability of digital processes to convincingly depict the material effects deliberately suppressed by Eisenman in his built work has led to the abandonment of abstract form in favor of the visceral articulation of environments.

Of course, Eisenman's use of the terms analog and digital implies much more than a degree of allegiance to computer-based design processes. He described analog projects as indices of abstract information in physical form, by definition intimately tied to problems of legibility and meaning. Such indexical operations have been crucial to Eisenman's work throughout his career, both as a means to manipulate abstract form as well as to embed referential information within those forms. Digital projects, on the other hand, simply employ certain computational techniques with no clear relation to meaning or history. Clearly uncomfortable with such independence of form and content, Eisenman questioned the possibility of judgment and disciplinary identity in the absence of legibility.[5] For Eisenman, the real danger is not that digital processes will displace analog ones, but rather that in the use of digital processes, architecture may very well displace its own history.

Of the five presenters, Greg Lynn most directly extends the formal investigations of Peter Eisenman. Charting a course from work he began in Eisenman's office (especially on the Frankfurt Biocentrum and Cincinnati DAAP projects), Lynn demonstrated how his own work turns away from Eisenman's simple primitive forms (grids, cubes, bars, and el-forms) and geometrical transformations (rotations, scalings, doublings, etc.), in favor of calculus-based operations on complex primitives such as spline surfaces and blob (isometric polysurface) forms. Suggesting that Frankfurt and Cincinnati were "analog projects that wanted to be digital," Lynn portrayed his own work as the natural progression of Eisenman's formal manipulations into the digital age.

Wes Jones, who spent his time in Eisenman's office working on the more semantically driven Wexner Center for the Arts, labors in his own projects to "soup up" the representational effects of architectural form. Transforming architectural precedents ranging from Le Corbusier's chaise lounge to ordinary shipping containers, Jones employs this hot rod analogy as a means to manipulate legible forms toward what he termed MAYA—the "most advanced yet acceptable" level. Thus, Jones aspires to test but not transgress the perceived limits of the discipline.

In diverse projects such as a health spa in the Okavango delta in Botswana, a bar in New York's meatpacking district, a store fit-out for Issey Miyake, and an extreme skiing outpost in Alaska, Lindy Roy redirects Eisenman's formal manipulations to perpetrate elegant visual and tactile effects with materially specific elements such as fiber optic strands, translucent glass and plastic, and, at her Subwave installation at P.S. 1, even mist. Though her operational strategies are similar to Eisenman's,[6] Roy shifts attention away from the forms themselves toward their resultant atmospheric effects.

Like Roy, Thomas Leeser labors to directly engage visitors with visual effects. Where Eisenman utilizes outside information to manipulate form, Leeser indexes his projects' programs to articulate surface. Using digital technologies, Leeser inscribes his projects with ephemeral traces of program, creating vital environments that constantly change according to the actions of their occupants. Footsteps are temporarily recorded on digital floors, web use is translated onto the wall surfaces of an internet company, and dynamic structural loading is mapped into the truss work of a bridge through complex sensors linked to color-coded lighting. Often deployed within generic interiors, Leeser's projects constituted the conference's least formally exuberant but most legibly indexical designs.

In projects such as the Torus House and the Tel Aviv Museum of Art, Preston Scott Cohen, drawing upon extensive research of projective geometry and stereotomy, exhibits a predilection for formal manipulations akin to Greg Lynn's, though his interests lie not in the logic of complex surfaces but rather on the volumetric possibilities of traditional architectural space making. Like Eisenman, Cohen has also devoted considerable attention to the Italian baroque.[7] For Eisenman, these investigations serve as catalysts to foster a close reading of the architectural object. By contrast, Cohen deploys the lessons of the baroque to generate atmospheric effects best experienced through distracted attention.[8]

Though the above descriptions suggest a partitioning of the participants with Lynn, Cohen, and Jones as sympathetic to Eisenman's formal ambitions and Roy and Leeser setting out to contrast them, such an assessment would be disingenuous. Despite their superficial differences, and regardless of the undeniable strength of their respective investigations, each participant ultimately represents a predictable trajectory from Eisenman himself. Whether form is agitated according to complex computational procedures (Lynn, Cohen), semantic information (Jones, Leeser), or both (Roy), the primary mechanism of each of these practices, as with Eisenman's own, is the index—the instrumentalization of information to manipulate form and generate effects.[9] In other words, each participant leaves Eisenman's fundamental position on the primacy of formal manipulation, legibility, and indexicality effectively unchallenged.

In leaving Eisenman's intellectual project of indexicality intact, each protégé failed to deploy Eisenman's most potent technique—criticality. In his keynote address, Eisenman presented the history of architecture as serial patricide—each generation perpetrating critical displacements on what has come before. This genealogical model affords any discipline its specific history and maintains its autonomy from other cultural practices. But over the last thirty years, the so-called "critical project" has become not only more pervasive but also increasingly internalized and self-referential, transforming a revolutionary ethos into a formulaic technique. The resulting predictability elicits a perverse oxymoron—the status quo of the avant-garde. Or, in the words of Reyner Banham, "New shapes notwithstanding, it is still the same old architecture, in the sense that the architects involved have relied on their inherited sense of primacy in the building team, and have insisted that they alone shall determine the forms to be employed. Formalism it may be, but it remains formalism within the limits of a professional tradition."[10]

Banham's quip comes from his two-part essay "Stocktaking," of 1960, in which he railed against such narrow views of the profession. Under the heading Tradition, he placed those who espoused the "operational lore" of architecture, the set of techniques and habits that architects have maintained and passed down through generations of masters and pupils. Emphasis is placed on history, disciplinary autonomy, and the formal and representational properties of the objects produced. In contrast, Banham proposed Technology, a faction made up in large part of non-architects and specialists "ignorant of the lore of the operation," a group capable of "creat[ing] an Other Architecture by chance, as it were, out of apparent intelligence and the task of creating fit environments for human activities."[11]

Exchanging Banham's Tradition/Technology with contemporary terms—difficult/easy, critical/projective, indexical/diagrammatic, life/lifestyle—provides a fair assessment of the state of current debate.[12] As one camp circles the wagons in order to fend off onslaughts against architecture's autonomy, the other welcomes all comers to the party.

Alone among the participants at the conference, R. E. Somol has aligned himself with the latter group. Celebrating the possibilities of a more expansive field he writes, "One aspect of this reorientation would be to recognize (and possibly profit from) architecture's erosion by surrounding design fields, the slackening of the discipline, its dissolution into graphic, landscape, product, interior, fashion, and urban 'design.' All design fields are in the process of becoming-one. What's becoming 'out of place' is the role of disciplinarity in the communion of information technology and the virtuality of materials."[13]

A broader sampling of Eisenman's progeny could possibly have provoked such a debate. Architects such as Mark Wamble of Interloop Architects and Sarah Whiting of WW both spent time in Eisenman's office before setting off in directions remarkably different from the indexical investigations seen here. But in a cunning act of synecdoche, "The Shape of Things to Come" presented a single facet of the discipline as the whole of architectural culture, and in so doing severely limited the possibilities of the conference.

NOTES

1. At least one participant did read the work. See Sanford Kwinter's excellent review: "Kaddish (for an Architecture Not Born): Peter Eisenman's Guiseppe Terragni," *Bookforum* (Winter 2003): 13–16.
2. Alejandro Zaera-Polo had been invited as well, but cancelled at the last minute.
3. The conference was organized with a keynote address from Eisenman on Friday night, and presentations from the five invited architects and two panel discussions on Saturday. The three critics did not present but participated in both panel discussions.
4. An important exception is Jeffrey Kipnis's 1999 exhibition "Perfect Acts of Architecture," which featured works by Eisenman, Rem Koolhaas, Bernard Tschumi, Thom Mayne, and Daniel Libeskind. See the exhibition catalog *Perfect Acts of Architecture* (New York: MoMA, 1999).
5. Eisenman even questioned this lack of legibility in his own work, claiming that without the clear process of his earlier projects, he "did not know how to make the form" of the Naples proposal.
6. To generate the seductive forms of her projects, Roy indexes such diverse processes as Vidal Sassoon hair-cutting techniques, theoretical biology, and the formation of termite mounds.
7. As the only presenter never to have been employed in Eisenman's office, Cohen's relationship to Eisenman's historical teachings (and his difference from the other presenters) might be attributed to his having been Eisenman's student at Harvard.
8. For more on Cohen's relationship to the baroque and his production of atmospheric effects, see Sylvia Lavin, "The Three Faces of Tel Aviv," *A+U* 6: 405 (June 2004): 12–21. See also Cohen's own *Contested Symmetries and other Predicaments in Architecture* (New York: Princeton Architectural Press, 2001).
9. Stan Allen describes the index as "a series of clues pointing back to the event of design and the hand of the author. This is a fundamentally modern practice, reflecting a belief in the object's capacity to carry traces of its origin and making a corresponding belief in interpretation as unmasking a self-referential play of meaning." See his "Tracks, Traces, Tricks," in *ANY* 0 (May/June 1993): 10. See also Rosalind Krauss, "Notes on the Index: Seventies Art in America," *October* 3 (Spring 1977): 68–81; and "Notes on the Index: Seventies Art in America, Part 2" *October* 4 (Autumn 1977): 58–67, texts which Eisenman cited in his keynote address as influential to his own understanding of the term.
10. Reyner Banham, "Stocktaking" *The Architectural Review* 127 (Feb 1960). Reprinted in Mary Banham, ed., *A Critic Writes: Essay by Reyner Banham* (Berkeley: Univ of California Press, 1996): 54.
11. Ibid., 61.
12. For a historical perspective, Marshall McLuhan's terms hot/cool (invoked at this conference by R. E. Somol), form/function, and even *Moderne/Ancien* may be added to the list.
13. R. E. Somol, "In the Wake of *Assemblage*," *Assemblage* 41 (April 2000): 93.

Return of the Living Dead: Archigram and Architecture's Monstrous Media

2008

Fig. 5.1 Front cover of *Archigram* 4 (1964). Designed by Warren Chalk.

As the Modern Movement died in 1939, so too did this neo-functionalism of Archigram die in 1968.
– Peter Eisenman

Forty years on, architecture remains haunted by the specters of the '60s. Surely you've felt them rustling in a late-night studio or whispering in a darkened lecture hall. The ghosts lurk in the shadows of our newest buildings and congregate in our schools. They creep into our conversations and possess our pundits. Lately, they have been reported swimming in the pixilated haze of our computer screens. Watch closely—with the right kind of eyes, you might catch a glimpse as these restless spirits charge contemporary work with the necrotic aura of another place, another time.

Normally, we write off these spectral sightings as influence, genealogy, precedent, or quotation. Rarely is the nefarious potential of supernatural activity examined or even admitted. Before the twentieth century, the spirits of the past generally were understood to be harmless, beneficial, or even essential. Past practitioners worked to ensure the presence of ancient ghosts in contemporary work while audiences and critics applauded their achievements. Even as later historians detected historical phantoms in the supposedly pure work of the 1920s and '30s, their presence generally was accepted as part and parcel to legitimate creative practice.

But in the 1960s, as a deep suspicion of the status quo developed through all facets of cultural production, new forms of supernatural activity were unearthed. Its subversive power comes clearly into focus in the grainy black and white of George Romero's 1968 classic, *Night of the Living Dead.* Much already has been said about the film's astute commentary on the turbulent 1960s. Produced by inexperienced filmmakers on a shoestring budget, the film deployed campy dialogue and cartoonish effects to raise serious questions about racial and gender stereotypes, senseless violence, blind conformance, the politics of resistance, and other pressing issues of the day. Such pointed critique was made possible in large part by the filmmaker's canny choice of supernatural menace. The Night was plagued neither by the traditional ethereality of ghosts nor by the uncomplicated corporeality of monsters. Instead, Romero unleashed a relentless horde of zombies.

Both living and dead, human and beast, familiar and undeniably other, zombies inhabit the unruly space between categories and demonstrate the transformative potential lurking within us all.[1] The zombie is the ordinary individual transformed by and absorbed into the faceless mob. Maintaining the material existence left behind by their spectral cousins, zombies pose a more immediate threat than disembodied spirits. Ghosts merely scare us, zombies bite.

While ghosts and spirits generally are considered part of the natural order, their zombie counterparts usually are the product of human intervention and science gone awry (Romero's zombies, for example, were caused by radiation from a failed NASA satellite). The message is clear: too much technology leads to disaster—we experiment at everyone's peril. Yet in architecture as elsewhere, such advice is rarely heeded, particularly in periods of cultural upheaval like the 1960s. Driven by a pervasive revolutionary *zeitgeist,* radical upstarts in England, Italy, Austria, and elsewhere unleashed projects and polemics that shook the discipline to its core and left in their wake a series of unbuilt and unbuildable aberrations—the architectural undead.[2]

Abominable works like Ron Herron's Walking City, Superstudio's Continuous Monument, and Hans Hollein's Aircraft Carrier City are a far cry from the friendly ghosts that merely haunt the work of others. More real than the virtual buildings they are said merely to represent, these subversive projects ply their effects in this world, not the next. Despite the efforts of our most vigilant critical exorcists, these architectural zombies keep coming back, and no body of work has been more impressive in its consistent refusal to just lie down and die than that of Archigram.

By most accounts dead and buried by the end of the 1960s, Archigram has since been resurrected by countless critics and historians to stand as both ally and impediment to all of the major ideological debates of the last forty years. The group and its output has been deployed as a means to resuscitate the "true" spirit of modernism, to challenge its most revered proponents, to demonstrate both the virtue and inefficacy of the avant-garde, to fend off and usher in the rising tides of postmodernism, and to shore up and attack a host of stylistic and typological trends. Indeed, since the group burst onto the scene in the early 1960s, it has become impossible to stake an architectural position without having a position on Archigram, even if that position is to denounce or suppress them.

Today, a burgeoning digital avant-garde bears striking similarities to the neo-avant-garde of Archigram's generation, embracing, as did their '60s forebears, cutting edge technology, extra-disciplinary expertise, and experimentation with non-traditional media. Understanding Archigram's monstrous incursions into architecture—a world until the '60s understood to be made up exclusively of buildings—proves particularly useful to twenty-first-century practitioners at work concocting contemporary digital demons. As Archigram's iconoclastic projects, publications, and polemics were reviled by the orthodox standard bearers of the '60s, so too does the work of today's digital generation draw fearful condemnations from the establishment. But what was true forty years ago remains the case today: These outrageous works suggests not the dissolution of the discipline but rather demonstrate that architecture is a restless spirit capable of animating material, minds, and media far beyond buildings.

*

In nine and one half eponymous issues released from 1961 to 1974, Archigram took advantage of the highly reconfigurable space of the printed page to manipulate forms, juxtapose elements, and orchestrate architectural experiments impossible in other media. Defying the scalar, temporal, and spatial limitations of built form, individual projects by Archigram members, their allies, and their heroes stand alongside contemporary products and comic book images and are blurred together by shaped texts and captions that run with abandon across the pages. Such techniques effectively erase hierarchical differences between these diverse elements and actors, encapsulated in the Archigram mantra first voiced in Issue 3: "It's all the same."[3]

We see these techniques in every issue of the magazine. In *Archigram* 1, textual information is employed not to describe architectural objects, but rather to loosen architectural possibility from built form. Throughout the sheet, Peter Cook's handwritten captions follow and peel away from the contours of projects by Mike Webb, Timothy Tinker, David Greene and others, in some cases the words written across the buildings in a form of editorial graffiti. In these and other techniques, the *Archigrams* differ radically from traditional architectural publication. In their pages, the aim is never simply to document or describe. Rather, projects and products are transformed into an alternative architectural milieu, a presentation of a future world fundamentally different from the present one.

One possible future is narrated in *Archigram* 4, the famous "Zoom Issue" of 1964. Here, the group adopts their trademark comic book style in a strip that intricately syncopates a dialog-rich plot (collaged together from contemporary DC space comics), captionless futuristic skylines (drawn by Ron Herron), and critical exegesis from comely female commentators (avatars of contributing Archigrammers). These latter elements link the space comic back to contemporary architectural discourse in "a two-way exchange between space comic imagery and the more advanced 'real' concepts and prophesies----- Geodesic nets, pneumatic tubes, plastic domes and bubbles."[4]

Other issues push the magazine further into territory unavailable to contemporary construction. *Archigram* 5 employs dissipative strategies that erase long-held distinctions between architecture and the city and introduces seminal projects such as Cook's Plug-In City, Herron's Walking City, and Dennis Crompton's Computor City. *Archigram* 6 further undermines the linear sequence of traditional print media with a clever choreography of narrative threads. For Issues 7 and 8, binding is abandoned altogether and with it, the fixed sequence of print media.

As linear narrative is left behind in the magazine, concurrent Archigram projects abandon traditional architectural form. Peter Cook's "Metamorphosis: Sequence of Domestic Change" chronicles a dissolution of architecture from "Straight Bits" in 1960 to "Becoming Almost Ethereal" by 1985. Architecture as static form imbued with representational meaning vanishes and is replaced with an ever-updated kit of gadgetry geared to enhance human life. Other projects push this transformative agenda even further. Mike Webb's Suit-a-loon, Warren Chalk and David Greene's Electronic Tomato, and Chalk's Bathamatic all abandon architecture as a representational vehicle and instead expand the possibilities of architectural performance.

Yet as *Archigram* moved toward its swan song, their unconstrained optimism began to show signs of decay. Mike Webb's "Capsulized Freak Out," featured in *Archigram* 8, hints at the precarious possibility of the dissolution of autonomous human subjects into technologically enhanced cyborgs. He writes, "The organic birth-death-life-earth-heaven-God is no longer valid. ...You merely: take it away, eat it, drive it, fuck it. ...Plug in to any or all. Switch on and be serviced. Finished, full, switch off -- doesn't matter because: 2. It's all the same. ...The pill and the plastic liver have ended the concern that we are all part of some wonderful inevitable natural process."[5] For Webb, "It's all the same" has come full circle. No longer the liberating slogan of a fully interchangeable, technological utopia, the flattening of hierarchy into unbridled recombinatory potential reveals its darker side. In sweeping away time-honored differences—between buildings and media, between vacuum cleaners and space capsules, between the actual and the virtual—Archigram opens the possibility of eradicating the differences between the human and non-human. Like Romero's contemporaneous zombies, Archigram's bold step into a technological future suggests a fundamental transformation of human subjectivity.

*

Through the middle 1960s, Archigram's provocative drawings, influential teaching, and seemingly boundless energy made them heroes in London student circles and persistent irritants to the academic status quo, drawing glowing praise and breathless derision in near equal measure. Reyner Banham's "A Clip-On Architecture" is the earliest serious study of the group's output and remains a seminal resource.[6] Building on the revisionist arguments of his influential *Theory and Design in the First Machine Age*,[7] Banham provided Archigram with a coherent genealogy of "anti-formal," "indeterminate," and "endless" precedents while using the group to take obvious if *sotto voce* pot shots at the monumental figures and tendencies of orthodox modernism.

By 1967, the group's threat to the course of mainstream modernism was clear, drawing a curt dismissal from no less a figure than Sigfried Giedion. Further direct and indirect condemnations from the old guard came from Constantine Doxiadis, Peter Hall, Denise Scott Brown, the Smithsons, and others.[8] The critiques are similar in their dismissal of the group's output as fantastical, untenable, and/or anti-humanistic and in their adherence to an earlier, orthodox position in line with CIAM, Team X, and conventional urban planning.[9] Warren Chalk's "Owing to Lack of Interest, Tomorrow Has Been Cancelled" offers a rebuttal to such criticism that underscores Archigram's interest in experimenting in alternative media:

> It isn't necessary to be dreary to make a point, or to be profound to have something to say; some of the greatest insights in the world accompany a joke. And many of the mind-blowing ideas about futures in never-never-lands have originated off the pages of comic books and science fiction picture backs. Cartoons help us to discover the hidden realities of life, where straighter communications may fail.[10]

Chalk's title captures the distinct waning of interest in optimistic "futures in never-never-lands" that followed the events of May 1968, as the pressing issues of an increasingly turbulent present came to dominate the international scene. While the historians stepped in to take stock and summarize what was widely perceived to be a closed chapter in the history of architecture, new critical journals, steeped in the theoretical language of the Frankfurt School and the New Left, took up a different agenda. In Italy, *Contropiano* launched the strident political critiques of Antonio Negri and Manfredo Tafuri. In France, *Utopie* offered a venue for the socialist positions of Jean Baudrillard and Henri Lefebvre. But it was in the American journal *Oppositions*, founded in 1973 by Peter Eisenman, Kenneth Frampton, and Mario Gandelsonas, that continental thinking was to find its most potent architectural incubator. Here, the seeds of the more theoretical strains of architectural postmodernism were sown by a new generation of revisionist thinkers that positioned themselves unequivocally against Archigram's (and Banham's) technological progressivism.

Eisenman elucidated his position in "Post-Functionalism," a 1976 editorial.[11] Foreclosing the possibility of an "English Revisionist Functionalist" return to bygone modernist tendencies, Eisenman argues that modernism in architecture had not yet even occurred. He writes,

> Deriving from a non-humanistic attitude toward the relationship of an individual to his physical environment, [modernism] breaks with the historical past, both with the ways of viewing man as a subject and...with the ethical positivism of form and function. Thus, it cannot be related to functionalism. It is probably for this reason that modernism up to now has not been elaborated in architecture.

While modernism successfully had been adopted in painting, literature, and music, it had not developed in architecture because the discipline had yet to engage the "non-objective," "non-narrative," and "a-temporal" qualities that marked the shift from humanism to modernism in other fields and signaled the movement's fundamental condition: "a displacement of man away from the center of his world." To finally bring about architectural modernism, Eisenman argued for the abandonment of the form/function dialectic (and its outmoded humanism) in favor of a "new, modern dialectic" of "transformation" and "decomposition" located entirely within the problem of autonomous form.

Once again, we see the central concern turning around the nature of subjectivity. Giedion, Doxiadis, and other orthodox critics saw Archigram's experiments with technology and alternative media as anti-humanistic threats to modernist achievement, threats which Mike Webb's "Capsulized Freak Out" seemed to recognize. For Banham, Archigram's technologically enhanced environments provided the playground for a modern *homo ludens*, the idealized "man at play" first theorized by Johan Huizinga.[12] For Eisenman, the ambition of both camps to place the human subject at "the center of his world" advanced not a modernist position but rather a nostalgic maintenance of traditional humanism. Alongside the vanguard of the post-'68 generation, he saw no place in the contemporary context for adherence to such an outmoded view of subjectivity.

Through the late 1960s and into the '70s, this battle for the subject raged across the cultural landscape.[13] And whether it was waged in the streets of Paris, the pages of *Oppositions*, or in the gory scenes of *Night of the Living Dead*, it was the stable humanist subject that generally came out the loser. For Archigram, this meant a distinct falling out of favor with architectural culture. By the mid-'70s, their last pamphlet had been printed, their only commission had been cancelled, their offices closed, their ranks dispersed, and their consistent presence in the architectural press faded to obscurity. The dearth of Archigram literature that ensued after 1975 is best reflected in an extensive bibliography on the group compiled by the library of the Architectural Association in London, which contains no entries for the period of 1976 through 1986, and only a handful through 1994.[14]

That year saw the opening of a major traveling exhibition, *Archigram: Experimental Architecture, 1961–1974* and an explosion of interest in the group has continued unabated into the present.[15] The causes of this renewed interest are varied and perhaps impossible to pin down specifically, though certain trends certainly helped to create a receptive audience. Barry Curtis cites the success of Richard Rogers and British High Tech as a catalyst, while William Menking saw fit to deploy Archigram as an alternative to the nostalgic "malling of 42nd Street" in New York and other saccharine Pomo confections.[16] In the middle 1990s, architectural postmodernism began to show signs of strain, as architects and critics began to evoke, after nearly twenty years of measured avoidance, the term "new."[17] This new architecture was marked by a slow but steady shift away from the overtly theoretical '80s into a more technologically inspired '90s, as well as the slow disintegration of the "uneasy alliance" between Peter Eisenman and Rem Koolhaas.[18]

Even during his association with Eisenman's Institute of Architecture and Urban Studies in the 1970s, Koolhaas never subscribed to the suppression of Archigram so central to Eisenman's autonomous position. His influential "Exodus, or The Voluntary Prisoners of Architecture" of 1972 was a dystopian Archigram redux, their genial technophilia here gone feral, their playful sexuality now hardcore. Breakthrough OMA projects of the early '90s—the Kunsthal Rotterdam, the Jussieu Library, and the Mediatheque in Karlsruhe—maintained similar affiliations to the British team in their brash juxtaposition of formal and programmatic elements toward subversively social rather than overtly configurational ends.

If in the 1990s one branch of the discipline turned their attention toward the manic accumulations of program characterized in Koolhaas's work, another embraced a technophilia not seen since Archigram's celebration of space-age componentry in the 1960s. The advent of digital design technologies saw architectural studios of all stripes leapfrog from T-squared Ludditism to the forefront of Information Age experimentation. In more advanced practices, this move ushered in a wave of virtual, digital projects that, like Archigram's, proved too ambitious to fabricate but too influential to dismiss (both despite valiant efforts by dedicated proponents and detractors). Whether aligned with the programmatic aims of the Koolhaas camp or the technologically enhanced inheritors of autonomous form, both arms of the late-twentieth-century architectural vanguard could claim Archigram as their rightful forebear.

As works by members of the digital set garner increasing attention within the discipline, we see many of the old arguments again coming to the fore. In an eerie echo of Archigram's reception, today's vanguard are celebrated for leaving the shackles of built form behind as often as they are chastised for advancing monstrous aberrations of architecture. In either case, building-generated effects take center stage, with those produced in other media garnering either extended justification or out-of-hand dismissal. The organization of so many debates across the built/unbuilt divide, today as in the 1960s, leaves the specific tactics, strategies, and relations to material practices beyond the building industry but nonetheless proper to architecture under-examined and ripe for further study. Directing our attention here can elucidate architecture's long-standing attentiveness toward and expertise with the complex dynamics that issue from the accumulation, dispersal, and interpenetration of media, opening new possibilities for understanding both historical and contemporary projects as well as the subjectivities that engage them.

*

With remarkable consistency, treatments of Archigram tend to conclude by discussing the potential dissolution of architecture in the face of advanced technology.[19] Whether this marks the ultimate failure of the Archigram project or a still attainable mandate to be assumed by a present or future vanguard remains an open question as too many contemporary conversations slide into a century-old debate over the efficacy of the avant-garde. While pundits on the right maintain a purist disavowal for the unbuilt fantasies of Archigram and the inheritors of their tradition, critics on the left readily attack the few built examples that have emerged (Beaubourg, the Seattle Library, Kunsthaus Graz) as complicit monuments to architectural tradition in spite of their supposed anti-monumental, revolutionary ambitions. Such bickering offers little to contemporary discourse.

Architects long have suffered from a self-perpetuated, chauvinistic stance toward materials. Despite periodic attempts to correct this backward view, we tend to hold bricks and mortar, and to a lesser extent glass and steel, in exalted positions. This view artificially foregrounds permanent buildings as the sole area of our expertise even as their execution falls increasingly outside our control. Further compounding these anxieties is the widely held agreement with Walter Benjamin that buildings are best experienced in a state of distracted attention—even if we manage to pull one together, properly critical culture is encouraged not to take notice.

Yet regardless of whether they ultimately are built, all architectural projects are actualized first as drawings, writings, models, gestures, and speeches long before their instantiation in built form. And it is here, in the materially specific realm of paper and pixels, that architects ply some of their most potent effects. Indeed, architecture is present in print as surely as it is in the enduring stones of the Acropolis, though it is perhaps only now, after a century of engagement with contemporary media, that we are able to notice it there. Understanding architecture not as a class of buildings but rather as an emergent effect that issues from a range of media reveals the *Archigrams* and their monstrous progeny neither as a dangerous threat to disciplinarity nor as a disappointing reminder of our inefficacy, but rather as offering the clearest indicator of the discipline's unparalleled expertise in the contemporary mediated milieu. Though they may call for a reconsideration of the nature of modernism, the essence of architecture, or even the constitution of human subjectivity, these mutant experiments do not signal the dissolution of architecture. Rather, they offer a means to understand that architecture's most enduring strengths obtain where we least expected to find them—in the array of less durable but equally potent materials beyond building.

NOTES

1. Zombies thus prove particularly well suited to the complex cultural climate of the 1960s. In Romero's classic, their presence upsets all the usual tropes. Unable to fend off their relentless attack, good guys succumb to the zombie horde and damsels in distress are killed off one by one. The unlikely survivor/hero, a resourceful black man in an otherwise hapless white cast, falls victim to a trigger-happy posse too eager to save the day. Robbed of a traditional happy ending and shaken by unprecedented gore, the audience is left to ponder why, exactly, everything seemed to go wrong.
2. I am indebted to N. Katherine Hayles for suggesting to me the equivalence of unbuilt architecture and the undead. See our "Virtual Architecture, Actual Media," 174–99 in this volume, which develops many of the themes outlined here.
3. *Archigram* 3 "Expendability" (Autumn 1963): np.
4. *Archigram* 4 "The Zoom Issue" (Spring/Summer 1964): 4.
5. Mike Webb, "Capsulized Freak Out" in *Archigram* 8 "Milanogram" (1968): np.
6. Reyner Banham, "A Clip-On Architecture." *Design Quarterly* 63 (1965): entire issue.
7. Reyner Banham, *Theory and Design in the First Machine Age* (London: Architectural Press, 1960).
8. See Sigfried Giedion, *Space, Time, and Architecture*, 5th ed. (Cambridge: Harvard Univ. Press, 1967): 586; Constantine Doxiadis, *Encyclopedia Britannica Book of the Year, 1968* (London: Encyclopedia Britannica,

1968): 68; Peter Hall, "Monumental Follies," *New Society* (Oct 1968): 602–603; Denise Scott Brown, "Little Magazines in Architecture and Urbanism," *Journal of the American Institute of Town Planning* 34: 4 (1968): 223–32; and Alison and Peter Smithson, *Without Rhetoric: An Architectural Aesthetic, 1955–1972* (Cambridge: MIT Press, 1973): 78. Many of these protests, along with Giedion's cited above, are outlined in Charles Jencks, *Modern Movements in Architecture* (London: Penguin Books, 1973): 291–92.

9. The group similarly was dismissed by later historians. Manfredo Tafuri saw them as overly idealistic (*Modern Architecture* (New York: Abrams, 1976): 383), Kenneth Frampton categorizes them among an "ambivalent" group that failed to adhere to his concept of Critical Regionalism (*Modern Architecture: A Critical History* (London: Thames and Hudson, 1992): 280–313), and Spiro Kostof found their efforts unfashionable and out of touch with contextualism and tradition (*A History of Architecture* [1985] [London: Oxford University Press, 2nd ed., 1995]: 748).
10. Warren Chalk, "Owing to Lack of Interest, Tomorrow Has Been Cancelled" *Architectural Design* (Sept. 1969).
11. Peter Eisenman, "Post-Functionalism," *Oppositions* 6 (1976): i–iii.
12. Banham outlines this version of the modern subject and its relation to Archigram in *Megastructure: Urban Futures of the Recent Past* (New York: Harper and Row, 1976): 84–103.
13. A raft of publication has been devoted to the subject of 1960s cultural theory. Two excellent surveys, written from opposing points of view, are Luc Ferry and Alain Renaut, *French Philosophy of the Sixties: An Essay on Antihumanism* [1986], translated by Mary Schackenberg Cattani (Amherst: The University of Massachusetts Press, 1990) and François Cusset, *French Theory: How Foucault, Derrida, Deleuze, and Co. Transformed the Intellectual Life of the United States* [2003], translated by Jeff Fort (Minneapolis: Univ. of Minnesota Press, 2008).
14. The bibliography is available online at http://www.aaschool.ac.uk/library/documents/archigram.pdf. Accessed 8 August 2008.
15. The show opened in Vienna in February 1994 and by 2005 had traveled to Paris, Zurich, Hamburg, Manchester, New York, Ithaca, Pasadena, San Francisco, Seattle, Milan, Brussels, Rotterdam, Winnipeg, Chicago, Taipei, and Tokyo. Four catalogs have been released: *Archigram,* ed. Alain Guiheux (Paris: Editions du Centre Georges Pompidou, 1994; *A Guide to Archigram 1961–74,* ed. Dennis Crompton (London: Academy Editions, 1994); *Concerning Archigram,* ed. Dennis Crompton (London: Archigram Archives, 1998); and *Archigram: Experimental Architecture 1961–1974,* ed. Dennis Crompton (Tokyo: PIE Books, 2005).
16. Barry Curtis, "A Necessary Irritant" and William Menking, "Archigram: Welcome to New York" both in Crompton, *Concerning Archigram,* 25–79 and 160–67.
17. Jeffrey Kipnis provides an important polemic in "Towards a New Architecture," in *Folding in Architecture,* ed. Greg Lynn (London: Academy Editions, 1993).
18. Kipnis discusses the nature of the Koolhaas/Eisenman relationship in the early 1990s in "Recent Koolhaas," *El Croquis* 79 (1996): 26.
19. This tactic echoes Banham's famous closing to *Theory and Design in the First Machine Age* and is employed (sometimes with a direct quotation) in Curtis's "Archigram: A Necessary Irritant"; Hadas Steiner's *Beyond Archigram: The Structure of Circulation* (London: Routledge, 2009); Simon Sadler's *Archigram: Architecture without Architecture* (Cambridge: MIT Press, 2005); and elsewhere.

A Confederacy of Heretics

2013

Fig. 6.1 *A Confederacy of Heretics*, curated by Todd Gannon, Ewan Branda, and Andrew Zago. SCI-Arc Gallery, Los Angeles, 2013.

A *Confederacy of Heretics* examines the explosion of activity associated with the Architecture Gallery, Los Angeles's first gallery dedicated exclusively to architecture. Instigated by Thom Mayne in the autumn of 1979, the Architecture Gallery staged ten exhibitions in as many weeks by both young and established Los Angeles practitioners, featuring the work of Eugene Kupper, Roland Coate Jr., Frederick Fisher, Frank Dimster, Frank Gehry, Peter de Bretteville, Morphosis (Thom Mayne and Michael Rotondi), Studio Works (Craig Hodgetts and Robert Mangurian), and Eric Owen Moss. Another young architect, Coy Howard, opened the events with a lecture at the Southern California Institute of Architecture, which hosted talks by each exhibiting architect. In an unprecedented move by the popular press, the events were chronicled in weekly reviews by the critic John Dreyfuss in the *Los Angeles Times.*

Commonly understood today as a set of beliefs or practices in conflict with prevailing dogma, the word *heresy* derives from the Greek αἵρεσις, meaning choice. In classical antiquity, the term also signified a period during which a young philosopher would examine various schools of thought to determine his future way of life.[1] These inflections neatly capture the ambitions and attitudes held by the architects at the center of this presentation. Some had grown weary with what they viewed as the stale orthodoxies of the establishment, and saw their work as a distinct challenge to the status quo. Others were less strident, and experimented with a diverse range of historical sources as potential platforms from which to develop their individual idioms. Others still struck out in bold new directions, drawing inspiration and techniques from the art world, literature, and other sources. Such wide-ranging activities defy any attempt to portray these architects as members of a coherent group or "L.A. School."[2] More correctly, the Architecture Gallery constitutes one of many loose, temporary confederacies into which these architects entered during their formative years. Here, the heretics found strength in numbers, and the impact of their efforts was felt across Los Angeles and around the world.

Gathering an array of original drawings, models, photographs, video recordings, and commentary alongside new assessments by current scholars, *A Confederacy of Heretics* aims neither to canonize the participating architects nor to consecrate their unorthodox activities. Rather, the exhibition re-examines the early work of some of Los Angeles's most well-known architects, charts the development of their most potent design techniques, and documents a crucial turning point in Los Angeles architecture, a time when Angeleno architecture culture shifted from working local variations on imported themes to exporting highly original disciplinary innovations with global reach. Taken together, the exhibition, symposium, and catalog that comprise *A Confederacy of Heretics* offer a unique lens through which to analyze a pivotal moment in the development of late twentieth-century architecture.

The Architecture Gallery opened in October 1979, a time when the continued viability of orthodox modernism was being contested in Los Angeles and around the world. Not only had architecture by then witnessed the passing of most of its modern pioneers,[3] but the tumultuous socio-political events of the 1960s had shaken the field to its core. By the end of the '70s, architecture's most advanced practitioners had long been developing alternative modes of inquiry. Theoretical projects, as opposed to commissioned buildings, had become widespread vehicles of disciplinary innovation, and a rift had opened between those committed to viable commercial practices and those dedicated to seemingly antithetical disciplinary pursuits and personal ambitions.

Much of this latter work addressed what many understood to be a "loss of center" in the cultural milieu, the apparent result of critical attacks on the foundational tenets of Western humanism by proponents of post-structuralist theory and deconstruction.[4] Critics from inside and outside the field called the unifying dogma of modernism in question,[5] and architects set off in pursuit of wildly divergent agendas. Simultaneously in the mid-1960s, the Archigram group attempted to recuperate modernism's links to technology, Robert Venturi waxed poetical about his taste for complexity and contradiction, and Aldo Rossi sought refuge in symbolic forms and collective memory. Within a few years, Venturi and his partner Denise Scott Brown had made their way west to learn from Las Vegas and other pop and vernacular phenomena. Taking a more academic approach to signs and signification, critics such as George Baird and Charles Jencks sought to establish a new ground for architectural production in language. By the late '70s, Léon Krier, Colin Rowe, and Fred Koetter had made compelling cases for the appropriation of historical forms alongside equally impassioned pleas for a renewed attentiveness to architecture's irreducible essence from the likes of Peter Eisenman, Daniel Libeskind, and Bernard Tschumi, among others.[6] Each of these varied agendas drew strong and devoted followings whose output atomized the unified approach of modernism into an unruly constellation of competing alternatives for a postmodern world without a center.

Los Angeles architects of the period were not immune to this widespread suspicion of orthodoxy, and at the Architecture Gallery and elsewhere, they pursued radical new trajectories. But where their counterparts on the East Coast and in Europe tended to characterize the loss of center as a burden or tragedy, the predominant reaction among Southern California architects was a sense of liberation. Such a response might have been expected in Los Angeles, which for generations had made a virtue of its peripheral status with respect to more established (and establishment) centers to the north and east.[7] Since at least the 1880s, Los Angeles architects had exploited the city's distance from established centers to develop idiosyncratic variations on imported styles, as evidenced by the Newsom brothers with Queen Anne, the Greene brothers with Arts and Crafts, and Schindler, Neutra, and the Case Study group with orthodox modernism. In the late 1970s, the city that had perfected the periphery was the ideal place to speculate on how to organize a world suddenly bereft of the notion of center.

Concentrating primarily on younger practices operating outside the commercial mainstream, the Architecture Gallery showcased fringe members of an already peripheral disciplinary culture. But where like-minded apostates to orthodoxy in other parts of the world tended to band together in groups such as *La Tendenza* in Italy or the Institute for Architecture and Urban Studies in New York, architects in Los Angeles eschewed such collective endeavors in favor of the individual pursuit of personal and idiosyncratic agendas. In his lecture for the Architecture Gallery series, Eric Owen Moss articulated his view of the situation:

> The problem that we face in doing architecture and in defining ourselves for ourselves is, finally, a personal and individual one. There have been many, over eons of time, who have attempted to deal with that kind of fundamental irrationality in a collective sense, to try to develop an order, an underneath, a platform which seems to make the finitude of the individual a little bit more palatable and coherent and intelligible, to define a context which is broader than the individual and which will support and in fact ameliorate the problem.

Though he observed that the Pythagorians and, later, the Russian Constructivists had managed to find a sense of order collectively, Moss saw no such option available to his own generation: "It will finally be my opinion that any sort of effort, on a collective level, is, at least for us, at this point in time, impossible. These kinds of searches have to be carried out on an individual level."[8]

The wide array of approaches on display at the Architecture Gallery attested to each architect's commitment to his own personal ambitions and underscores the inability of any collective label to adequately account for their activities. Nonetheless, certain shared tendencies can be discerned. Most do not encompass the entire group, but rather loosely organize the participants into overlapping clusters of interest. A majority of these architects, for example, shared a distinctly pragmatic frame of mind and a willingness to take on commissions, such as garage renovations and small residential additions, which more established practitioners might have considered economically unfeasible or intellectually irrelevant. Several, including Eugene Kupper, Frank Dimster, and Roland Coate, grounded their endeavors in disciplinary fundamentals such as archetypal forms, functional performance, and attentiveness to the exigencies of the building site. Many, including Frank Gehry, Frederick Fisher, and Thom Mayne and Michael Rotondi of Morphosis, experimented with vernacular elements and materials, particularly in their residential projects. A critical reassessment of disciplinary conventions also colors much of the work on display. With the 2-4-6-8 House, for example, Mayne and Rotondi took a small project as an opportunity to perpetrate a wholesale reinvention of the conventions of construction documentation. In now iconic drawings, they outlined the building's tectonic elements and construction sequence in excruciating detail, carefully delineating even the simplest connections in an almost comically thorough sequence of axonometrics [**Fig. 6.2**]. In this, the architects slid from reimagining fundamentals to another common tendency—the expenditure of unreasonable, even unnecessary, effort. Craig Hodgetts and Robert Mangurian's voluminous production of drawings and models for the South Side Settlement House is another case in point [**Fig. 6.3**], as are many of the artifacts in the present exhibition. As Ray Kappe remarked, "the drawing...almost became a thing in itself for a lot of these guys. ...Robert and Craig were just drawing the hell out of projects. Obviously, [this was] not necessary for construction; obviously not necessary, even, to understand the building."[9] Kappe's observation is valid, but fails to recognize the more radical proposition, widely espoused by younger architects of the period, that buildings were not always necessary to understand the architecture.

Rhetoric such as this, though part and parcel to East Coast architecture discourse, was rare in Los Angeles, where production typically trumped polemic. Hodgetts, Howard, and Rotondi later recounted that much of the motivation for their elaborate drawings and models had to do with the sheer pleasure of making them.[10] Love of the game notwithstanding, these labor-intensive artifacts had an additional benefit: they made for arresting publications. A widely shared ambition among these architects was a dogged pursuit of local and national design awards. Particularly prized was recognition by the *P/A* Awards, the annual competition held by *Progressive Architecture* magazine. Each of the architects in the exhibition devoted significant effort to *P/A* Award submissions, and their projects were consistently found among the winners from the mid-1970s onward. Coy Howard later elaborated on his method:

> The way you won *P/A* Awards is you would draw like you were a maniac. ...All these young people were obsessive, and they're just going to draw this thing and draw this thing and draw this thing. They're so totally passionate about architecture that [the jury] just *has* to give you an award.[11]

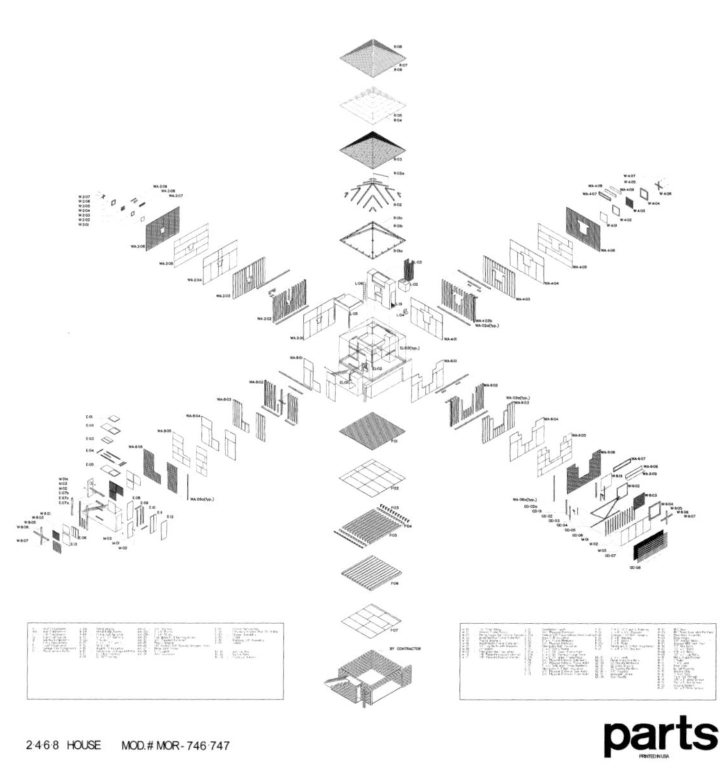

Fig. 6.2 Morphosis, 2-4-6-8 House (Los Angeles, 1978). Parts axonometric.

Fig. 6.3 Studio Works, South Side Settlement (Columbus, Ohio, 1975–80). Interior perspective.

As with the theoretical significance of their work, most of the architects downplayed the promotional aspects of their activities. Howard's recollections are typical: "everybody probably saw it differently. I didn't do [drawings] for the *P/A* Awards. I mean, I did them and then used them in the *P/A* Awards, but I didn't do them for the *P/A* Awards."[12] For Howard, as for all of the participating architects, architecture was much more than a career. It was a way of life.[13]

*

It is important to recognize that the Architecture Gallery did not occur in isolation. More symptom than cause, the events took place at a time when the city's architectural community had been working diligently to raise the level of public discourse and to make its activities known to broader national and global audiences. Through the 1970s, architectural exhibitions, lectures, and conferences occurred in Los Angeles with increasing frequency. And while many of these early efforts would not broach significant influence beyond the city limits, their increasing volume and sophistication brought important attention to highly original new work and would prove a crucial catalyst for the Architectural Gallery.

Events often were sponsored by one of the three new schools of architecture that recently had been launched as alternatives to established programs at the University of Southern California and Cal Poly San Luis Obispo. The UCLA School of Architecture and Urban Planning opened its doors in 1964 under the direction of founding dean Harvey Perloff, and from the start took a distinctly anti-orthodox tack. By the late 1960s, Archigram members Ron Herron, Warren Chalk, and Peter Cook were teaching in the program. In 1970, the school launched a master's degree program directed by Tim Vreeland. Formerly an associate with Louis Kahn in Philadelphia, Vreeland brought with him close ties to East Coast architectural personalities and debates. By the early '70s, he had recruited Kupper, Hodgetts, and Howard, a recent graduate of UCLA's planning program, as faculty members. Charles Jencks, at the time a rising star on the international scene, began making regular visits to the school in 1974.

In 1968, Ray Kappe was invited to lead an architecture program within the newly created School of Environmental Design at Cal Poly Pomona. A victim of his own success (the program grew from twenty-five to two hundred students in just three years), Kappe soon came into conflict with the dean over the size of the program.[14] In 1972, Kappe left Cal Poly with six of its faculty members and roughly fifty of its students. Twenty-five additional students joined the group and in September, The New School, officially the Southern California Institute of Architecture (SCI-Arc), was opened in a Santa Monica warehouse. In addition to founding faculty members Ray and Shelly Kappe, Ahde Lahti, Thom Mayne, Bill Simonian, Glen Small, and Jim Stafford, Architecture Gallery participants Eric Owen Moss, Roland Coate, and Frank Gehry were soon teaching at this unorthodox "school without a curriculum." Michael Rotondi, who would later assume the directorship of the school, was a member of the first graduating class in 1973 and joined the faculty the following year.[15]

These new institutions quickly amplified the volume of architectural discourse in Los Angeles. In 1973, SCI-Arc launched its Wednesday-night Design Forum lecture series, which drew local as well as national and international personalities from the outset.[16] The following year, UCLA convened an important conference designed specifically to insinuate a West Coast presence into ongoing East Coast debates. "Four Days in May," also known as "White and Gray Meet Silver," was conceived by Vreeland in collaboration with Hodgetts, Kupper, Anthony Lumsden, and Cesar Pelli. The group invited representatives of the well-known White vs. Gray debates, with the five Los Angeles architects acting as counterparts to the five core representatives of the opposed East Coast factions.[17] The Los Angeles participants, dubbed the Silvers,[18] did not present any work at the conference, which focused on the ideological and stylistic differences between the neo-modernist Whites and the postmodernist Grays. According to Hodgetts, the event "was more about putting UCLA on the map, I think, than trying to identify a group."[19] The Silvers put their own work center stage two years later when UCLA convened a sequel with "Four Days in April." Hodgetts did not participate, but the group swelled to six members for that presentation, adding Frank Dimster and Paul Kennon in his place.

Contrasting their White and Gray counterparts, who pursued highly formalized agendas through small private commissions, the Silvers directed their efforts primarily toward large-scale commercial projects. Major achievements, such as Pelli's Pacific Design Center [**Fig. 6.4**], Lumsden's Manufacturers Bank building, and Dimster's Houston Center tower, for example, each were completed under the auspices of large corporate firms (Gruen, DMJM, and Pereira, respectively) where each architect functioned as design director.[20] These and other projects were characterized by slick

Fig. 6.4 Cesar Pelli for Gruen Associates. Pacific Design Center (Los Angeles, 1975).

glass envelopes reminiscent of recent projects by Japanese architect Kisho Kurakawa as well as Norman Foster's groundbreaking corporate facilities for Willis Faber and Dumas and IBM. A vaguely English attitude was further signaled by Vreeland's invocation of the group's use of a pragmatic "style for the job," a catchphrase previously associated with the work of James Stirling in the 1960s.[21]

The Silvers' unapologetic commitment to the mainstream brought pointed criticism from invited respondents at the 1976 conference. Charles Jencks noted the ironies of what he labeled "silver-plated capitalism." Esther McCoy, Charles Moore, and David Gebhard each questioned the lack of regional specificity to the work, and John Hejduk worried that in the presented projects, "high technology is generally wrapped up in high romanticism, with the danger that it could lead to totalitarianism." Stirling, for his part, saw the work as little more than "chic packaging," to which Pelli demurred, "All of our projects are way below the level of people such as Stirling."[22]

Such criticism, as well as Pelli's feeble response, demonstrates the continued hegemony of orthodox values over architectural culture in the mid-1970s. Carefully tailored compositions of elements, sensitively knitted to their sites and inflected by a postwar suspicion of capitalism, remained the norm, and the radicalism of projects such as Pelli's Pacific Design Center, Lumsden's scheme for the Lugano Convention Center, or Kupper's UCLA Extension Building went unacknowledged. Yet in their abandonment of traditional part-to-whole coherence for ambiguously scaled figures and open-ended systems, these projects signaled far more aggressive moves away from orthodoxy than concurrent work by Stirling, the Grays, or even—Eisenman's and Hejduk's polemics notwithstanding—the Whites. Unfortunately, the Silvers would not continue to meet after the 1976 conference, their later corporate works failed to live up to the promise of early achievements, and the episode was soon largely forgotten. Nonetheless, the Silvers made a lasting impact on architectural discourse in Los Angeles by generating significant architectural debate—and whetting an appetite for further conversation—in a city that previously simply hadn't had any.[23]

The following month, another group of Los Angeles architects debuted in an exhibition at the Pacific Design Center. *Twelve Los Angeles Architects* was initiated by Bernard Zimmerman and organized by students at Cal Poly Pomona. The exhibition featured the work of established local practitioners Roland Coate Jr., Daniel Dworsky, Craig Ellwood, Frank Gehry, Ray Kappe, John Lautner, Jerrold Lomax, Tony Lumsden, Leroy Miller, Cesar Pelli, James Pulliam, and Zimmerman himself. Like the Silvers, the L.A. Twelve had been assembled as a local response to out-of-town groups (specifically the New York Five and the Chicago Seven), and its organizers saw in the Twelve a similar commitment to mainstream, as opposed to vanguard, practice.[24] With projects ranging from elegant Miesian assemblages by Ellwood to stripped down commercial facilities by Zimmerman and Lomax to exuberant residential projects by Kappe and Lautner, there was little formal or stylistic commonality across the group.[25] A series of twelve monthly lectures was staged at the Pacific Design Center in 1978, but the group had ceased to meet regularly the previous year.[26] Ultimately, like the Silvers before them, the L.A. Twelve never developed beyond a parochial phenomenon.[27] While many of the participating architects continued to produce significant projects (the bulk of them in an unapologetically orthodox idiom), their collective activities generated little of lasting influence.

Two additional exhibitions warrant specific mention. In January 1978, Otis College of Art and Design hosted *America Now: Drawing towards a More Modern Architecture*, a condensed re-presentation of exhibitions held at the Cooper Hewitt Museum and the Drawing Center in New York the previous year.[28] In a polemical catalog essay, curator Robert A. M. Stern argued that modernism had favored "polytechnicians" over poets and had dissipated the power and importance of drawing by, among other reasons, favoring conceptual axonometric projections over perceptual perspectival renderings. For Stern, the recent renewed interest in architectural drawing coincided with a waning adherence to the tenets of modernism and signaled a shift away from "the poverty of orthodox modern architecture" to a far richer postmodern poetry.[29]

Though Stern's critique was baldly tilted toward his own stylistic predilections, his belief that architects sought to advance beyond the strictures of orthodox modernism through drawing was widely shared. That same January, Coy Howard assembled a collection of drawings by local architects at the Los Angeles Institute of Contemporary Art. *Architectural Views: Physical Fact, Psychic Effect* featured works by Richard Aldriedge, Frederick Fisher, Eugene Kupper, Studio Works, and Howard himself that went well beyond the representation of buildings to mine the medium of drawing for untapped potential. Howard remembered his own motivations as follows:

> It basically grew out of [a feeling that] "I don't know if what I'm doing here is of any value, but let me test and see if I can come to understand what I'm trying to do architecturally in terms of the drawing." So, the drawings became this incredible vehicle...I would study them and study them and study them, and try to invent different techniques to try to discover the sensibility that I wanted in the buildings which I wasn't sure was there. So, doing those drawings was absolutely pivotal for me in developing my aesthetic.[30]

An array of techniques was on view at the exhibition. Studio Works hung a neat row of tiny, carefully mounted pen-and-ink sketches that clearly enumerated the functional and organizational elements of their scheme for Nicollet Island in Minneapolis. Across the room, a series of evocative collages of their South Side Settlement House, assembled in part from Mangurian's meticulous construction documents, offered little in the way of technical clarity but an abundance of emotional impact. Howard's work displayed a similar breadth of investigation. Two carefully inked images of his exhibition design for the 1976 Scythian Gold exhibition at LACMA contrasted an enormous and highly expressive perspective drawing of his Rinaldi House mounted directly

Fig. 6.5 Coy Howard, Rinaldi Residence (Los Angeles, 1978).

to the wall with long, dynamically arrayed strips of masking tape [**Fig. 6.5**].[31] Kupper hung a series of six axonometrics of his UCLA Extension project as well as ink and colored-pencil studies of his house for Harry Nilsson. Fisher's large-scale rendered site plan of his scheme for Machu Picchu also was fixed directly to the wall with tape, while Aldriedge's careful perspective drawings in ink and watercolor were fastidiously mounted. In each case, the work on the wall went far beyond the mere representation and planning of a future building to stand as self-sufficient works of architecture in their own right. Far more emphatically than previous presentations, the LAICA exhibition demonstrated the radical potential of alternative techniques being developed in Los Angeles.

By the late 1970s, such wide-ranging activity had begun to draw attention from local, national, and international audiences, with increasing interest going to younger practitioners. In addition to coverage in the *P/A* Awards, projects by Architecture Gallery participants such as Coate's Alexander House, Morphosis's Villas Florestas, and Moss's Morganstern warehouse received extended reviews.[32] Peter de Bretteville, Hodgetts, Mangurian, and Howard were included among the "Forty under Forty" list of significant young architects Robert A. M. Stern compiled for the Japanese journal *A+U* in 1977.[33] In 1978, *A+U* dedicated the bulk of its April issue to a survey of young Los Angeles architects assembled by Michael Franklin Ross.[34] As with previous group presentations, this collection was stylistically and programmatically diverse, held together by little more than a common desire to move beyond the International Style toward what Ross tentatively referred to as a "possibly-post-modern" interest in "indulgent complexity."[35] Unbuilt projects predominated, though recently completed buildings such as Helmut Schulitz's high-tech residence in Coldwater Canyon, Moss's Playa del Rey triplex, and Morphosis' small Delmer addition in Venice demonstrated the viability of alternative approaches. For Ross, the work represented "a restless desire to do something more, something special, something that isn't just another repetition of what has gone before, but in some small way expands the realm of possibilities for architecture and for the people who experience it."[36] This widely read presentation drew significant attention to the younger generation from outside Southern California, and, despite Ross's attempts to disprove any collective ambitions, established the notion of a coherent group of young Los Angeles architects in the minds of many observers in the city and beyond.

By the end of the decade new local journals such as *L.A. Architect*, the monthly newsletter of the AIA's Southern California Chapter, and *Archetype*, an independent effort launched by San Francisco-based architect Mark Mack, brought additional coverage, and provided important platforms from which to broadcast activities and ideas. But it was the writing of *Los Angeles Times* architecture critic John Dreyfuss that would prove particularly significant to the Architecture Gallery. Dreyfuss, the son of the noted industrial engineer Henry Dreyfuss, joined the *Times* in 1966 and became its architecture and design critic ten years later. Often critical of the city's downtown architectural establishment, he devoted significant attention to new projects by unorthodox Westsiders in the late 1970s.[37] Eric Moss remembers a "genuinely interested, genuinely supportive guy. ...he was open, and he was sympathetic, and he didn't come with an ideological perspective. As far as I could tell, he was just looking for ideas, looking for new stuff, looking for interesting characters."[38]

Dreyfuss took particular interest in the house Frank Gehry built for himself in Santa Monica in the summer of 1978 [**Fig. 6.6**], and in a long article in the *Times* carefully outlined the architect's unorthodox intentions and design process, the house's basic organization strategy, and described salient effects such as the perspectival illusions created by varied wall heights along the building's south façade.[39] Setting up his readers for a positive response, Dreyfuss also described a number of skeptical neighbors, including Santa Monica's mayor, who had been won over after visiting the house and learning

Fig. 6.6 Frank Gehry, Gehry House (Santa Monica, 1978).

of the architect's intentions firsthand. Dreyfuss's article was the first sustained treatment of Gehry's house in either the popular or professional press, but it was far from the last. The house was soon featured across the architectural literature and national newspapers, and even found its way into *People* magazine and a cover story on American architects in *Time*.[40]

Drawing inspiration from the work of local artists Charles Arnoldi and Ed Moses, among others, Gehry wrapped his unassuming Santa Monica house in a complex assemblage of glass, galvanized metal, unfinished plywood, and chain link. Inside, he stripped away finishes to reveal the bare studs and lath beneath. Formerly exterior surfaces were recast as unlikely interior elements, and typical interior spaces such as kitchen and dining were placed outside the original house, with an asphalt floor amplifying the ambiguities of the new enclosure. The house represented a bold departure from both modern and postmodern orthodoxies and marked a significant breakthrough in Gehry's development. With it, the architect established a line of exploration he would develop over the next decade.

Gehry also used the house to take aim at prevailing tendencies on the East Coast. In his lecture for the Architecture Gallery series, he joked that a model of the house made for a 1979 exhibition in New York was assembled with a deliberate lack of traditional craft with the express purpose of "upsetting the people in New York, who are very precise about architecture." He went on to articulate a more serious statement of his personal interests:

> There is a certain fascination with something not looking designed. I feel that a lot of buildings, a lot of architecture, a lot of work, has that "designed" look—that everything is in place. I am really trying to get away from that, to look more like it was less contrived. Now maybe, in fact, it ends up being more contrived, but I hope not.[41]

Gehry's taste for carefully careless, fragmentary compositions executed in straightforward vernacular materials would become a hallmark of Los Angeles architecture through the 1980s and '90s, leading many critics to see the architect as a trailblazer and father figure for the younger generation. In truth, the relationship was much more of a two-way street, and Gehry clearly drew off the energy of his younger colleagues.[42] But few would disagree that the house marked a spectacular achievement for Los Angeles architecture. With it, Gehry was launched into the international spotlight, and a parade of onlookers soon descended on Los Angeles's West Side for a closer look.

*

In the summer of 1978, a thirty-four-year-old Thom Mayne returned to Los Angeles after a year at Harvard. On the East Coast, Mayne had collected a graduate degree and "realigned" himself after a several years of deep involvement at SCI-Arc.[43] Michael Rotondi picked him up at LAX and drove straight to Frank Gehry's not-yet-completed house in Santa Monica. For Mayne, "It was just a startle, I'll never forget it. I had been in Boston and [it was] just dead. I was this L.A. kid...it was an enjoyable year, but there was just no way

I could possibly live in Boston. ...I really had a new appreciation for L.A. and the kind of freedom I had here."[44]

Rotondi and Mayne quickly set to work on two new projects, a garage renovation in Venice and a small single-family house in Tijuana. In contrast to the more stringent functionalism of earlier Morphosis projects such as the Sequoia School (which had begun as Rotondi's thesis at SCI-Arc) and the Stirlingesque Reidel Medical Building, the 2-4-6-8 and Mexico II houses were composed of centralized, symmetrical volumes capped by pyramidal roofs. 2-4-6-8's iconic progression of foursquare windows was articulated in bright yellow, blue, and red, with bands of pink concrete block running through the base. According to Rotondi, SCI-Arc director Ray Kappe was not pleased with their swerve away from more orthodox methodologies: "Kappe was really pissed off at us when we did that one because it had bright colors. He thought we were selling out to Aldo Rossi. ...Everybody was just trying things out. And Ray was Ray. He was a modernist, but with an open mind—but closed when he thought we were giving in to postmodernism."[45]

Kappe's paradoxical stance—open to change but committed to orthodox values—was a key catalyst for the Architecture Gallery. As younger faculty like Mayne, Rotondi, and Moss developed their positions, their architecture veered further from the status quo of Kappe's generation. By the late 1970s, a distinctly adversarial relationship had taken shape. As Mayne recalled,

> At that time...Bernard Zimmerman, Ray Kappe, and a group of could-have-been, wannabe Case Study guys...they owned the city. And we were going, "No, we don't buy it." We were going somewhere. It was very much part of the SCI-Arc dialogue. We used to have some fantastic, really robust conversations and disagreements about where we were going, about just what we stood for.[46]

For Mayne, the modernist project was exhausted. "The people I studied under, Pierre Koenig, et cetera, that was the end, that was the last group. ...[ours] was a group that was starting to redefine things."[47] Soon after Mayne's return to Los Angeles, an opportunity to publicly stake out alternative positions presented itself.

Ray and Shelly Kappe took a sabbatical during the 1978–79 school year and remained away through the summer. By the time they returned, Mayne had organized the fall's Design Forum lecture series. His recollection of exactly how the events came together is vague: "I can't remember. It was my turn, or they asked me to do the lecture series—we took turns doing that."[48] Kappe recalled something more calculated:

> I was on sabbatical when they put that thing together. ...I came back to kind of a surprise. ... I get back and Thom Mayne says to me, "We put together a program with guys who are doing architecture." He names the people and I said, "I do architecture, why aren't I on the list?" So, it was a set-up. It was a time when both Eric [Moss] and Thom were just starting to move to a new place."[49]

That new place had little room for members of Kappe's generation. For the lectures, Mayne chose younger practitioners with the exception of Gehry, whose radical new projects aligned him more with Mayne's generation than his own, and Coate, with whom Mayne had collaborated in the early 1970s. Most were teaching at either SCI-Arc or UCLA, with Dimster and De Bretteville representing USC. Mayne drew participants from both the Silvers (Kupper, Dimster) and the L.A. Twelve (Gehry, Coate), choosing the most idiosyncratic characters from each previous group. The series' title, "Current L.A.: 10 Viewpoints," foregrounded the individualistic nature of each practice over any notions of shared methodology. An exhibition to accompany each of the nine lectures was soon added to the agenda, with Mayne's sparsely furnished home and studio in Venice serving as the venue. Coy Howard, who would not exhibit his work, was slated to give two lectures bookending the series. Each of the SCI-Arc lectures was videotaped and screened on a small black-and-white monitor in the gallery.[50]

By any metric, it was a heterogeneous assemblage, and, despite its lack of approval from SCI-Arc's director, it seemed to align with the school's experimental mandate. Moss later characterized it as a natural development of SCI-Arc's unorthodox pedagogy—and the failure of its founders to fully deliver on its initial promise:

> If you set something up as a departure and then try to teach something that was no departure at all...the opportunity for departure manifests itself. I would say, in retrospect, that these shows would be a manifestation. The train had left the station, you know? First you made the station, and then you made the train, and then, finally, it took off.[51]

Howard delivered his opening talk—equal parts criticism of the establishment and poetic meditation of the nature of beauty—on 3 October. Kupper's exhibition opened the following Tuesday. The next morning, two articles by John Dreyfuss appeared in the *Los Angeles Times*. The first outlined the series of exhibitions as a whole; the second offered a specific treatment of Kupper's installation.[52]

How Dreyfuss came to write about the shows is unclear. Mayne recalls the journalist contacting him with a request to see Kupper's exhibition, and then insisting, against Mayne's initial disagreement, that he produce weekly reviews of remaining shows.[53] Rotondi, who worked closely with Mayne to organize the events, remembers a discussion "to see if we could get Dreyfuss to write about [the shows], which he did."[54] Regardless of the motivating circumstances, Dreyfuss's contribution was crucial. With illustrations by *Times* photographer Mary Frampton and others, the reviews certainly were responsible for the steadily increasing—and largely non-professional—traffic in the gallery as the weeks progressed.[55] The articles also changed the tenor of disciplinary conversation in Los Angeles. For the participating architects, they afforded a heightened sense of significance to their ongoing experiments. For the city's architectural establishment—many of whom had close ties with the paper's owners—the attention, which meant a corresponding lack of coverage for their own output, was cause for concern. Dreyfuss soon found himself in conflict with the paper's editors, and after 1983 architectural reviews in the paper would be taken over by Sam Hall Kaplan, a critic who did not share Dreyfuss's sympathy for the younger generation.

Nonetheless, the buzz generated by the exhibitions would continue unabated into the 1980s. As Dreyfuss put it, they "catalyzed a significant segment of the Los Angeles architectural community, precipitating a steamy brew of respect, anger, pride, jealousy, excitement, and interest."[56] Dreyfuss's concluding article, which appears to respond directly to criticism he received from establishment architects, outlined an accurate prediction of developments in Los Angeles architecture through the 1980s. As architects in the exhibition—particularly Gehry, Moss, and Morphosis—rose in significance, many established practitioners indeed were "left by the wayside in terms of being movers and shakers in their profession."[57] With the Architecture Gallery, the youngsters emphatically put the city's graying establishment on notice, and their "obscure, theatrical, and trendy" output would soon become synonymous with cutting-edge architecture in Los Angeles.[58]

NOTES

1. The theologian Heinrich Schlier outlines "the *hairesis* of the philosopher, which in antiquity always includes the choice of a distinct *bios* [way of life]" in Gerhard Kittels, ed., *Theological Dictionary of the New Testament*, vol. 1 (London: Eerdmans, 1964): 180–82. For more developed discussions of heresy's relationship to the construction of the self, see *Heresy and Identity in Late Antiquity*, eds. Eduard Iricinschi and Holger M. Zellentin (Tübingen: Mohr Siebeck, 2008). On the concept's relationship to modernity, see Peter Gay, *Modernism: The Lure of Heresy from Beckett to Baudelaire and Beyond* (New York: W.W. Norton, 2008).
2. There were several attempts to bring together these and other Los Angeles architects under a single banner in the late 1970s and early '80s. Charles Jencks claims the label "L.A. School" was invented by a group of architects that convened a series of meetings at the Biltmore Hotel in 1981. See his "LA Style / LA School," *AA Files* 5 (1983): 90. In *Heteropolis: Los Angeles, the Riots, and the Strange Beauty of Hetero-architecture* (London: Academy Editions, 1993): 132, n. 9, he lists the group's instigators as George Rand, Gene Summers, and himself, and participating architects as Roland Coate, Peter de Bretteville, Frank Gehry, Craig Hodgetts, Coy Howard, Eugene Kupper, Tony Lumsden, Thom Mayne, Robert Mangurian, Charles Moore, Cesar Pelli, Stefanos Polyzoides, Michael Rotondi, Tim Vreeland, and Buzz Yudell.
3. The twenty years preceding the Architecture Gallery saw the deaths of Frank Lloyd Wright (1959), Le Corbusier (1965), Mies van der Rohe (1969), Walter Gropius (1969), Louis Kahn (1974), and Alvar Aalto (1976). Los Angeles also lost a large share of notable personalities, including A. C. Martin (1960), Welton Becket (1969), Richard Neutra (1970), Lloyd Wright (1978), Charles Eames (1978), and A. Quincy Jones (1979).
4. Among the most influential of these attacks is Jacques Derrida's essay, "Structure, Sign, and Play in the Discourse of the Human Sciences," delivered as a lecture at Johns Hopkins University in 1966 and translated into English in Derrida, *Writing and Difference* (Chicago: University of Chicago Press, 1978): 278–93.
5. Damaging critiques include Jane Jacobs's *The Death and Life of American Cities* (New York: Random House, 1961) and Manfredo Tafuri's "Toward a Critique of Architectural Ideology" [1969], in *Architecture Theory since 1968*, ed. K. Michael Hays (Cambridge: MIT Press, 1998): 6–35.
6. See *Archigram*, ed. Peter Cook (London: The Architectural Press, 1973), which collects much of the material published in the group's eponymous pamphlet from 1961–70; Aldo Rossi, *The Architecture of the City* [1966](New York: MIT Press, 1982); Venturi, *Complexity and Contradiction in Architecture* (New York: Museum of Modern Art, 1966); Venturi, Scott Brown, and Steven Izenour, *Learning from Las Vegas* (Cambridge: MIT Press, 1972); Baird, "'La Dimension Amoureuse' in Architecture," in *Meaning in Architecture*, eds. Baird and Jencks (New York: George Braziller, 1969); Jencks, *The Language of Post-Modern Architecture* (New York: Rizzoli, 1977); Maurice Culot and Krier, "The Only Path for Architecture," *Oppositions* 14 (Fall 1978); Rowe and Koetter, *Collage City* (Cambridge: MIT Press, 1978); Eisenman, "Aspects of Modernism: Maison Dom-ino and the Self-Referential Sign," *Oppositions* 15/16 (Winter/Spring 1979); Libeskind, "'*Deus ex Machina*'/'*Machina ex Deo*': Aldo Rossi's Theater of the World," *Oppositions* 21 (Summer 1980); and Tschumi, "The Architectural Paradox," *Studio International* (Sept–Oct 1975).
7. Carey McWilliams's classic study, *Southern California: An Island on the Land* [1946] (Salt Lake City: Gibbs Smith, 2010), provides an excellent account of such activities throughout the city's history. I offer my own musings about the peripheral nature of Los Angeles architecture in "Downtown" [2007]

reprinted in *LA Forum Reader*, eds. Rob Berry, Victor Jones, Michael Sweeney, Mimi Zeiger, and Chava Danielson, Joe Day, Thurman Grant, Duane McLemore (New York: Actar, 2018): 176–78.

8. Eric Owen Moss, 5 December 1979. "*Eric Owen Moss: Armageddon or Polynesian Contextualism, Part One.*" SCI-Arc Media Archive. Southern California Institute of Architecture.
9. Ray Kappe, interview with the author. Los Angeles, 29 June 2012.
10. Personal interviews with the author, Summer 2012.
11. Coy Howard, interview with the author and Ewan Branda. Los Angeles, 16 May 2012.
12. Ibid.
13. Importantly, that way of life was widely understood to be specifically architectural. Though Howard and Frank Gehry both maintained close ties with and drew significant inspiration from the Los Angeles art scene, these and other participating architects ultimately maintained clear disciplinary boundaries between art and architecture. Eugene Kupper and Roland Coate, for example, were and remain avid painters, but they operated for the most part independently of the Los Angeles arts community. While both attempted early on to use the medium to inform their architectural ambitions, each ultimately saw painting as a distinct alternative to architectural practice. Coate, in the end, chose painting, and closed his architectural practice in 1983 to devote himself to painting full-time. Kupper chose architecture, and largely suspended painting through the 1970s and early '80s.
14. Kappe had wished to cap enrollment at 250, but the dean, while Kappe was away, decided to increase to 350 students. Ray Kappe, "SCI-Arc History," unpublished manuscript, collection of the author.
15. Architecture Gallery participants Robert Mangurian, Coy Howard, Craig Hodgetts, and Frederick Fisher also had joined the faculty at SCI-Arc by the early 1980s.
16. In addition, Shelly Kappe hosted regular panel discussions at the school through the 1970s on topics ranging from "women in architecture" to "the role of the large office" to the "construction industry gap." More speculative topics, such as "Alternative Architectural Practices" and "Which Way to the Future?" also were featured. SCI-Arc video-taped the lectures from an early date and the collection recently has been digitized and made available online. See the SCI-Arc Media Archive, https://www.youtube.com/sciarcmediaarchive.
17. The White position was held by the "New York Five" (Peter Eisenman, Michael Graves, Charles Gwathmey, John Hejduk, and Richard Meier) and was galvanized in the influential publication, *Five Architects* (New York: Oxford University Press, 1972). A collection of critical responses to this work from five "Grays," Allan Greenberg, Romaldo Giurgola, Charles Moore, Jacquelin Robertson, and Robert Stern, appeared in "Five on Five," *Architectural Forum* (May 1973): 46–57. Participants at UCLA included Werner Seligmann, Michael Graves, Peter Eisenman, Charles Moore, Richard Meier, Robert A. M. Stern, Giovanni Pasanella, T. Merrill Prentice, Charles Gwathmey, Richard Weinstein, and Jaquelin Robertson, with Colin Rowe (White) and Vincent Scully (Gray) each giving lectures. The event was reviewed in "White, Gray, Silver, Crimson," *Progressive Architecture* (July 1974): 28, 30, 32. A year later, the Japanese magazine *A+U* devoted an entire issue to the White vs. Gray phenomenon. See "White and Gray: Eleven Modern Architects," *Architecture + Urbanism* (April 1975). Coy Howard was commissioned to make a film of the event, but at the time of this writing, a copy has not been located.
18. Most accounts claim the name had to do with the slick, glass-and-steel aesthetic espoused by most of the group. According to Charles Jencks, the moniker also had to do with the fact the each of the architects drove a silver BMW. (Charles Jencks, telephone interview with the author, Los Angeles and London, 30 May 2012.) Hodgetts contested this assertion in a later interview with the author.
19. Craig Hodgetts, interview with the author. Los Angeles, 5 Mar 2012.

20. Eugene Kupper, who ran a small private practice, stands as a significant exception to the corporate character of the Silvers. Frank Dimster left Pereira to set up his own small practice in 1975.
21. See Reyner Banham, "The Style for the Job," *New Statesman* (14 Feb 1964): 261.
22. These quotations, and Vreeland's above, are from Peter Papademetriou, "Images from a Silver Screen," *Progressive Architecture* (Oct 1976): 70–77. Stirling had given a keynote lecture to kick off the April events at UCLA.
23. Cf. Jencks "The Los Angeles Silvers: Tim Vreeland, Anthony Lumsden, Frank Dimster, Eugene Kupper, Cesar Pelli, Paul Kennon," *Architecture and Urbanism* 70 (Oct 1976): 14. Hodgetts offered a similar assessment in a 2012 interview with the author.
24. "They might be said to exemplify the highest ideals of the architectural mainstream. Their crusade... is to illustrate their conviction that the profession of architecture can without overthrowing its traditional values successfully serve the interests of the marketplace." Nicholas Pyle, "Foreword," in *Twelve Los Angeles Architects*, eds. N. Charles Slert and James Harter (Pomona: Cal Poly Pomona, 1978): vi.
25. The catalog accounted for this by dividing the architects into four categories: The Expressionalists (Coate, Lumsden, and Pelli), the Constructionalists (Ellwood and Kappe), the Rationalists (Dworsky, Lomax, Miller, Pulliam, and Zimmerman), and the Experimentalists (Gehry and Lautner). See Slert and Harter, *Twelve Los Angeles Architects.*
26. This inaction drew harsh criticism from *Los Angeles Times* critic John Dreyfuss. See his "Comment," in Slert and Harter, *Twelve Los Angeles Architects*, iii–iv.
27. "And Then There Were Twelve...The Los Angeles 12," *Architectural Record* (Aug 1976), appears to be the lone national publication on the group.
28. The exhibitions, curated by Robert A. M. Stern (at the Drawing Center) and Richard Oliver (at the Cooper-Hewitt) showcased a diversity of work by Charles Moore, Stanley Tigerman, Michael Graves, Robert Venturi, John Hejduk, Peter Eisenman, Coy Howard, and Franklin Israel, among others.
29. See Robert A. M. Stern, ed., "America Now: Drawing towards a More Modern Architecture," *A.D. Profiles* 6 (June 1977): 383. Local critics held similar views. The following year, Anne Luise Buerger remarked, "When the Modern Movement appeared as corporate architecture in the United States, architectural drawing suffered the consequences of a corporate specialization that too often combined division of labor with division of spirit." See "Art and Architecture: Drawing them Together," *L.A. Architect* (Feb 1978): np.
30. Coy Howard, interview with the author and Ewan Branda. Los Angeles, 16 May 2012. In a small publication on the show, other participants offered their own observations on drawing. Fisher: "Drawing serves the two aspects of design: analysis and synthesis. It facilitates dissection of a building in abstract or real terms, and replicates the selective focus of thoughtful perception." Kupper: "Architectural drawings can serve the direct purpose of technical communication, but they can also be an expression of architectural theory. Architecture is a potential of the creative spirit, not another name for real estate or construction." Aldriedge: "With my drawings I am trying to catch a glance of the moods, emotions, and ancient memories that may exist behind the architecture." Hodgetts and Mangurian, with tongues firmly planted in cheeks, flatly state, "Drawings are a minor part of our process." See "Architectural Views: Physical Fact, Psychic Effect," *L.A. Architect* (Feb 1978): np.
31. Curved polycarbonate panels that lay strewn on the floor beneath the image were in fact a framework which could be assembled into a cylinder. The drawing—a 360-degree view of the interior of the house—could be mounted inside the cylinder to afford a viewer willing to climb inside an immersive, kinesthetic preview of the proposed space.

32. See Thomas Hines, "Coate," *Progressive Architecture* (Aug 1976): 58–61; Esther McCoy, "Everyman's Casa," *Progressive Architecture* (July 1978): 76–79; and David Morton, "Look Again: Morganstern Warehouse," *Progressive Architecture* (Jun 1979): 66–69.
33. See Stern, "40 under 40," *Architecture and Urbanism* 73 (Jan 1977): 17–142. The issue also included a synopsis of recent architectural activities in Los Angeles. See Panos Koulermos, "Los Angeles," ibid., 11–12.
34. See Michael Franklin Ross, "Young, Los Angeles and Possibly-Post-Modern, Architects," *Architecture and Urbanism* 90 (April 1978): 83–154. The represented practices were Chris Dawson & David Brindle, Ronald Filson, Arthur Golding, Coy Howard, Charles Lagreco, Douglas Meyer, Morphosis, Eric Owen Moss & James Stafford, James Porter, Michael Franklin Ross, and Helmut Schulitz.
35. Ibid., 84.
36. Ibid., 85.
37. Cf. "Job Center Does its Job—and Architecture Excels," *Los Angeles Times* (23 Jan 1977), on Gehry's UCLA Placement and Career Planning Center; "Pavilion: Crater with a Stage at Bottom," *Los Angeles Times* (15 May 1977), on Gehry's Concord Pavilion; and "An Unlikely Dash of Exuberance," *Los Angeles Times* (22 Oct 1978), on Moss's Morganstern Warehouse. Dreyfuss's reviewed both Stern's Otis exhibition and Howard's LAICA exhibition in "Architects: Insights into the Sketches," *Los Angeles Times* (30 Jan 1978): E1, E5.
38. Eric Owen Moss, interview with the author, Ewan Branda, and Andrew Zago. Culver City, CA, 7 Jun 2012.
39. Dreyfuss, "Gehry's Artful House Offends, Baffles, Angers his Neighbors," *Los Angeles Times* (23 July 1978).
40. See Sally Koris, "Renegade Frank Gehry Has Torn Up His House—and the Book of Architecture," *People* (5 Mar 1979) and Robert Hughes, "Doing Their Own Thing," *Time* (8 Jan 1979).
41. Frank O. Gehry, 7 November 1979. "Frank O Gehry Part One." SCI-Arc Media Archive.
42. Coy Howard saw in Gehry's occasional invitations to younger architects to meet for discussions at his studio deliberate attempts by the older architect to insinuate himself into ongoing conversations among the younger generation. Howard's reaction to the oft-uttered label, "the Gehry kids," was unequivocal: "It's the other way around. Gehry's our kid, in actual fact." Coy Howard, interview with the author and Ewan Branda. Los Angeles, 16 May 2012.
43. As Mayne had been involved in running the graduate program at SCI-Arc but did not hold a master's degree himself, the school granted him a sabbatical to attend the program at Harvard.
44. Thom Mayne, interview with the author. Culver City, CA, 14 July 2012.
45. Michael Rotondi, interview with the author and Ewan Branda. Los Angeles, 13 Jun 2012.
46. Thom Mayne, interview with the author and Ewan Branda. Culver City, CA, 5 Mar 2012.
47. Ibid.
48. Thom Mayne, interview with the author and Ewan Branda. Culver City, CA, 14 July 2012.
49. Ray Kappe, interview with the author. Los Angeles, 29 Jun 2012. Shelly Kappe was incensed by Mayne's move, and in a 2012 conversation with the author insisted that the exhibitions were a renegade action that should not be considered official SCI-Arc events.
50. Nearly all the lectures are now available online at the SCI-Arc Media Archive. At the time of writing, only Coate's lecture and Howard's concluding talk have not been located.
51. Eric Owen Moss, interview with the author, Ewan Branda, and Andrew Zago. Culver City, CA, 7 June 2012.
52. See "One-Week Shows by 11 Architects" and "Kupper Employs Dual Process," *Los Angeles Times* (11 Oct 1979): C25, 26, 28.

53 Thom Mayne, interview with the author. Culver City, CA, 5 Mar 2012.

54. Michael Rotondi, interview with the author and Ewan Branda. Los Angeles, 13 June 2012.

55. According to Mayne, the comedian and art patron Steve Martin dutifully checked out the new offerings every Saturday. Martin would later purchase Coate's Alexander House in Montecito. Thom Mayne, interview with the author and Ewan Branda. Culver City, 14 July 2012.

56. Dreyfuss, "Gallery Stirs Up Architects," *Los Angeles Times* (12 Dec 1979): E26.

57. Ibid.

58. Howard offered this description to Dreyfuss in a 1979 interview. Ibid.

Pragmatic Radicalism, Aesthetic Bliss, and other L.A. Stories

2014

Fig. 7.1 *A New Scuplturalism*. Museum of Contemporary Art, Los Angeles, 2013. General view.

Last June, two weeks late and amid a welter of controversy, an exhibition ostensibly titled *A New Sculpturalism: Contemporary Architecture from Southern California* opened at the Museum of Contemporary Art's (MOCA) Geffen Contemporary gallery in Los Angeles. Part of Pacific Standard Time Presents: Modern Architecture in L.A., a series of exhibitions and related events sponsored by the Getty,[1] *A New Sculpturalism* focused on built work by Los Angeles architects from the last twenty-five years, and was nearly unraveled by an embarrassing tussle between a faltering institution wishing to appeal to the general public and a skittish architectural community desperate for rigorous critical attention. In the end, the exhibition offered disappointingly little to its constituencies. MOCA publicly rehearsed its familiar pattern of dysfunction, the exhibition-going public received eye candy where it could have found edification, and the participating architects missed out on opportunities to productively assess their recent past and to nurture new audiences for the immediate future.

A MUDDLE AT MOCA

When the Pacific Standard Time Presents lineup was first announced in September 2012, *A New Sculpturalism* appeared poised to answer the Getty Research Institute's sweeping historical overview, *Overdrive: L.A. Constructs the Future, 1940–1990,* with an emphatically contemporary conclusion.[2] MOCA received the largest grant from the Getty Foundation ($445,000) and scheduled the latest opening date (2 June) of the eleven exhibitions.[3] Press materials promised "the first scholarly and extensive examination of the prolific and often radical built forms that characterize buildings designed in Southern California during the last twenty-five years" and to showcase "emerging and younger talent" with a collection of pavilions designed by "less established firms in L.A."[4] Having jettisoned its curator of architecture and design in 2009, the museum tapped Christopher Mount, a former curator at the Museum of Modern Art in New York and former executive director of the Pasadena Museum of California Art. The announcement was a welcome respite from the controversies that had plagued MOCA in recent years,[5] and seemed to signal that the embattled institution had set a new curatorial course.

Unfortunately, that optimism was short-lived. Just a month ahead of the scheduled opening, following weeks of lurid gossip in the architectural community, the *Los Angeles Times* confirmed that Frank Gehry had pulled out of the show, citing discomfort with its "trivialization" of his work.[6] The same article recounted Mount's fears that, owing to budgetary concerns, the entire exhibition would be canceled. Rampant speculation ensued: the show was off, then it was back on, but without Mount. The scope and venue would change. Thom Mayne had stepped in to curate. Neither MOCA nor the Getty could be reached for comment.

The rumor mill churned unceasingly. Even participants in the exhibition were unsure what would happen. Given MOCA's recent troubles, the collapse of not just the show but also the entire institution seemed within the realm of possibility. Nonetheless, there appeared to be ongoing activity related to the exhibition at Morphosis, SCI-Arc, and at least some of the offices that had been commissioned to build pavilions for the show. Anticipation—if not always for the exhibition, then at least for the next tawdry detail—swelled.

The day before *A New Sculpturalism* was due to open, the *Los Angeles Times* assured its readers that the show was on and Gehry was back in, having been "coaxed by Thom Mayne," who claimed to be acting not as a curator but as some sort of "facilitator." The article confirmed that MOCA would remain the venue and Mount the curator, despite Gehry's quoted explanation that he had returned only because Mount had been replaced (at Gehry's request) by Mayne.[7]

Confusion was amplified when the exhibition finally opened two weeks later. On the title banner outside the Gehry-designed Geffen Contemporary, the show's original title had been scratched out and replaced with "Contemporary Californian Architects." Inside, the gallery wall offered a third option: "Contemporary Architecture Comes from Southern California." Further muddling the situation, the wall text assigned only the "original concept" to Mount. Installation and production were credited to Stray Dog Café, with Anne Marie Burke listed as the project manager. No mention was made of any involvement by Mayne, but those in the know recognized Stray Dog Café as the obfuscating label on the facade of the Morphosis studio back in the 1980s, and were familiar with Burke's long tenure as Morphosis's communications director.

The exhibition's installation was equally puzzling. Despite being housed in the cavernous side gallery at the Geffen, it felt strangely insignificant. To access the space, visitors had to tiptoe through a field of several thousand crumbling clay figures installed in the main gallery by Swiss artist Urs Fischer.[8] Beyond this unceremonious vestibule, visitors were greeted by three pavilions—by Tom Wiscombe Design, PATTERNS, and Atelier Manferdini—before being deflected into a vast collection of often poorly lit models and drawings. The show included a broad sampling of internationally recognized names, including Eric Owen Moss and Neil Denari, lesser-known local firms such as Brooks + Scarpa, and "younger" practices such as Griffin Enright and Predock Frane. A large model of Morphosis's Phare Tower proposal for Paris loomed near the center of the space, part of a wide selection of the firm's earlier projects on display throughout the room. Dashed lines painted on the floor loosely divided exhibited projects into oddly conventional programmatic categories.[9] Projected images of buildings flashed on curved panels overhead, while a recording of commentary by the exhibiting architects echoed throughout the space. Gehry's contribution—a suite of presentation materials from his second-place scheme for the National Museum of China competition—was detached from the side gallery altogether. To find it, visitors had to leave the space and again negotiate Fischer's clay-figure labyrinth.

Following several conflicting accounts of Mayne's involvement, it became clear that Mount remained curator in name only, and that Mayne's team had reimagined the installation from scratch. Though Mount's initial selection of firms remained almost unchanged, his intent to include only built projects was abandoned and the focus of the exhibition shifted toward drawings and models.[10] Mayne's intervention certainly improved the largely superficial affair that MOCA appeared poised to deliver, but the failure to clarify Mount's casual sampling of firms and, worse, to offer a substantive alternative to his concept of "sculpturalism," left many of the show's initial shortcomings glaringly intact.

Naturally, the critics pounced. *Los Angeles Times* architecture critic Christopher Hawthorne derided Mount's notion of sculpturalism as "supremely narrow...singling out form and aesthetics at the expense of all the other ways that buildings are made and operate in contemporary Los Angeles." True to his dependably negative stance toward Mayne, Hawthorne also attacked the installation's banal organization and leveled accusations of insularity, not just at Mayne, but at the entire "architectural ruling class in Los Angeles." The show, he intoned, was "unapologetically a celebration of white-male architecture, floating in a bubble of its own making, hardly pausing even to glance in the direction of contemporary Los Angeles and its cultural complexity."[11]

Some of Hawthorne's indictments rang true. Sculpturalism is, no doubt, a crude and clumsy concept. It adds very little to a discussion of Los Angeles's vibrant tradition of formal, material, and tectonic innovation, and instead brands the manic diversity of the city's architectural output over the last three decades with a single, woefully inadequate slogan. Mount was rightly, if inelegantly, taken to task for it by the architects. Hawthorne was also right in pointing out that Los Angeles's predominately white, predominately male, architectural community has been inattentive to its historically homogeneous and privileged demographics. But it is unwise to imply that overt references to topics such as race and gender (or "ecology" and "public interest design") are necessary components of an architectural exhibition, and downright foolhardy to understand the show's "insular" architecture as somehow divorced from Los Angeles's "cultural complexity." Hawthorne is too attentive a student of the city's (and, one hopes, architecture's) long history of productively private cliques to be permitted such a lazy assertion.

As the impact of the so-called "L.A. School" and countless other groups here and elsewhere attests, small, self-contained communities of formally obsessive architects have a far better track record of producing lasting political and cultural effects than even the most earnestly "engaged" practitioners. The error of *A New Sculpturalism* was not an excess of aesthetics and insularity, but rather an inadequate assessment of just how aesthetically diverse and tribal Los Angeles architecture has become.

RADICALISM REDUX

By the end of the 1980s, the bad-boy iconoclasm conjured a decade earlier by Gehry, Mayne, Moss, and other L.A. offices had matured into a formidable, and for some, even profitable, mode of professional practice. As offices grew and young assistants craved independence, a generation of fledgling practices was spawned. In 1991, the newly formed Los Angeles Forum for Architecture and Urban Design assembled a broad cross-section of these new firms in its first major publication, *Experimental Architecture in Los Angeles.*[12] Some in the collection, including Josh Schweitzer (ex-Gehry) and Michele Saee (ex-Morphosis), delivered idiosyncratic single-family houses and bespoke restaurant interiors to L.A.'s Westside in the familiar idioms of their mentors. Others, such as Victoria Casasco, dabbled in overtly postmodernist themes, while Charles and Elizabeth Lee returned to a more orthodox, modernist idiom. A few, including Neil Denari, the Central Office of Architecture, and AKS Runo, devoted significant energy to ambitious speculative projects and painstaking drawings and models, which projected the more visionary aspects of the previous generation into bold new territory.

Alongside this proliferation of stylistic and tectonic diversity, a significant number of Los Angeles architects turned their attention toward the city's urban fabric and the unique structures of public and private life it engendered. In 1999, John Chase, Margaret Crawford, and John Kaliski released *Everyday Urbanism,* also through the L.A. Forum.[13] The everyday urbanists paid particular attention to low-income neighborhoods such as Watts and East L.A., and favored vibrant street life, ethnic and economic diversity, and do-it-yourself initiatives over the automobile-centered and developer-driven affluence that underpinned many of the Westside experimentalists. Complementing these urban initiatives was an unabashed enthusiasm for Los Angeles's peculiar, anonymous architecture. Chase's 2000 anthology, *Glitter Stucco and Dumpster Diving,* is perhaps the most serious attempt to plumb L.A.'s quirky vernacular underbelly, offering an important treatment of the midcentury "dingbat," the city's pervasive stucco-box-on-stilts apartment typology that has served as an organizational template and ideological scapegoat for L.A. architects since the 1950s.[14]

Through the 1990s, these varied strains of L.A. architecture were producing new work at a rapid pace. Concurrently, the Westside client base of artists, entrepreneurs, and post-'68 hooligans that the older architects had seduced through the 1970s and '80s had given way to a well-heeled creative class eager to stake a claim (and often, to turn a fast buck) in the now trendy enclaves of Venice, Santa Monica, and Silver Lake. Intoxicated by skyrocketing real-estate values, a generation of amateur speculators and unimaginative copycats set to work converting hard-won disciplinary achievements into viable commercial products. A particularly effective tactic hybridized the full-custom idiosyncrasy of the experimental residence with the vulgar efficiency of the everyday dingbat. Eames chairs, Nelson lamps, and fashionable couples were arranged and photographed in white-walled and alarmingly interchangeable interiors throughout the formerly grungy neighborhoods that had sustained the eccentricities of the earlier generation. By the end of the decade, a huge swath of Los Angeles had been made over, recast as a homogeneous, high-dollar, postradical *Dwell*-scape.

With potent lines of development thus largely exhausted of disciplinary interest, many L.A. architects turned their attention to more unconventional approaches. Greg Lynn's arrival in the mid-1990s brought intensive digital design and fabrication research and an expansive catalog of novel forms and materials, while Gehry's experiments with CATIA software demonstrated how unprecedented formal complexity could be deployed in commercial practice. Equipped with this formidable computational arsenal, Gehry's work began to shift from the figural aggregations he explored through the early 1980s—for example, the California Aerospace Museum near downtown and the Schnabel House in Brentwood—toward the more voluptuous, curvilinear forms of the Team Disney Building in Anaheim and the Disney Concert Hall. Moss and Morphosis also changed course through the '90s, with the manic articulation of the former's Gary Group Building and the latter's Crawford House giving way to a more gestural abstraction apparent in Moss's Stealth Building in Culver City and Morphosis's Diamond Ranch High School.

At the turn of the millennium, another cabal of young architects began to come into its own. Freshly graduated from progressive programs at Columbia and UCLA, thirty-something practitioners such as Hernán Díaz Alonso, Jason Payne, and others espoused few of L.A.'s familiar mannerisms and instead adopted more intellectualized, East Coast concerns that traced their aesthetic and ideological roots largely through Greg Lynn to Peter Eisenman. Steeped in digital production and fabrication techniques, their working methods quickly displaced the painstaking handicraft espoused by older architects, and the mechanistic, ad hoc assemblages of the late twentieth century gave way to smooth, shiny, and increasingly cornerless compositions developed in the virtual space of 3D modeling and animation software.

A TALE OF (AT LEAST) TWO CITIES

All of these strands of development (if not all of these architects) were represented in *A New Sculpturalism,* and any number of frameworks might have been deployed to elucidate them. Unfortunately, the exhibition elided significant differences in favor of portraying Los Angeles architects as one big, happy family. This genealogical ambition was reinforced by the "Professional Timeline" published in the exhibition catalog, which tracks the emergence of new firms from older ones in a disciplinary family tree.[15] This diagram is particularly revealing when compared to the revised version prepared for the gallery guides. The original—multicolored and somewhat difficult to decipher—attempts to illustrate the complex, overlapping trajectories through which many L.A. practices developed. The revised version is much clearer, but in pruning Mount's original tree, it reduces the complex lineage of each practice to a single source. The revised version also highlights five firms (Gehry Partners, Morphosis Architects, Eric Owen Moss Architects, Hodgetts + Fung, and Greg Lynn Form) as apparently more significant than the others, but offers no insight as to why that might be the case. Stranger still, well-known developments such as Craig Hodgetts's exit from Studio Works in 1983 and Michael Rotondi's from Morphosis in 1991 pass unacknowledged. The agenda, as with the exhibition itself, seems to be one of tidy, if inaccurate, simplification.

Problematic though they may be, the timelines could have offered a framework with which to engage the exhibited work. Arranged more strategically, the exhibition could have illustrated how the various master/protégé relationships introduced by the timelines played out. Unfortunately, the typologically organized installation largely canceled the possibility of such comparisons, and ultimately favored passive consumption over engaged scrutiny.

Despite the overriding impression of continuity advanced by *A New Sculpturalism,* few could miss the anomalous note struck by Lynn's work at the far end of the hall [**Fig. 7.2**]. The playful, brightly colored plastic of his Blob Wall and Toy Furniture contrasted with the slick, predominantly monochrome models elsewhere in the exhibition, while the mirrored surface of Lynn's Sociópolis Housing Block answered the show's overarching tone of self-seriousness with the twinkling insouciance of costume jewelry. Three medusoid Numinous Lamps floated overhead to complete the scene. Where much of the work in the exhibition pointed deferentially to previous generations, Lynn's stood irreverently independent, pointing forward to an alternative L.A. agenda that is just now coming into focus.

Fig. 7.2 *A New Sculpturalism*. Museum of Contemporary Art, Los Angeles, 2013. Installation of projects by Greg Lynn Form.

Further hints of what this agenda might hold were provided by the three pavilions at the opposite end of the hall. Tom Wiscombe's untitled scheme explored his interest in both the tectonics of composite materials and the spatial effects of complex volumes and surfaces [**Fig. 7.3**]. Three impossibly thin black panels, constructed of a water-based polymer with carbon- and glass-fiber reinforcing, leaned toward each other to form a loose pyramid. Strange, trefoil shapes appeared to have been pushed through each panel from the outside. Inside, a momentary sense of stable centrality was quickly undone by the intrusion of these trefoil shapes, which seemed to insist that occupants move to the perimeter, where a series of elegant interstitial spaces defined the puckered zone between the surface of the panel and the mass of the impacted shapes. Taken together, these peripheral spaces implied a kind of nascent ambulatory, which reasserted the initial feeling of centrality and set in motion the next cycle of alternating centrifugal and centripetal sensations.

A few steps beyond, PATTERNS' Textile Room also experimented with the tectonic and affective possibilities of synthetic materials [**Fig. 7.4**]. Black carbon fiber and yellow aramid filaments were stretched taught around a

Fig. 7.3 Tom Wiscombe Design, MOCA Pavilion, 2013.

multisided steel frame with video images (culled from popular films shot in Los Angeles) calibrated to and projected on the pavilion's radially patterned surfaces by media artist Casey Reas. As seen in an online video clip, the effect is mesmerizing.[16] But as installed, with a cacophony of other objects competing for attention, the intended effect largely evaporated into the surrounding milieu. PATTERN's investment in advanced material and fabrication technology also underwhelmed. Relegated to the role of cladding and dematerialized by the projections, the robotically laminated surfaces were overpowered by the blunt physicality of steel-frame structure, particularly on the interior, where large, bolted connection plates reminded visitors that, regardless of the technical and affective achievements of the cladding, conventional construction remained at the heart of the endeavor.[17]

Fig. 7.4 PATTERNS, Textile Room, 2013.

The final pavilion, Tempera, by Atelier Manferdini, distilled various strands of the firm's recent preoccupations with tessellated geometries and painterly surface effects into a beguiling cocktail of affective fancy [**Fig. 7.5**]. The scheme comprised a cubic volume tilted up and pried open to reveal a florid interior, with a cascade of color spilling onto the adjacent floor and wall. On the exterior, floral excrescences bloomed from meticulously detailed aluminum panels. Within, all indication of tectonic craft was effaced to foreground a billowing graphic printed on the aluminum panels and punctuated with an array of inset mirrored disks. At first, the mirrors appeared as perforations in the printed panels that gave way to a strange inner layer of additional printed surfaces. Drawing closer, visitors discovered through their own unexpected reflections that they were already immersed in that inner space, which produced (at least in me) a jarring shock that failed to dissipate even after the trick had been discovered.

The three pavilions combined with Lynn's projects to bracket the main body of the exhibition with a kind of plastic exuberance that I suspect lay at the heart of Mount's notion of sculpturalism. Despite its last-minute erasure, this reductive term hung stubbornly over the work in the show, particularly the anomalous offerings at the periphery. The installation's deadpan categorizations—"pavilions" and "research"—and the pavilions' lack of programmatic

Fig. 7.5 Atelier Manferdini, Tempera, 2013.

specificity only reinforced the possibility of their being seen as less than fully architectural, or worse, as *merely sculptural*. Thus, the installation inadvertently rehearsed exactly the trivialization for which Mount had been sidelined. Even worse, I overheard a few visitors reverse this implied hierarchy, parsing the show into the "sculptural," that is, complicated, interesting, and the "architectural"—ordinary, boring.

These unfortunate side effects notwithstanding, partitioning Lynn's "research" and the three pavilions from the rest of the exhibition highlighted an important swerve in recent L.A. architecture. Whereas these works were developed largely unencumbered by the stultifying realities of commercial practice and quotidian use, most of the other projects in the exhibition are remarkable primarily for their artful engagement of exactly those constraints. Indeed, it was through inventive wrangling with unbuildable sites, inflexible construction systems, and unreasonable budgets that L.A.'s architects secured some of their greatest achievements, ultimately inventing the receptive audience so necessary for their continued success. The tactical facility exhibited by so many in a context so unforgiving gave rise to the unique tradition of architectural innovation that *A New Sculpturalism* celebrated but ultimately failed to articulate. Let's call it *pragmatic radicalism.* Such inventiveness is not unique to Los Angeles, but this city's disciplinary culture has evolved a distinctive valence of that quality. Pragmatic radicalism is the attitude that brought world-class architecture to the back alleys of Venice and the blank warehouses of Culver City and launched Los Angeles architecture into the international spotlight.

LEARNING FROM *LOLITA*

As *A New Sculpturalism* demonstrated, pragmatic radicalism's potent tincture of ardent individualism, ad hoc ingenuity, critical skepticism, and unbridled ambition is occasionally fouled by debilitating bouts of anti-intellectualism and brooding insecurity, and is dangerously easy to dilute with slipshod execution, lazy imitation, and commercial opportunism. But under the right circumstances, it can sweep away the banal contingencies of the everyday, driving to the root of architecture (as radicalism's etymology dictates) to unleash primal, exhilarating effects one might refer to as *aesthetic bliss.* The phrase comes from Vladimir Nabokov, who coined it in 1956 to describe his literary ambitions. *"Lolita,"* he writes, "has no moral in tow. For me, a work of fiction exists only insofar as it affords me what I shall bluntly call aesthetic bliss, that is a sense of being somehow, somewhere, connected with other states of being where art (curiosity, tenderness, kindness, ecstasy) is the norm. There are not many such books."[18] There are not many such buildings, either. Most have a moral in tow. That moral may have to do with the program, budget, or even bombastic ambition to advertise an architect's carefully constructed alterity. Whatever its source, such moralism always undermines the irreducibly architectural.

Just about all of the projects in *A New Sculpturalism* wore their aesthetic agendas on their sleeves, but only a few rose to that elusive state of aesthetic bliss. Manferdini's pavilion did, as did Wiscombe's, in a different way. I also noticed that blissful quality in Lynn's plastic aggregations, in Coy Howard's rich accretions of graphite, and in Johnston Marklee's curious building masses. I saw it elsewhere in the exhibition too, but I also saw plenty of projects that missed the mark. Some were solid examples of proficient professional practice—respectable buildings to be sure, but out of place in a major museum show. Others were the architectural equivalents of what Nabakov referred to as "didactic fiction" and "topical trash."[19]

By mixing important innovations so casually with later, frankly derivative examples, *A New Sculpturalism* inadvertently demonstrated that the pragmatic radicalism that proliferated in Los Angeles in the 1980s and '90s *used to be* an effective vehicle with which to pursue aesthetic bliss, and that today, this formidable attitude has skidded well past the point of diminishing returns and largely disintegrated into a collection of stylistic clichés. Indeed, Gehry, Mayne, Moss, and the other early innovators of the manner have long since moved on to more productive ways of working. While I look forward to the offerings the elder generation has in store, I will be keeping a closer eye on the largely untested inventions of Lynn and the younger generation, who have diverged even more sharply from L.A.'s now conventionalized mode of radicalism. Had *A New Sculpturalism* directed more attention to differences rather than similarities, the exhibition could have clarified the many important distinctions among contemporary L.A. architects and offered an opportunity for both professional and popular audiences to cultivate their receptivity to the rarefied inflections of aesthetic bliss. That it did neither should be seen as a dereliction of institutional duty that this city and our field can ill afford to repeat.

NOTES

1. The PSTP initiative provided sizeable grants to eight institutions in support of eleven exhibitions that examined Los Angeles architecture from 1940 to 1990. Grantees, in addition to MOCA, included the Southern California Institute of Architecture, where I cocurated, with Ewan Branda and Andrew Zago, the exhibition, *A Confederacy of Heretics*.
2. See *Overdrive: L.A. Constructs the Future, 1940–1990*, Wim de Wit and Christopher Alexander, eds. (Los Angeles: Getty Research Institute, 2013).
3. SCI-Arc's exhibition opened first, on 29 March 2013, with the Getty's and LACMA's opening just over a week later. Grants for the other exhibitions ranged from $260,000 to $430,000.
4. Press release for "Pacific Standard Time Presents: Modern Architecture in L.A.," 27 September 2012. MOCA invited twelve firms to submit proposals for pavilions to be included in the show, of which three were executed. The proposals are documented in the exhibition catalog. See Christopher Mount, *A New Sculpturalism: Contemporary Architecture in Los Angeles* (New York: Skira Rizzoli, 2013): 234–55.
5. See Bob Colacello, "How Do You Solve a Problem like MOCA?," *Vanity Fair* (March 2013).
6. Christopher Hawthorne, "MOCA's 'A New Sculpturalism' Faces Uncertain Future without Gehry," *Los Angeles Times* (3 May 2013).
7. Mike Boehm, "Frank Gehry Back in MOCA Architecture Show, Coaxed by Thom Mayne," *Los Angeles Times* (1 June 2013).
8. MOCA had commissioned Ball Nogues Studio to design and install an entry pavilion, but budgetary and scheduling issues in the months leading up to the exhibition forced its last-minute cancellation. Ball Nogues's proposal would not have changed the path through the Fischer installation.
9. Moving past the pavilions to the opposite end of the hall, visitors first encountered residential projects, then housing, commercial, civic/governmental, cultural, educational, and "research" projects.
10. Mount's initial selection of architects and his general ambitions for the show were made available several weeks ahead of the exhibition's scheduled opening by the early release of the exhibition catalog.
11. Christopher Hawthorne, "Review: MOCA's Revamped Architecture Show a Model of Insularity," *Los Angeles Times* (29 June 2013).

12. *Experimental Architecture in Los Angeles*, eds. Aaron Betsky, John Chase, and Leon Whiteson (New York: Rizzoli, 1991). Frank Gehry provided an approving introduction.
13. John Chase, Margaret Crawford, and John Kaliski, *Everyday Urbanism*, (New York: Monacelli, 1999).
14. John Chase, *Glitter Stucco and Dumpster Diving: Reflections on Building Production in the Vernacular City* (London: Verso, 2000). Chase's book builds on a long tradition of campy connoisseurship, which stretches back through UCLA's two postmodernist Charleses (Moore and Jencks) at least to Denise Scott Brown, who "discovered" the Santa Monica Pier for serious architectural consideration while teaching at UCLA in the mid-1960s.
15. Mount, *New Sculpturalism*, 230–31.
16. "Textile Room 03 Full," http://vimeo.com/71997211.
17. An earlier version of the scheme employed an additional interior skin of stretched filaments that concealed the steel structure and the video projectors. Unfortunately, budgetary constraints foreclosed this more provocative proposal. See Mount, *New Sculpturalism*, 252.
18. Vladimir Nabokov, "On a Book Entitled *Lolita*," in *Lolita* [1955] (New York: Vintage International, 1997): 314–15.
19. Ibid.

Facts and Effects: Oyler Wu's Pendulum Plane

2009

Fig. 8.1 Oyler Wu Collaborative, Pendulum Plane (Los Angeles, 2008).

Upon entering the new L.A. Forum gallery on Hollywood Boulevard, one's attention is drawn immediately upward to a curious network of aluminum tubing floating overhead. Viewed on end, the work resembles an enormous prehistoric crustacean, its many-jointed legs poised to scoop unwary prey into its ominous maw. Attempting to avoid the clutches of this beast, most proceed along the edges of the space, always with a watchful eye cocked toward the ceiling. This oblique vantage point cancels zoomorphic readings to favor science fiction. Perhaps we have happened upon a fleet of spacecraft about to deploy or an alien machine of uncertain intent. In any case, Oyler Wu's Pendulum Plane fills the room with an eerie tension. The work obviously does *something*—something that might commence at any moment—but what, exactly, remains unclear.

Repeat visitors encounter clues that reveal the project's more beneficent aspects. Often, dangling appendages appear to have plucked artworks from the gallery wall and drawn them forward for closer inspection. Occasionally, slender arms seem to have just lifted electronic equipment into position to project light and sound through the space. I cannot be certain but I believe I once witnessed, from the corner of my eye, a lone tentacle ease silently down to steady a teetering piece of sculpture.

When the gallery is occupied the Pendulum Plane sways almost imperceptibly—*pulsates* is a better word—adding another hint of vitality to the scene. Yet for its obvious capability of movement, few have seen it actually move. Instead, we experience a gentle insistence that coaxes us on from one item to the next.

While a visitor's attention easily is fixed on artworks thus presented, eyes are inevitably drawn upward along graceful curves into the network above. Some have deemed this a distraction, a presentation in competition rather than complicity with curatorial intent. In a sense, these criticisms are valid. No matter how compelling the exhibition, a significant amount of time is given over to contemplating the uncanny scene overhead. I will not take sides on the intractable popularity contest between artworks and the places in which they are displayed. (Suffice it to say I am fickle; I award my allegiance on a case-by-case basis.) Instead, I will use this space to probe a simpler question, one concerned less with interdisciplinary hierarchies and more with tendencies deeply entrenched in our field.

*

Past architecture routinely directed our attention upward. Think of the intricate tracery of a Gothic cathedral, the dazzling *trompes l'oeil* of baroque Rome, or the shimmering vaults of the Crystal Palace. In the past, the impact of architecture could be attributed in large part to a work's capacity to compel us to look up. Of course, contemporary architecture continues to trade in these aerial effects, but the focus of attention has shifted. Next time you see a recent work in print or in person, notice where your eyes are drawn. Whether Herzog and de Meuron's taut planes or Frank Gehry's billowing curtains, the vertical surfaces most often catch our eyes. Overhead horizontals routinely recede. In more quotidian spaces, this preference for the vertical is even more pronounced. Look up. Odds are your eyes were greeted by a cacophony of structural, mechanical, and electrical equipment. If you are at home, a blank surface likely met your gaze. Now lower your eyes to the walls. See the difference? Whether an environment tickles or tortures, its most potent effects typically issue from upright elements. Nowhere is this dominance of the vertical over the horizontal more pronounced than in exhibition spaces, where habit and convention have conditioned us to seek interest only on or between the walls. The question more to the point, then, is this: When did architects stop paying attention to the ceiling?

One might begin by searching for clues in the transition from past theocentric cultures to the anthropocentric worldview we know as humanism.[1] As collective attention shifted from spiritual matters to more worldly concerns, architectural interests followed. From the fourteenth to the eighteenth centuries, the field's most aggressive experimentation migrated from the transcendent vaulting of religious spaces to the complex plans and representational facades of secular commissions. By the end of the nineteenth century, modernism had begun to complicate the situation, with new technologies dissipating traditional modes of material expression. Today, the transition is in large part complete. We have, *en masse,* averted our eyes from the heavens to the earth.

Colin Rowe traced this shift in tectonic terms in his 1947 essay, "The Mathematics of the Ideal Villa." Tallying the similarities and differences between Palladio's Villa Foscari and Le Corbusier's Villa Stein, Rowe noticed that the point-supported free plan, for all the compositional freedom it afforded, deprived Le Corbusier of the volumetric possibilities available to Palladio's traditional bearing-wall construction. He writes:

> In other words, free plan for free section; but the limitations of the new system are quite as exacting as those of the old; and, as though the solid wall structure had been turned on its side, with the former complexities of section and subtleties of elevation now transposed to the plan, there may be here some reason for Palladio's choice of plan and Le Corbusier's choice of elevations as being the documents, in each case, most illustrative of elementary mathematical regulation.[2]

Thus, Palladio's sculpted cellular enclosures give way to Corbusier's fluid, sandwiched spaces; where lofty domes once focused our attention skyward, flat slabs now deflect it to the periphery. Today, expressive as well as economic concerns drive the prevalence of trabeated systems over vaulted construction, cementing this shift in emphasis across the discipline. Vertical surfaces have stepped into the spotlight while overhead elements have slipped to the outer reaches of our perception.

With all of us no longer paying attention, the ceiling was freed to take on other tasks. Mechanical equipment, which most of us prefer neither to see nor hear, long has found solace there. Consider, for example, the theater. Since the classical period, its arsenal of mechanical tackle has been located well above eye level, tucked surreptitiously if not always invisibly behind the proscenium. As these clever contraptions lowered props and even actors in and out of the scene, we spectators learned to see through them, to suspend disbelief and imagine the spectacles before us were achieved unaided. Artificial sound and lighting equipment eventually took their own posts in the shadows, placed with the knowledge that special effects work best when their source remains unknown.

In other environments the situation is similar. The spaces over our heads have become nothing if not more populated with equipment. More accurately, the spaces over our heads have become nothing *because* they are more populated with equipment. As more stuff clutters the spaces above us, we grow more comfortable not noticing it there, effectively eliminating overhead elements from our awareness. Once the playground of the most potent architectural effects, the ceiling has become the invisible realm of equipment specifically designed to operate below the threshold of our attention.

One last observation from Rowe before returning to Hollywood: In his influential two-part essay "Transparency: Literal and Phenomenal," co-written with Robert Slutzky, a meticulous step-by-step analysis teases two categories of effects out of painting and architecture.[3] As the first text plays out, their bias becomes clear: the literal transparency they find in Moholy-Nagy photomontages and at Walter Gropius's Bauhaus pales in comparison to the phenomenal transparencies that animate Léger's canvasses and Le Corbusier's Villa Stein. By the end of the second essay, the authors' initial attention to paintings and plans gives way to an analysis that unfolds entirely on vertical building surfaces, reaching its crescendo in serial diagrams of Michelangelo's unbuilt façade for the church of San Lorenzo in Florence. In a masterful sleight of hand, Rowe and Slutzky conflate architecture with painting then collapse it into diagram, effectively dematerializing built form into oscillating pattern. For present purposes, their preference for pattern is less a concern than their identification of two classes of effects bent on dematerialization. Both literal and phenomenal transparency work to undermine the material presence of the walls on which they operate, and mark yet another step in a history of architecture unfolding through systematic dematerialization.

A précis of that history might run as follows: The stone ceilings of the past drew our attention ever upward, belying their chthonic weight with pattern, pendentives, and illusionistic paint. Later, a shift from spiritual to secular concerns found expression in new material and tectonic configurations, and our disciplinary attention slid from ceiling to wall. Out of work, ceilings offered their vacant surfaces to mechanical equipment and got involved in the production of subliminal environmental effects. Vertical surfaces, in turn, stepped to the fore to take on increased expressive and representational responsibilities. In time, these surfaces registered increasing dematerializations, as modernists pursued both literal and phenomenal transparencies. With contemporary practice increasingly focused on digital media and the production of ambient effects, dematerializations have become more pronounced, and architecture emerges as a field seemingly committed to staging its own disappearance.

This trajectory reveals our tendency to see through gallery architecture not as a special condition but rather as an aggravated occurrence of symptoms already prevalent in the field. Gallery ceilings, long abandoned to lighting and equipment, uniformly fail to hold our attention and whether or not we share Rowe's preference for walls that act like paintings, gallery walls always take a back seat to the real thing. With our attention thus captured by exhibited artworks, the enclosing architecture effectively is vaporized. Of course, this is patently untrue *in fact*, but *in effect* it is difficult to deny.

*

In their ambition to create a "dense aesthetic or visual field," the architects of the Pendulum Plane cleave to this historical trajectory. Operating somewhere beyond the surface of materials, Oyler Wu's intended effect is akin to Rowe and Slutzky's phenomenal transparency, though in Hollywood, complex composition is intended to produce atmospheric spatial allusion rather than an oscillating catalog of patterns. Their approach to the functional problem of staging exhibitions, on the other hand, moves the Pendulum Plane beyond this architectural lineage and invites comparisons to theater design. As a mechanical device bent on the flexible accommodation of changing exhibitions, the work functions akin to the equipment in a theatrical fly space. And while the work's direct contact with exhibited works of art might call forth comparisons to art framing, its attitude toward exhibitions suggests a stronger analogy to proscenia and theatrical curtains. Each move marks a significant contribution to the field; we shall examine them in turn.

Theatrical curtains engender effects so potent we rarely notice them. Most obviously, these heavy fabrics mask backstage preparations, but carefully controlled movement transforms these perfunctory screens into crucial performers. Drawn closed in advance of the show, the curtain's quiet presence builds anticipation for the impending action. Eased aside, the curtain reinforces the proscenium arch like a matte to a frame, smoothing the transition between the quotidian world of the spectator and rarefied space of the spectacle beyond. Of course, our access to this space is fleeting. Swept closed at the finale, the curtain erases the illusion it revealed, deflecting our attention to the rising din of an audience already making its way to the exits.

Fly-space equipment is similarly specific. Generally lightweight and exhibiting an air of ad-hoc flexibility, catwalks, cables, and jerry-rigged components hover above the stage to indicate the sober efficiency and no-nonsense functionality required of the artifice below. We have all at some point craved a glimpse of this mysterious world. Some wish to mingle with actors, aficionados, and VIPs, others long to examine the intricate equipment that makes it all possible. Either way, backstage beckons with the allure of forbidden intimacy, an allure only heightened when our advances are thwarted.

The Pendulum Plane collapses these elements into a single milieu, then offers us all a backstage pass. Its various configurations stage effects that range from the height of artifice to a frank baring of the device, at times choreographing a dizzying oscillation between the two. But while theater curtains and equipment operate best at the edge of our perception, in Hollywood, the Pendulum Plane's insistent material presence moves it to center stage. Deploy the end modules symmetrically and leave the rest retracted to produce a metalized version of the traditional stage—the lead pair perfectly will resemble a drawn curtain while the knotted mass of the remaining panels will provide an abstracted intimation of the fly space beyond. Lower all the edges to produce a continuous curtain suited to stylized procession. Lighting from above amplifies the energy, as intricate shadows dance on the white walls beyond. (I eagerly await the space's first fashion show. It will be a stunner.) Deploy the piece asymmetrically for the backstage effect, with an ad-hoc assemblage of thin members dangling print works like props in a play.

To date, my favorite show was *Who Is in Charge Here: Authority and Authoritarianism,* a collection of experimental media art masterfully installed by Anne Bray and Sara Daleiden.[4] Attaching both projectors and screens to the Pendulum Plane, Bray and Daleiden opened virtual worlds not only on the gallery walls but also hologram-like in the center of the space. A cacophony of soundtracks heightened the uncanny effect, delimiting loose aural precincts within the visually continuous space. A cunning placement of projectors completed the scene. Some hung at eye level from the Pendulum Plane while others were perched on white bases at the perimeter. Power cords tumbled

Fig. 8.2 Oyler Wu Collaborative, Pendulum Plane (Los Angeles, 2008).

to the floor and slithered off in search of electricity. This frank presentation of electronic equipment offered a perfect material contrast to the flickering virtual scene; many visitors scrutinized the whirring mechanisms with an intensity equal to that afforded the imagery. While the show staged each piece to allow ample space for individual immersion, peripatetic eyes inevitably veered from projected images to projecting equipment and back again, then traced sinewy power cords from the floor up into the aluminum network above. On view for only a single weekend, this incredible installation integrated the Pendulum Plane into an ensemble that perfectly merged illusory artifice with behind-the-scenes access and set a high bar for future curators.

For all these salutary associations, the intended effect of a "dense field" remains elusive. Since its installation, the piece most often has been folded horizontally, often cruelly impaled by light fixtures added by others after the fact.[5] In this configuration, the edges are too crisp, the arrangement too regular, the individual elements too large, and the overall scale too small to produce a convincing field. Deployed in greater numbers, the elements might emerge as a field, and unfolding the frames asymmetrically improves the situation somewhat, but to my eye, the careful polish of the aluminum surfaces and the deft precision of their assembly call attention to individual elements and trump a more unified reading.[6] While the work may fall short of its architects' intended effects, its exquisite execution, robust physicality, and legible systematicity more than compensate with long-term rewards for sustained attention.

Timid curators and insecure artists no doubt will take issue with the Pendulum Plane. It is big, bold, difficult to light, and more difficult to ignore. It flaunts its physicality when it should cede attention to exhibited artworks. Such traits generally are seen as deficiencies in gallery design—even the competition juries expressed reservations about the work's potential hostility to exhibited artworks—and to date, most exhibitors have attempted to ignore rather than engage the piece. As demonstrated by *Who Is in Charge Here,* such concerns amply are offset by other, more daring, curatorial possibilities. Beyond these, the work's specifically architectural contributions secure its place among Los Angeles's most significant interventions in recent memory.

First among these is Oyler Wu's brilliant reassertion of the ceiling as fertile territory for experimentation. Architecture for too long has diverted its attention laterally. Of course, overhead ambiguity can engender powerful effects and vertical surfaces continue to satisfy, but I, for one, am thrilled to have fresh impetus to look up.

Next is the firm's cunning deployment of a mechanical device neither as invisible agent nor inert sign but rather as an active performer within the spatial milieu. The move forecloses the possibility of reading the Pendulum Plane solely on autonomous, aesthetic terms, and the work's direct engagement with exhibited content, along with its wide range of potential configurations, ensures a lively, participatory dialog between art, architecture, and visitors.

Finally, a nod to the firm's reassertion of architecture's physicality without resorting to outdated attitudes toward materials. Too often, architects understand materials as dumb containers into which we pour our ideas, inert substrates that either predetermine actions (the stance of the "truth to materials" set) or foreclose possibilities (a naïve view sometimes advanced by the digital generation). Such attitudes fail to recognize an important distinction between physicality and materiality. Physicality signifies the raw attributes of objects in the world. Any object exhibits a potentially infinite number of traits, ranging from the reflective qualities of its surface to the configuration of its molecular components. Objects are too complex, our perceptions too limited, to register them all. Materiality names the phenomenon that draws our attention to a meaningful few; it is the fleeting interaction between a physical object, a perceiving subject, and the context in which they interact. As pointed out by N. Katherine Hayles,

> Because materiality in this view is bound up with the text's context, it cannot be specified in advance, as if it existed independent of content. Rather, it is an *emergent* property. What constitutes the materiality of a given text will always be a matter of interpretation and critical debate; what some readers see as physical properties brought into play may not appear so to other readers.[7]

Though Hayles here refers to the materiality of literary texts, her observations are equally pertinent in an architectural context.[8] In either field, physicality is an infinite collection of *facts,* while materiality is a vacillating *effect.* It is the coordination of objects and attention that transforms stone from weighty to weightless, glass from glowing to gauzy to gone. To control it requires careful calibration, and its efficacy will always be open to interpretation.

Today, contemporary architecture maintains a tiresome feud between those intoxicated by the hallucinatory potential of the digital and those still seduced by outdated material myths. To a generation of architects grown impatient with digitally driven works that fail to deliver on the promise of their presentations as well as with nostalgic pleas to retreat to our supposedly real roots, Oyler Wu offers a productive alternative. With a rare virtuosity in both actual and virtual construction, the firm takes seriously the physical constraints of materials while simultaneously capitalizing upon the formal possibilities made available by contemporary digital techniques. But their more important innovation lies in understanding that materiality does not lie wholly within the object, but rather emerges from its promiscuous interactions with context. Where others mistakenly assume a seamless translation from the digital to the physical, Oyler Wu carefully calibrates the exchange. With meticulous attention paid not just to the objects they construct, but also to the particular contexts they inhabit as well as the array of subjects and objects with which their work interacts, Oyler Wu engages the full repertoire of elements that constitute architecture's materiality. Through masterful technique, tireless experimentation, and plain hard work, they conjure base physical facts into material effects of the highest order.

NOTES

1. Peter Eisenman has devoted considerable attention to this topic, as well as to the struggle to produce a subsequent shift from humanism to modernism in architecture. See, for example, his essays in *Eisenman Inside Out: Selected Writings* 1963–1988 (New Haven: Yale University Press, 2004), in particular the Introduction, ii–xv; "Aspects of Modernism: Maison Dom-ino and the Self-referential Sign" [1980], 111–20; and "The End of the Classical; The End of the Beginning, the End of the End" [1984], 152–68.
2. Colin Rowe, "The Mathematics of the Ideal Villa" [1947], in T*he Mathematics of the Ideal Villa and Other Essays* (Cambridge, MIT Press, 1976): 12.
3. Colin Rowe and Robert Slutzky, "Transparency: Literal and Phenomenal" [written 1955–56, first published 1963], in *The Mathematics of the Ideal Villa,* 159–83, and "Transparency: Literal and Phenomenal, Part 2" *Perspecta* 13/14 (first published 1971): 287–301. Both are reprinted in *The Light Construction Reader,* ed. Todd Gannon (New York: Monacelli Press, 2002).
4. The exhibition was curated by Bray as part of *Hollywould...* , the Freewaves 2008 festival. See www.freewaves.org.
5. Budgetary and schedule concerns precluded the architects from participating in the lighting design. While these clumsy additions satisfy a crucial functional requirement and can be reconfigured, I share the architects' frustration with them and remain hopeful that a more thoughtful lighting scenario is forthcoming.
6. The work's calibration to display all panels at a uniform height further detracts. While an amazing technical achievement, the crisp horizontals and clear cadences thus achieved suggest a tight regimentation of figures rather than the loose affiliations of a field.
7. N. Katherine Hayles, *My Mother Was a Computer* (Chicago: University of Chicago Press, 2005): 104. Emphasis in the original.
8. Elsewhere, Hayles and I have developed this point in architectural terms. See our "Virtual Architecture, Actual Media," 174–99 in this volume.

Of Raspberries, Rawhide, and Rhetoric

2012

Fig. 9.1 Hirsuta (Jason Payne), *Rawhide: The New Shingle Style*, SCI-Arc Gallery (Los Angeles, 2011).

Last summer, the SCI-Arc Gallery hosted *Rawhide: The New Shingle Style,* by Hirsuta, the Los Angeles-based practice led by Jason Payne. The exhibition consisted of a single model and a full-scale section of the roof of Raspberry Fields, the firm's soon-to-be-completed project for a house in northern Utah. While the roof fragment offered a compelling preview of the project's acclaimed shingled surface, the architect's cunning aggregation of unlikely associations in both the exhibition and the project it illustrated augured a provocative renovation of a remote schoolhouse as well as the rhetorical tendencies of contemporary architectural discourse.

The Raspberry Fields project will covert a century-old wooden schoolhouse into a new residence for an owner who plans to cultivate raspberries in the surrounding landscape. Differential weathering on the otherwise symmetrical building inspired the firm's proposal. On its southwest side, the schoolhouse bears the scars of decades of harsh winter storms and searing summer sun; what remains of the wood roof and siding is grotesquely twisted and deformed. The siding on the northeast, shielded from direct sun and prevailing weather patterns, appears much as it must have when first installed.

To change the program from school to residence, the architects expanded the southeast end of the building along a tight curve in plan, making the entire structure appear to list precariously to one side and lending a strange plasticity to an otherwise straightforward form. New interior elements are arranged according to what Payne terms "a nuanced play of symmetry-making and breaking...in the age-old compositional play that pits idiosyncrasy against balance." On the exterior, the architect's "formal-geometrical project" is left behind and the "affective material qualities of wood" take center stage. Custom cedar shingles designed to amplify their natural weathering will be used to resheath all exterior surfaces the structure. Cut considerably longer than standard shingles, left unfixed at their lower ends, and stained on their undersides in a palette of rich colors, the new shingles will weather and warp more rapidly than the original siding. Over time, exterior surfaces will diverge in character across the building's central axis, with the more harshly exposed surfaces to the southwest becoming tangled, scruffy, and polychromatic while those to the more protected northeast remain more or less uniform.

These dual tendencies extend to the architect's description of the project. For every nod to contemporary formal complexity and its fastidious articulation, there also seems to be an equal and opposite appeal to vernacular associations and accidental effects. In fact, a tally of these associations shows a distinct leaning toward the latter. Presentation materials on Hirsuta's website, for instance, feature just one citation of *à la mode* cultural practices (Vidal Sassoon hairstyling techniques) but a whole herd of livestock. And while the building profile and the site plan reveal the telltale sweeps of digital modeling software, the project is gabled, wooden, and, in perhaps its most iconoclastic move, *brown.* I should point out that the gable is not one of those ironic, Monopoly-house gables currently fashionable in Europe, nor one of those dreamy metaphysical gables of Japanese derivation. But as its distorted massing attests, neither is it a typical vernacular gable; its associations lie elsewhere. The wood shingling is similarly ambiguous. Though extravagantly curled, it makes no overt attempt to appear artificial. Nonetheless, and despite its earth tones, one cannot accurately describe it as natural. As with the gable, a range of associations is suggested, but their ambiguity forecloses any determined categorical allegiance. These unlikely intersections of the contemporary and the commonplace, the straightforward and the strange, locate Raspberry Fields in an undecidable space and have elicited a deep fascination for the scheme since it was first published in 2008.

The SCI-Arc exhibition gave Payne an opportunity to test certain of the project's techniques and effects at full scale and focused attention on a major reconsideration of the initial design. As the project originally was conceived, all of the custom shingles were to be straight when first applied to the schoolhouse, with their eventual distortion left, as before, to natural weathering. This presented significant dilemmas, as there would be no immediate evidence of the architect's design intention upon completion of the building, nor any way to guarantee that weathering would cause the shingles to curve in the carefully composed manner depicted in widely publicized models and drawings. After a period of anxious debate within his studio, Payne decided to pre-curl the shingles in order to "kick-start" their deformation. For the exhibition fragment, individual shingles were heated in a steam-filled container, then hand-bent around a curved formwork and allowed to cool. The pre-curled shingles were then applied to the wood roof frame and meticulously composed to produce the final configuration in the gallery. A similar process will be employed on the southwest-facing wall and roof surfaces on site in Utah.

Payne's decision to valorize "artificial" composition over "natural" process is laudable and consistent with his initial concept. The obvious imprint of the designer's hand introduces a destabilizing ambiguity into any understanding of the building's surface, and over time, the rich play between compositional artifice and natural weathering will only become more complex. Payne's decision also calls into question some of the more irritating tendencies in recent architecture—both the knee-jerk valorization of indexical processes as well as the disingenuous attempts to diminish or deny their role. Raspberry Fields promiscuously mingles authorial intention with stochastic effects, expanding contemporary ambitions without ceding the valuable conceptual ground gained through previous experimentation with process-based design techniques.

The installation's title further signals the architect's ambition to broaden current conversations about architectural surfaces. As Payne makes clear in a short text written for the exhibition, the title "Rawhide" foregrounds the project's animalistic associations. Rejecting the architectural "skin" as "a rather well-worn path...no longer particularly interesting underfoot," Payne advances the notion of the building surface as "hide" in order to "push the dialogue of cladding toward an expanded array of associations and models less well-known to the discipline." He continues:

> Possible interpretations abound: where the skin is bald and shaven, the hide retains its thick fur. If the skin's geometry is immediately and completely apparent, that of the hide only flirts with visibility,

> and only then after the luster and texture of its hairiness has been combed through. Skins are thin, so thin as to be insufficient unto themselves, requiring the "bones" underneath to carry some of the load. Never mind that with hides; whether they require underlying structure or not is of little consequence to their luscious external reading. A good hide feels entirely self-sufficient, such that their prostration on a floor becomes the center of a room's attention. Nothing more is required.[1]

Though technically a part of a larger whole, the full-scale fragment was strangely complete unto itself.[2] Its bilateral symmetry, pronounced spine, and naturalistic profile gave it a distinctly biomorphic aspect, while its furry exterior, earthy hue, and musky scent added more visceral, faunal qualities. Viewed from the mezzanine above the gallery, the project's unmistakably bovine posture came clearly into focus. Payne confirmed these associations during a public gallery talk with Eric Owen Moss, and admitted to studying the form of cows reclining in a pasture to determine the shape of the building.

To further interrogate what he calls "the becoming-animal of architecture," Payne recently led a seminar of SCI-Arc graduate students in a series of formal investigations with actual cowhides. He initially planned to display the reconfigured hides alongside the roof fragment as part of the exhibition, which could have opened a provocative dialogue between the "becoming-animal" of architecture and the "becoming-architecture" of animals. Unfortunately, the idea was abandoned.

While the title "Rawhide" and the cowhides make clear Payne's desire to expand contemporary architectural conversations, his subtitle, "The New Shingle Style," betrayed a countervailing ambition to engage historical ideas within the disciplinary fold. Curiously, this overt historical association receives no specific mention in the gallery guide, even though Payne's reference to the shingle style is a far more provocative move in contemporary architecture than swerves into the animalistic and the affective. These latter themes have been recurrent subjects of discussion among Payne's contemporaries for some time, most significantly in the exhibition *Matters of Sensation*, curated by Marcelo Spina and Georgina Huljich at Artists Space in New York in 2008, which included the model of Raspberry Fields shown at SCI-Arc. The shingle style, on the other hand, seems wholly anathema to Payne's generation; indeed, the topic has found little traction among young architects since the 1970s. Even to postulate a "new" shingle style is not new. Vincent Scully, the original chronicler of the shingle style, outlined a new version in 1974. In *The Shingle Style Today: or, The Historian's Revenge,* the historian traces the reemergence of nineteenth-century themes in works by Robert Venturi and others from the late 1950s to the 1970s.[3] Scully's language is curiously echoed by Payne. In a gallery talk at SCI-Arc, Payne claimed that his project "is not meant to reinvigorate [the shingle style] into a new movement, it's really just meant to swerve it, to turn its direction." Compare this with Scully: "The young architect, no less than [Harold] Bloom's 'strong poet,' inevitably fastens on the work of his chosen precursor, purposely 'misreads' it, and finally 'swerves' from it to create a new field of action for his own design."[4] Indeed, the two seem to have suffered from a similar weariness with the labors of their early careers, though the causes were almost exactly opposite. Scully writes:

> When most of the architects of the late [eighteen]eighties reacted against the Shingle Style it was toward the bright, light, geometric purity of more classicizing forms that they turned. While writing *The Shingle Style* I was not immune to such feelings, and each night I found myself leafing through the early volumes of Le Corbusier's *Oeuvre complète* with stupefied absorption. The thin, tense, hyper-intelligent forms were apparently the relief I needed from shingle fuzz, plastic intersections, and infinite spatial variety.[5]

Payne:

> I was becoming increasingly dissatisfied with working with smooth, bald surfaces, hence, the hair. I started searching for ways to reinvest an otherwise clean, bare surface with qualities that would have to do with material dynamics, effects, and so on.[6]

Payne also engages with a period that has been almost wholly absent from contemporary, as well as modernist, discourse—the picturesque. From the house's disintegrating cladding to the architect's attentiveness to visual composition and his recent musings on installing the exhibited roof fragment as a folly on site in Utah, echoes of the picturesque are everywhere apparent at Raspberry Fields, though Payne is careful never to allow them to develop into fully articulated quotations. Planned manipulations of the surrounding landscape recall the vast earthworks undertaken by Capability Brown and other landscape designers of the eighteenth and nineteenth centuries, and

Payne even borrows one of Brown's most potent techniques—the ha-ha—to produce expansive vistas unimpeded by fences, roads, or other visual clutter. More broadly, the interest of Payne and many of his contemporaries in architecture's affective potential and emotional sensibility in general resonates distinctly with the rhetoric of picturesque practitioners and theorists.

In spite of these potent alignments, direct engagement with picturesque ideas has been almost nonexistent in twenty-first-century architecture. Indeed, avoidance of the movement and its tendencies has been endemic in advanced architectural circles for most of the past century, and vehement opposition has been part of its history since the idea was introduced in the late eighteenth-century writings of Uvedale Price, Richard Payne Knight, and Humphry Repton. Early attacks often centered on the movement's anti-classicism, its emphasis on surfaces over structure, and its predilection for asymmetrical building plans.[7] Sylvia Lavin has argued persuasively that architects and historians of the modern period deliberately suppressed the picturesque, painting the movement as a kind of scapegoat and "sacrificing" it to atone for the purported crimes of preceding centuries.[8] When picturesque ideas were resurrected as Townscape by Nikolaus Pevsner and the editors of the *Architectural Review* in the 1940s and '50s, the younger generation of British architects and critics reacted with venomous derision.[9] Similarly, during the Whites versus Grays debates of the 1970s, picturesque tendencies adopted by the latter faction were roundly dismissed by the former.

Though opposed to Townscape's nostalgia, Colin Rowe undertook an important examination of picturesque vocabulary in the 1950s. His essay, "Character and Composition," investigates the sudden appearance of "composition books" in the early twentieth century and traces their ideological sources to the historical literature of the eighteenth and nineteenth centuries. Rowe elucidates an ongoing debate between a classically inspired line of thinking and more painterly ambitions, which pits geometrical order against compositional play, academic convention against individual license, and determinate objects against atmospheric effects. To revisit the essay today is to encounter passages startlingly resonant with contemporary concerns. Rowe writes: "The Picturesque was now found to be emphasizing the pleasure of the eye, rather than the rational existence of the object. It had aimed to produce 'effect,' and, if by means of certain visual stimuli, it had induced an atmosphere in which certain states of mind were possible, its success was assured."[10]

In another passage, Rowe could have been writing of the designers of Raspberry Fields as easily as he was of mid-nineteenth century Gothic Revivalists: "They came to envisage [character] as the product of specific circumstances, as the vindicating evidence of a genuine interaction between a given individual, given material conditions, and a given cultural milieu. Character became a quality to be extracted. It was implicit in the limiting data of the problem, from them it was to be educed and through them revealed."[11]

Even his closing lines could be read as a summary of the past thirty years of vanguard architectural practice, and not simply of nineteenth-century architecture:

> Perhaps at no time other than the late eighteenth century has architectural thought been confronted with so explosive an idea [as character]; and certainly no other architectural explosion can have created so portentous a vacuum. Limitless experiment was justified by the emergency, the wildest nonconformity flourished exotically among the debris. New experiences were stimulated by the chaos, new energies released by the confusion; both by arbitrary choice and pressure of circumstances, new conceptions of form were generated. By the demand for character, order was atomized. ...It is an idea which, by emphasizing the particular, the personal, and the curious, will always vitiate system; and it is, perhaps, the fundamental demand which typifies the architecture of the nineteenth century.[12]

When one reads passages such as these, the unacknowledged picturesqueness of Raspberry Fields come clearly into focus, as do the sources of recent tensions between today's advanced practitioners and the process-based design strategies they employ. Rowe's analysis demonstrates that concerns with "the particular, the personal, and the curious" long have come into conflict with universalizing, systematic approaches. In the eighteenth and nineteenth centuries, the application of increasingly formulaic classical principles was met with resistance by the individualist efforts of picturesque architects. In the twentieth century, the formulaic application of modernist principles was countered by the neo-picturesque of the Townscape movement and various expressionist and regionalist approaches. In each case, the pursuit of "character" through "composition" offered a means to reassert the individual subjectivity of the architect in the face of totalizing systems and idealized concepts. Payne—particularly in his decision to design a deliberately "weathered" exterior—exhibits similar tendencies. Unwilling to leave Raspberry Fields's signature effects entirely to the vagaries of the natural elements, the architect carefully composed its woolly surface. After revisiting Rowe, Payne's shift in strategy begins to look like an attempt to ensure that his finished work will be imbued with something akin to character.

As Payne and others of his generation seek refuge today from the barren systemization of digital processes by engaging in promiscuous dalliances with fashion, film, and even farm animals, the need to develop specific vocabularies with which to articulate their efforts becomes increasingly pressing. For too long, the discourse surrounding this work has been hamstrung by anxiety, vagueness, and a veritable school of red herrings imported from parallel cultural practices. Turning away from such distractions and toward the long-overlooked achievements of the picturesque makes available a wealth of highly refined concepts with which to advance current conversations on surface articulation, asymmetrical configuration, atmospheric effects, subjective moods, and other contemporary themes rooted in pre-modern sensibilities. By subtly directing attention toward the picturesque, Payne's efforts at SCI-Arc and in northern Utah offer much more than a welcome respite from computational processes; they also suggest a potent rethinking of the vocabulary of contemporary architectural conversations.

NOTES

1. See Payne, "Rawhide: The New Shingle Style," np., in the gallery guide published by SCI-Arc for the exhibition.
2. Many gallery visitors noticed this effect, prompting Payne to consider another significant change. Originally, the shingles and framing installed at the gallery were to be shipped to Utah for reuse in the building renovation. At the time of this writing, Payne was "considering constructing the piece as-is on the site, as a kind of folly." Jason Payne, email communication with the author, 25 Oct 2011.
3. See Vincent Scully, *The Shingle Style Today, or the Historian's Revenge* (New York: George Braziller, 1974). Scully's pioneering work on the shingle style is *The Shingle Style and the Stick Style* (New Haven: Yale University Press, 1955).
4. Scully, *The Shingle Style Today*, 2. Scully relies heavily on Bloom's concept of swerving, or "misprision," which he articulates in *The Anxiety of Influence: A Theory of Poetry* (Oxford: Oxford University Press, 1973).
5. Ibid., 38.
6. Jason Payne, SCI-Arc gallery talk, 29 July 2011.
7. For a solid account of historical suppressions of the picturesque, as well as for a good overview of the topic and its literature, see John Macarthur, *The Picturesque: Architecture, Disgust, and Other Irregularities* (London: Routledge, 2007).
8. Sylvia Lavin, "Sacrifice and the Garden: Watelet's "Essai sur les jardins" and the Space of the Picturesque," *Assemblage* 28 (Dec 1995): 17–19.

9. Reyner Banham outlines these events and their attendant literature in "The Revenge of the Picturesque: English Architectural Polemics, 1945–1965," in *Concerning Architecture: Essays on Architectural Writers and Writing presented to Nikolaus Pevsner*, ed. John Summerson (London: Allen Lane, 1968): 265–73.
10. Colin Rowe, "Character and Composition; or Some Vicissitudes of Architectural Vocabulary in the Nineteenth Century," in *The Mathematics of the Ideal Villa and Other Essays* (Cambridge: MIT Press, 1976): 71. The essay originally was written in 1953–54, and first was published in *Oppositions* 2 (Jan 1974).
11. Ibid., 72.
12. Ibid., 80.

Experiment and Crime

2010

Fig. 10.1 PATTERNS, Prism Gallery (Los Angeles, 2010).

In a recent lecture at the Southern California Institute of Architecture, Marcelo Spina compared the working method of PATTERNS, the Los Angeles-based architectural practice he leads with his partner-in-crime Georgina Huljich, to the deviant expertise of Dexter Morgan, the serial killer with a conscience played by Michael C. Hall in the hit American television series *Dexter*.

As the story goes, Dexter is a mild-mannered blood spatter analyst with the Miami Police Department by day, and a vigilante serial killer by night. Clearly an accomplished master at his day job, Dexter deploys broad technical expertise, a keen eye for detail, and cutting-edge technology (puns are difficult to avoid here) to solve seemingly unsolvable crimes, often providing the crucial forensic evidence required to bring a killer to justice. His impeccable standing within the department is mirrored by his picture-perfect home life—suburban bungalow, beautiful wife, precocious children—you get the idea.

Hidden behind this carefully crafted façade lies Dexter's "dark passenger," a deep psychological wound he sustained as a child that drives him to pursue his nefarious nocturnal activities. Of course, Dexter is no remorseless killer. He plies his trade according to a virtuous "code" imparted him by his stepfather, a deceased homicide detective. Only those deserving death in the eyes of the code—murderous outlaws who have eluded the criminal justice system—are worthy of a date with Dexter's knives. Lucky for us viewers, suitable victims are thick on the ground in Dexter's Miami, and our lovable hero-villain dispatches them weekly with careful planning, expert technique, and (again, the puns) masterful execution. Equal parts egghead technician, quirky homebody, and aberrant monster, Dexter disciplines his deviant urges with formidable technical skill to perpetrate, episode after episode, the perfect crime.

Spina's parallel is both clever and apt. Like Dexter, Spina and Huljich were immersed in the most advanced techniques and technologies of their field, training first at the National University of Rosario (both of them), then Columbia (Spina) and UCLA (Huljich). Like Dexter, they enjoy close family ties to disciplinary fieldwork (Spina's brother Maxi is also an architect and frequent collaborator). And like Dexter, PATTERNS marshals their expert training to pursue unorthodox creative ambitions. Where Dexter uses crime-solving expertise to commit crimes, PATTERNS deploys facile technique to perpetrate aberrant subversions of architectural convention.

While their work is formally and programmatically diverse, certain trends (patterns?) emerge. Let's call it the PATTERNS M.O. A consistent tactic begins with a stable modernist geometry (a gridded frame, a linear field, a static volume) and moves it through a series of transformations—anomalous perhaps, but always deliberate and systematic—to infect elemental primitives with fluid dynamism. Walls and floors warp into one another (Jujuy Redux, FyF House), grids bubble and stretch into complex patterns (Unibodies, Manifold Dubai), courtyards spin into blurred vortices (Ningbo Coil, Chengdu Office Park).

Early works point to the exuberance to come. At Jujuy 2056 [**Fig. 10.2**], for example, the public face of an otherwise straightforward residential block is formed by stretching walls and slabs past their concrete frame, then splicing them at alternating floors. This simple move transforms discrete

Fig. 10.2 PATTERNS, Jujuy 2056 (Rosario, 2003).

a sinuous ribbon that grows increasingly divergent as it snakes skyward. This ribbon is no mere ornamental flourish, however; it was achieved through a canny manipulation of conventional structure. The projecting vertical walls act as cantilevered beams to support the extended floor slabs, producing an atectonic effect through a clever rethinking of structural necessity. The side elevation offers another clue that a cunning intelligence is at work. Here, small punched windows appear to have slid across the brick façade, as if inexorably drawn toward the dynamism at the street. The bare concrete left in their wake suggests intentional scars in the building skin—signature tears left behind by a master's scalpel.

Later works are more aggressive in their desecration of architectural bodies and lend credence to suspicions of ritual scarring at Jujuy. At the Prism Gallery in Los Angeles [**Fig. 10.1**], a polycarbonate façade has been flayed into strips, an upper corner roughly bent back on itself. Lower strips are folded over and tethered to the street, while upper ones are peeled apart, stretched around a column, twisted horizontal, and secured to a protruding soffit. Moving closer to examine this macabre scene complicates initial suspicions of violent dismemberment. No entrails protrude from the open wounds, no fluid seeps at the seams. Instead, every edge is carefully finished, each joint lovingly detailed. Stranger still, this apparent mutilation reveals not the gory innards of a dissected corpse but rather gives way to the clean, well-lighted space of a contemporary gallery. Even more perverse, the space revealed is enclosed by a conventional commercial glazing system, a system unperturbed by the violence that has been visited upon the polycarbonate. This was no frenzied crime of passion, no blunt fragmentation or hackneyed collage. At Prism, disparate tectonic systems are riven, severed, and twisted apart only to be meticulously stitched back together again into an uneasy coherence that undermines decidable affiliation with either conventional or vanguard practice. There is no sign of struggle at this crime scene on Sunset Boulevard, only the mark of a controlled hand engaged in ghastly architectural experiment.

*

Today, *experimental* is the adjective of choice among young practices driven to unorthodox formal machinations. These firms tend to eschew conventional construction and quotidian commissions, choosing instead to wager on temporary installations, international competitions, and steady publication of their relentless output. The intellectual investment, technological requirements, and economic implications of experimental practice have most of the digital vanguard gravitating to teaching positions in the field's more progressive institutions. Formidable cabals orbit SCI-Arc, Columbia, the Architectural Association, and elsewhere, where they ply their deviant trade in plain sight.

The mantra of experimental research in most fields is "Fail Early, Fail Often." Testing limits it hopes one day to transgress, experimentation travels in close step with failure, producing far more dead ends than celebrated breakthroughs. Architectural innovation is no exception. Historically, a leaky roof in a famous work was a reliable clue that experimentation was afoot. In many of today's digitally fabricated installations, the liberal application of duct tape, zip ties, and aircraft cable offers ample evidence. Most of us have grown accustomed to seeing past these low-tech crutches in today's high-tech constructions, and routinely forgive the groaning seams, sagging cantilevers, and even outright collapses these quick fixes have failed to prevent.

Lazy critics make easy prey of such shortcomings, clumsily holding progressive experimentation to standards of permanence, stability, and polish normally reserved for high-end conventional construction. Such antagonism forecloses exactly the innovation these critics claim to desire. In order to move beyond it, convention's limitations must be challenged aggressively, tested to the point of failure. Superficial deficiencies are the inevitable side effects of groundbreaking work, and they indicate a lack of achievement only if the standards of past practice are the measure of future success. Of course, in experimental practice, the goal is not the rehearsal of precedent but rather the discovery of possibilities. Such a process always involves a degree of risk, and it is likely to leave a few corpses in its wake.[1]

Ironically, the work of PATTERNS rarely calls for such apology. Impeccable craft and meticulous polish hallmark their work at all scales, from the carefully cast Land Tiles at the Materials and Applications Gallery to their completed buildings in Rosario and Los Angeles. Further, where some members of the digital vanguard eschew any connection to disciplinary precedent, tectonic convention, or commercial construction in their relentless pursuit of the Brave New, PATTERNS consistently integrates the familiar into their unfamiliar output. Such incorporation of—but never capitulation to—the conventional sets PATTERNS apart from many in their generation. Not only does this operational promiscuity afford them significant advantages when moving ideas across scales, out of the laboratory, and into the field, it gives rise to complex forms of architectural coherence unavailable to more single-minded experimentation.

Take the Broad Café, an as-yet unrealized intervention developed for SCI-Arc in 2007 [**Fig. 10.3**]. The project is conceived as a complex linear system that develops quotidian counters and display cabinets into a system of wall-mounted and overhead elements that warp, bifurcate, stretch, and pucker to define both the café proper as well as an intimate gathering space on the mezzanine above. Contrasting these directional elements, an irregular grid introduces a syncopated rhythm across the linear trajectories. This cross-fertilization of two contradictory systems elicits an array of propitious effects. Tectonically, the grid breaks the continuous elements into discrete tiles manageable by available fabrication technologies and installation crews. Vertical tile edges and internal dimples afford structural rigidity to the individual panels as well as visual modulations ranging from soft highlights to deep shadows. The vertical fins also provide anchor points for attachment to a structural frame between the plastic panels and the existing concrete building.

Visually, the grid casts the prevalence of the initial linear reading into doubt. From certain vantage points, the project indeed appears as a laminar topology of directional flows. From others, a complex reticulated system dominates. Further complicating these readings, diagonal subdivisions in overhead openings resonate with the forking trunks emanating from the west wall as well as with a nascent diagonal mesh apparent in the easternmost panels. Neither the orthogonal grid, nor the rotated mesh, nor the linear flows

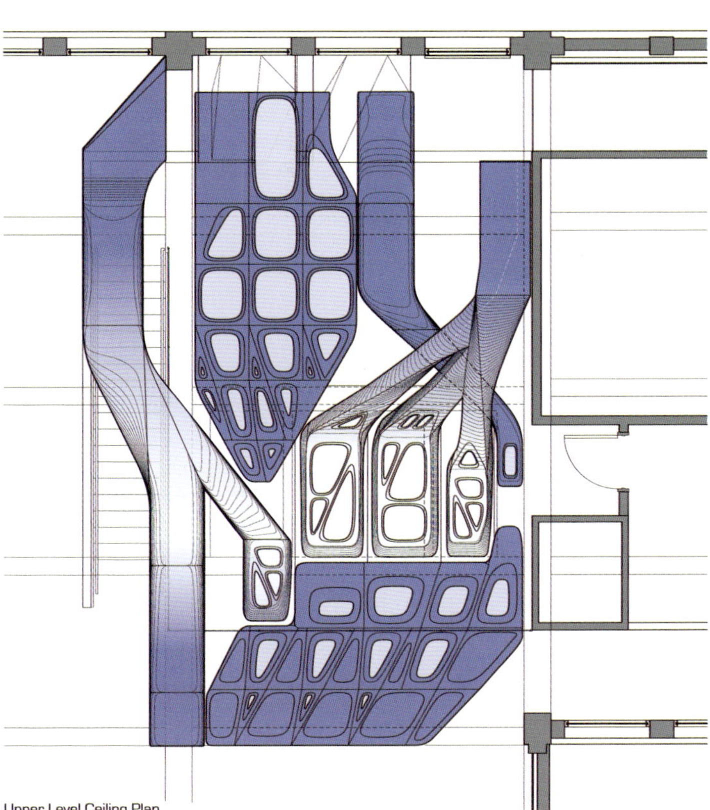

Fig. 10.3 PATTERNS, Broad Café (Los Angeles, 2007). Reflected ceiling plan.

emerges as a dominant system. Instead, interrelated organizations oscillate in a rich ambiguity that refuses to settle into a fixed hierarchy. Even the plastic intervention cannot easily be read as independent of the existing building. Beholden to yet divergent from the existing concrete building as well as from the carefully crafted steel framework that supports it, the intervention casts base building and exotic intervention, digital fabrication and quotidian construction, into uneasy confederations.

While the forms of the Broad Café are undeniably contemporary, strange resonances with conventional construction infiltrate its alien appearance. At times, the work takes on an almost Arts and Crafts flavor, its dimpled surface faintly recalling the ornamental coffers of a tin ceiling, its graceful curves the organic abstractions of Charles Rennie Mackintosh. Other associations are more menacing. Read against the gridded mullions of the existing building's

Fig. 10.4 PATTERNS, FyF Residence (Rosario, 2007).

Fig. 10.5 PATTERNS, Jujuy Redux (Rosario, 2012).

windows, PATTERNS's complexly subdivided apertures suggest diabolical mutation of the existing formal logic. Perhaps the Broad Café resulted from an affliction contracted by the building's concrete, some rare tectonic blistering that softened, discolored, and distended the existing material into a swollen, varicose lesion, possibly benign, but probably malignant.

PATTERNS's work abounds with similar combinations of the *de rigueur* and the deviant. In recent ground-up constructions like the FyF House [**Fig. 10.4**] and Jujuy Redux [**Fig. 10.5**], notice further infections of laminar topologies with reticulated tectonics. The former project braids a pair of discrete linear volumes into a contorted union. Surface tensions thus produced appear to delaminate the monolithic skin, revealing a contrasting structural grid within. In the latter work, conventional ribbon windows twist to merge with balcony handrails, causing herniated ridges to erupt across an otherwise smooth concrete facade.

A sustained examination of FyF undercuts the initial reading of discrete volumes structured by a continuous grid. On the garden façade, the twisting is confined to the pseudo-trellis on the right half of the house. To the left, a clean modernist box, reminiscent of the indifferent glazing at Prism, rests undisturbed by the left-side contortions. Jigsawed apertures only reinforce the division. Reading as deep punches in a thick mass, these openings offer no proportional relationship to the twisted grid on the right, nor does the thick wall afford a compelling affiliation with the thin veneer applied to the grid on the right. Similar dissonant pairings are apparent at the street façade, where an entry void divides the work into distinct halves. The left side is pliable—free to pinch at the entry and stretch at the garage—while the right stands taut and staunchly vertical, only a slight curve in plan replies to the supple undulations at left. Interior spaces, on the other hand, reinforce the initial reading of continuity. Reticulated glazing stitches disparate volumes together, and partitions find their place with little allegiance to the independent strands of the exterior. As at the Broad Café, no reading comes to dominate the others. Instead, the various systems oscillate in an uneasy tension that refuses to settle into a stable unity.

For all its experimentation with affiliated organizational systems, PATTERNS's work does not submit to easy alignment with familiar combinatorial practices such as collage, montage, assemblage, or more recent experiments with parasitic attachment.[2] While an appeal to the mash-up, that contemporary tincture of collage and montage, might account for the aggregated juxtapositions at Prism and FyF, each of these categories implies the distinct juxtaposition of independent elements. Some, like collage, draw attention to the disjunctive seams between composed fragments. Those that aim to erase seams, like the mash-up, nonetheless "emphasize by irony the distinct nature of the elements...and therefore the incoherent juxtapositions at work," as Jeffrey Kipnis has observed.[3] Indeed, an interpretation of PATTERNS's oeuvre wholly in terms of part-to-whole relationships ultimately fails to articulate a more cunning deviance at play in the work, nor does "incoherent juxtaposition" accurately capture the uneasy manner in which PATTERNS causes opposing organizational systems to cohere.

The startling array of dissonant effects—laminar and reticulated, topological and tectonic, contemporary and conventional—in projects like the Broad Café and Jujuy Redux does not arise from the simple aggregation of contrasting elements. Indeed, no single element in these works can be made to submit to decidable affiliation with one system or another. Instead, each project elicits these contrasting qualities from a single system. Broad's plastic panels are simultaneously vectoral and static, Jujuy's concrete spandrels both pliable and rigid. In these projects, PATTERNS does not splice disparate systems into uneasy wholes (as they do at Prism and FyF), but rather reengineers the formal DNA of a single system to expand its affective potential while maintaining its elemental integrity. Jujuy's herniated excrescences do not result from one body impacting another, like a pregnancy. Instead, disparate effects register in a single body to the point of transformative duress, like an abscess. The mode of experimentation here is not one of elemental combination but rather of festering contamination—the laminar afflicted with reticulation, the topological tainted by the tectonic, the contemporary corrupted by convention.

This shift in focus from the disjunctive manipulation of body parts to the intensive disturbance of bodily systems accounts for PATTERNS's unique ability to move beyond the "incoherent juxtaposition" of preexisting elements to the projection of novel strains of architectural coherence.[4] These felonious acts of architectural impropriety are perpetrated against two victims. On one hand, PATTERNS defiles mainstream practice with the topological deviance of the contemporary digital vanguard. On the other, they infect that same vanguard with a virulent dose of mainstream tectonic convention. In the end, these experimental crimes resonate less with Dexter, who takes great care to eradicate the evidence of his unscrupulous activities, than with mad scientists of nineteenth-century fiction. Prism and FyF align PATTERNS with the experimental tactics of Mary Shelley's Dr. Frankenstein, who meticulously sutured disparate parts into a seam-ridden and monstrous new whole. But at their most subversive, as at Jujuy Redux and the Broad Café, PATTERNS cleaves more closely to the techniques of H. G. Wells's Dr. Moreau, whose technical virtuosity at vivisection (in the original novel) and genetic experimentation (in the 1996 film adaptation) gave rise not to a singular monster, but rather to a teeming ecology of aberrant new species.

NOTES

1. These remarks undoubtedly will be construed as a blanket apology for faulty conceptions and slipshod construction. Many recent works have indeed suffered from careless planning and insufficient foresight, and rightly have been taken to task for it. My point here is not to absolve the vanguard of its tectonic sins. Rather, I am suggesting that the presence of last-minute bandages should not be taken as an automatic indication of irrelevance. As often as not (and as much as I'd prefer not to see them), these ad hoc additions alert us that limitations are being tested, that conventions are being challenged, that progress, however halting, is being made.
2. Nor can compliance with earlier categories such as Colin Rowe and Robert Slutzky's "phenomenal transparency" or Robert Venturi's "difficult whole" be sustained. Though resonances with these effects pervade the work, both ultimately appeal to a logic of traditional part-to-whole relationships, and in the end advance little more than clever elaborations of classical unity. Such reliance on traditional part-to-whole coherence comes up short when dealing with PATTERNS's more intensive compositional dynamics. See Colin Rowe and Robert Slutzky, "Transparency: Literal and Phenomenal" [written 1955–56, first published 1963], in *The Mathematics of the Ideal Villa Villa and Other Essays* (Cambridge, MIT Press, 1976); "Transparency: Literal and Phenomenal, Part 2," *Perspecta* 13/14 (1971); and Robert Venturi, *Complexity and Contradiction in Architecture* [1966] (New York: Museum of Modern Art, 1977).
3. Jeffrey Kipnis, "Towards a New Architecture," in *Folding in Architecture*, ed. Greg Lynn (London: Academy Editions, 1993): 48, n. 4. While Kipnis was referring here to "surrealist collage," his remarks are equally applicable to the logic of the mash-up.
4. These forms of coherence resonate distinctly with Kipnis's formulation of "intensive coherence," one of the new Five Points of Architecture he outlines in "Towards a New Architecture," 43. Here, Kipnis stressed the use of "smoothing operations" and other techniques to engender loose affiliations between an intervention and its context (offering Peter Eisenman's Columbus Convention Center, Frank Gehry's Vitra Design Museum, and Shoei Yoh's Odawara Sports Complex as examples) and incongruities between massing and section (as in Bahram Shirdel's Nara Convention Hall project), among other destabilizing formal effects. If PATTERNS had stopped at the similar contextual and spatial ambiguities we noticed at the FyF House and the Prism Gallery, we might conclude that they offer little more than stylish rehearsals of these now nearly twenty-year-old ambitions. Yet in their cunning development of *internal dissonances* within discrete building elements and formal systems, as well as in the careful attention paid to material and atmospheric effects, PATTERNS moves into territory largely unexplored in these earlier projects. For a related discussion of materiality and atmospherics, see my interview with Huljich and Spina, "Ouch or Ooooh? On 'Matters of Sensation,'" *Log* 17 (Fall 2009): 93–104.

Grand Gestures, Intelligent Plans

2013

Fig. 11.1 Tom Wright of WKK, Burj al Arab (Dubai, 1999).

I like buildings that encourage us to think and act differently. The best buildings embolden us to think new thoughts, to assume new postures, to imagine and exercise new kinds of freedom. The best buildings do much more than reimagine a specific place. They provoke us to reimagine ourselves.

Of course, most buildings don't encourage us to behave differently. They simply remind us to behave. In libraries we tend to get quieter, in nightclubs louder. Regardless of our faith, most of us will mind our manners in a church, mosque, or synagogue. Even the most progressive works tend to provoke easily anticipated conduct. The next time you visit that "significant contemporary museum" downtown, notice how quickly the tourists begin to shop and cognoscenti to sulk. Though I subscribe to and advocate the idea that new kinds of architecture can provoke new forms of behavior, I admit that it doesn't happen very often. And when it does, most of us tend not to notice.

In a perceptive 1978 essay, Robin Evans pointed out that one of the most significant developments in the history of architecture was the invention of the corridor.[1] This simple device imposed a radically new kind of order on buildings by separating the spaces in which we do things from the spaces through which we travel. Prior to the sixteenth century, Evans explains, buildings tended to be organized without such distinctions. Instead, rooms were connected directly to one another, with multiple doors linking an array of activities. These "matrix plans" set the stage for the chance encounters and lively social intercourse that characterized courtly life in renaissance Italy. Corridor plans, by contrast, isolate activities by linking rooms not directly to each other but rather to shared circulation routes. Corridor plans became the norm in Victorian England alongside new social values that placed a premium on privacy, efficiency, and isolated contemplation. While Evans did not claim a causal link between architectural plans and social mores, the curious correlation he discovered shed new light on the relationship between the organization of buildings and the kinds of activities likely to take place in them. Today, architects continue to prioritize privacy and isolation with corridor plans. In many cases, they are compelled to do so by building codes that mandate their use. The tendency even has spread to city planning, with highways and cul-de-sacs offering urban analogs to corridors and rooms. As many among us clamor for new forms of community, prevailing design conventions appear to foreclose them.

Which brings us to the hotel. As this catalog and the exhibition it accompanies demonstrate,[2] hotels routinely encourage guests to think and act differently, to assume new postures, to imagine and exercise new kinds of freedom. They do so by sanctioning social intercourse, promoting chance encounters, and re-contextualizing our most mundane and intimate activities. A well-designed hotel serves up both predictability and surprise in carefully prescribed doses, thus offering a potent model for reimagining social relations throughout the built environment. And like the humble corridor, its most effective techniques for doing so tend to operate below the threshold of our attention.

Any hotel's ability to project alternative social configurations has primarily to do with its guests. The fact that most guests don't know one another provides intimacy to strengthen nascent social bonds (think honeymoons) as well as vibrant communities within which to form new ones (think happy hour). A steady stream of new ideas is guaranteed by a constant influx of new guests, whose imminent departure necessitates that we act quickly if we are to take advantage of fleeting opportunities to interact.

Of course, many building types cater to anonymous and transient populations. But the hotel is unique in that its guests rehearse the quotidian activities of home within its walls. Performing familiar rituals such as sleeping, eating, grooming, and sex in a new setting, with novel ingredients and unfamiliar accoutrements, can cause us to experience these activities afresh, to notice their details differently, to imagine and attempt alternative configurations of the commonplace.

Hotel architecture often signals this transformative promise with the Grand Gesture. Think of the castellated massing of the Taj Mahal Palace Hotel in Mumbai, the soaring atrium of the Marriott Marquis in Atlanta, or the sweeping curves of the Fontainebleau in Miami. We find these forms throughout *Grand Hotel*, and most of us have succumbed to their powerful allure. Yet the efficacy of even the grandest gesture will dissipate with time. In order to ensure its progressive social program, a hotel also must perfect a less noticeable but far more affective element—the Intelligent Plan.

In a hotel, the purpose of the intelligent plan is twofold. First, it must mitigate the anti-social effects of transience and anonymity by offering an immediate sense of comfort, control, and security. Second, it must amplify the opportunities that transience and anonymity afford by offering easy access to diversion, chance, and community. A successful hotel often achieves the former by deploying something akin to the corridor plan to organize the individual spaces of the guest rooms and reception, and the latter with a variant of the matrix plan for the collective spaces of the lobby and lounges.

Privileging the individual over the collective, the corridor plan's strict efficiency can quickly impart a welcome sense of control to the guest. Once oriented and refreshed, the guest can confidently slip from the corridor plan's order to the excitement of social spaces organized according to the matrix plan. In each case, carefully calibrated atmospheric effects—light levels, background music, even ambient temperature—will set the tone. Well executed, these essential elements will ensure that the workings of the intelligent plan operate just below the threshold of one's attention.

Think back to your last hotel stay. You probably remember the grand gestures clearly: the stunning spaces, the elegant materials, the unusual forms. Your memory of salient atmospheric effects likely will be murkier but still available. Recalling the specifics of the plan—the route from street to shower, the location of the elevator—probably proves difficult, unless an element within that plan confiscated undue attention. Indeed, something as innocuous as a poorly placed towel bar can nullify the psychological benefits of a friction-free layout. Absent an intelligent plan, the seductive promises broadcast by grand gestures and amplified by atmospheric effects have little hope of being kept.

Recently I was reminded of both the ubiquity of the grand gesture as well as the power of the intelligent plan. An extended layover in Dubai provided the opportunity to visit the Burj al Arab. While there, my wife and I decided to splurge for the Culinary Flight. Described by the hotel's website as "a journey of pure gastronomic decadence," each course of the meal is served in a different space in the hotel. Courteous hotel staff met us in the lobby and escorted us from location to location, dutifully pointing out each of the hotel's opulent frills—cascading lobby fountain, gold-leaf interior columns, massive aquarium—along the way. This meticulous choreography, combined with a building plan that carefully demarcates each space from the next, left little for us to discover on our own. With so much attention lavished on the gestures and so little freedom afforded by the plan, the Burj al Arab offered little in the way of surprise, nearly nothing to nudge us off balance. For all the effort (and expense), the effect was curiously flat.

Not long after, I found myself in Las Vegas. The template for Dubai's decadent kitsch, here you will find the same self-conscious expense, the same meretricious luxury, the same penchant for over-the-top gesture. And here you will also find something conspicuously absent at the Burj al Arab: supremely intelligent plans. Where spaces in the Burj are carefully isolated from one another, in Vegas they elide seamlessly from one to the next. Indeed, even the most clumsily garish casino will reveal in its layout a virtuosic performance in advanced matrix planning. The best casino plans facilitate effortless transitions from street to slot machines, from buffet to blackjack table, from cocktail lounge to card room. More importantly, as R. E. Somol pointed out, they combine with immersive atmospheric effects to "establish a mood (a context) to allow the patron to construct a role as either high roller, swinging Rat Packer, or slumming voyeur."[3]

Though famous for the volume and impact of its grand gestures, Las Vegas has quietly and far more profitably exploited the transformative power of intelligent plans since its invention by Bugsy Siegel in the 1940s. Unfortunately, recent projects have undermined that power by betting too big on grand gestures. New York-New York and the Venetian, for example, employ what Somol called a "built-in redundancy" that refers back to an absent original. This nostalgic technique erases the potentiality of the casinos' planning and ultimately led the critic to an unfortunate conclusion: "What could one become in New York-New York except what one already is—a tourist?"[4]

As we know only too well, similar wagers on nostalgic gestures placed by architects and planners around the world have routinely failed to pay off. These efforts aim to turn us all into tourists, shuttled from attraction to attraction in an endless, and ultimately empty, pursuit of the next big thing (or, worse, of a past that never was). Paradoxically, if we are serious about designing an alternative world that privileges change over stasis, community over isolation, the truly new over the merely novel, the best way to start might just be to pack our bags and check in to the nearest Grand Hotel to troll for ideas. While there, we'll need to look past the easy impact of the grand gesture to see the far more radical potential of the intelligent plan.

NOTES

1. Robin Evans, "Figures, Doors, and Passages" [1978], in *Translations for Drawing to Building and Other Essays* (Cambridge: MIT Press, 1997): 55–91.
2. See *Grand Hotel*, eds. Jennifer M. Volland and Bruce Grenville (Vancouver: Vancouver Museum of Art, 2013).
3. R. E. Somol, "Start Spreading the News," *ANY* 21 (1997): 45.
4. Ibid.

Strange Loops

2017

Fig. 12.1 Abandoned railroad bed crossing Soda dry lake, Zzyzx, California.

> *Beautiful things...act like small tears in the surface of the world that pull us through to some vaster space. ...we find that we are standing in a different relation to the world than we were a moment before. It is not that we cease to stand at the center of the world, for we never stood there. It is that we cease to stand even at the center of our own world. We willingly cede our ground to the thing that stands before us.*
> *– Elaine Scarry* [1]

In his famous 1965 essay, "A Home Is Not a House," Reyner Banham argued for a shift away from traditional built form toward technologically assisted environmental performance. To make his case, he identified a fork in the road of architecture's prehistory:

> Man started with two basic ways of controlling environment: one by avoiding the issue and hiding under a rock, tree, tent, or roof (this led ultimately to architecture as we know it) and the other by actually interfering with the local meteorology, usually by means of a campfire, which, in a more polished form, might lead to the kind of situation now under discussion.[2]

With half a century's hindsight, Banham's partitioning proves less tidy than he made it seem. The tradition of hiding under a rock produces plenty of interference with the local (and global) meteorology, which we now track in terms of resource depletion, carbon footprints, heat islands, and other deleterious effects. At the same time, the technological means with which we interfere tend to produce their own forms of monumentality, as François Dallegret's exquisite drawings that accompanied Banham's essay made clear.

Banham structured some of his most well-known arguments as duels between competing ideologies such as aesthetics and ethics, tradition and technology, and style and performance. While he sometimes displayed a clear preference for the latter terms, more often he worked to uncover hints of "other" architectures that had less to do with abandoning one side for the other than with accounting for the paradoxical co-presence of contradictory ambitions in the built environment.[3]

Though Banham's search for alternatives was cut short by his untimely death in 1988, inventing "other" architectures that more nimbly negotiate the relationship between what we build, where we build it, and how we occupy it remains a pressing concern. As we become increasingly aware of humankind's culpability in the irreversible ecological effects associated with the Anthropocene, so too does considering our impact not only on our own probable futures but also on those of the myriad animal, vegetable, mineral, and other non-human entities affected by our actions.

Promising lines of thought will resist the easy partitioning of issues into dire choices (people versus planet, complacency versus action, oblivion versus salvation) and instead will acknowledge that the options outlined in such showdowns, like those in Banham's binaries, tend to curl back on themselves in complex feedback loops through which environments and their inhabitants co-construct one another. In these loops, oppositions do not finally settle into fixed hierarchies or resolve into dialectical syntheses. Rather, they reveal the imbrication of certainty and doubt, cause and effect, and beauty and justice in the uncanny co-existence of the human "us" and the non-human "other."

Such loops course through *Dark Ecology*, Timothy Morton's 2016 case for a new kind of ecological awareness. Though the effects of positive and negative feedback loops are well known in environmental literature,[4] Morton emphasizes the importance of *strange loops*, paradoxical structures that, like M. C. Escher's drawings, confound our understanding of the hierarchies that organize them.[5] He offers the simple act of starting a car as an example:

> Every time I start my car...I don't mean to harm Earth, let alone cause the Sixth Mass Extinction Event in the four-and-a-half billion-year history of life on this planet. ...Furthermore, I'm not harming Earth! My key turning is statistically meaningless. ...But go up a level and something very strange happens. When I scale up these actions to include billions of key turnings...harm to Earth is precisely what is happening. I am responsible as a member of this species for the Anthropocene.[6]

At varying scales of observation, our everyday actions prove both innocent and apocalyptic. Too often, pundits in the climate wars acknowledge just one metric and argue with half-truths. Yet, strictly speaking, the skeptics are correct—individuals and small groups exact a negligible toll on the environment. Of course, environmentalists are also correct—the human species causes undeniable damage to the planet. Unfortunately, neither side knows where to draw the line between innocence and culpability. Definitive answers to the most difficult questions elude us, so round and round it goes. Everybody's right; nobody wins.

In *Dark Ecology,* Morton attempts to break the logjam. Key to his argument is accepting that ecological awareness is *weird.* Etymologically, the term implies both looped structures and more familiar associations with the alien and strange. Rather than work to domesticate the world's weirdness (as Western thinking usually does), Morton exalts it. He revels in paradoxes—you are both individual and species, both part of the problem and not—encountered everywhere in ecological debates. He does so not to resolve contradictions, but rather, by showing that uncanny actions and paradoxical co-existences are less exceptions than the rule, to outline a future at one with the mystery and magic he finds throughout the world.

Morton draws heavily on the philosophical movement of object-oriented ontology (OOO),[7] in which he is a major voice, and devotes significant attention to the problem of causality. A succinct gloss concludes with a crucial claim:

> Object-oriented ontology holds that things exist in a profoundly "withdrawn" way. They cannot be splayed open and totally grasped by anything whatsoever, including themselves. You can't know a thing fully by thinking it or by eating it or by measuring it or by

> painting it. ...This means that the way things affect one another (causality) cannot be direct (mechanical), but rather [is] indirect and vicarious: causality is aesthetic.[8]

At first blush, Morton's claim may seem counterintuitive. Termites chomped on a wood beam and caused it to collapse. Case closed. OOO doesn't see it so simply. Graham Harman, generally regarded as the movement's founder, builds on the thought of Edmund Husserl and Martin Heidegger to understand the world in terms of *sensual objects,* which (following Husserl) are available to consciousness, and *real objects,* which (following Heidegger) cannot be known. For OOO, the most salient distinctions are not between subjects and objects (as in most Western philosophy), but rather between autonomous entities (real, but impossible to know) and relational ones (sensual, and available to consciousness).[9]

Think again about those termites. I'm willing to bet you know next to nothing about them, and not much more about the wood they chomped. Even expert entomologists and dendrologists are only capable of perceiving a tiny sliver of the roiling complexities we reductively label termites and wood. That sliver resides entirely in Harman's sensual realm. In the parlance of OOO, the real termites and the real wood are "withdrawn from access." You can't interact directly with them, and they can't interact directly with you. Neither can the termites interact directly with the wood, nor the wood with the termites, nor the termites and the wood with themselves. And yet, both the termites and the wood were altered by their meeting. This is possible because for OOO causality is indirect; reality is elsewhere.

This introduces a problem. Things clearly *happen,* even if we cannot fully know *how* they happen. The aesthetic dimension, Morton's version of Harman's sensual realm, accounts for the how of happening. It provides a way to understand that objects interact with one another (and with themselves) at a distance.[10] This is not to say that our termite-induced structural failure didn't happen but rather, paradoxically, that it happened without direct contact between the respective realities of the termites, the wood, and us, who must now deal with the shattered structural member in our kitchen. In other words, Morton's aesthetic dimension demonstrates that interactions between objects are profoundly weird. There is more going on in them than we can possibly know, and most of it happens beyond the sphere of our consciousness.[11]

However interesting it may be, possessing a philosophically sound account of causality is not normally a concern as we stretch an actual tarp over the actual hole in our termite-ridden roof. This makes philosophy easy to ignore, and most of the time most of us do so quite happily. This is too bad, for philosophy opens an invaluable window onto the most mysterious aspects of our world.

Think back to the day you decided to buy that house. As you walked into the light-bathed kitchen, its exposed beams drawing your eyes through glass walls to a lush garden beyond, something hit you—you love this place. What hit you? Certainly, it wasn't the house. Most of your contact with the house was incidental. Its surfaces directed photons toward your eyes, your weight caused its floors to deflect imperceptibly, et cetera. But for the most part the house just sat there unperturbed by your presence, and physically you were scarcely impacted by it. Yet somehow it had a profound effect on you. In fact, it was the house that hit you, but it did so without physically hitting you. It affected you *at a distance*. That is, it affected you aesthetically.

OOO helps us to see that that the world often operates more like art than machinery. There is more to causality than direct, "sensual" contact, as when a piston turns a crank or a termite eats a beam. Causality among "real" objects is indirect and extremely weird, as when a termite eats a beam or a work of architecture "moves you." Aesthetic causality, the kind that counts for OOO, is causality without contact.

By linking it so closely with causality, Morton seems to move aesthetics away from its traditional associations with beauty. In fact, he doesn't move it that far.[12] Consider his take on the causal ambiguities of beauty: "The basic issue with beauty is that it is ungraspable. I can't point directly to it and I can't decide whether it's me or the thing that is emanating beauty. ...Things influence one another such that they become entangled and smear together."[13] As with those billions of car ignitions, a weird looping structure undoes straightforward mechanical causality and calls into question the status of subjects and objects.[14] For Morton, these loops, and the flattened hierarchies that result from them, demand a wholesale reconsideration of philosophy, politics, and art. Through them, he aims to articulate, as opposed to camouflage, our paradoxical status as both perpetrators and victims of ecological crimes and to chart an alternative future through "ecognosis," his neologism for a fuller, more honest, and even joyous knowing of our place both in and as the world.[15]

Dark Ecology presents a daring alternative to mainstream ecological thinking. The intellectual investment, however, is substantial. For architects, it involves extended sojourns into territory beyond even the most ambitiously drawn disciplinary boundaries. Many won't be willing to make the trip. Fortunately, uncanny premonitions of Morton's ideas exist comfortably within the architectural ken, in Reyner Banham's late-career writings on the American desert.

In these little-discussed texts, Banham set out to make sense of the fascination, exhilaration, and befuddlement he felt in the Mojave and other western deserts. His is not the pristine, empty desert of popular imagination, but rather a "man-mauled" landscape literally shot through with evidence of human activity.[16] It is crisscrossed by freeways and power lines, pockmarked by rusted out cars and deserted campsites, and punctuated by odd "oases" like Baker, Zzyzx, and Las Vegas. All this adds to the desert's poetry, and some objects, such as the McMath-Pierce solar telescope in Arizona, exude a stunning sense of rightness and conviction. Banham's experience is far removed from Frank Lloyd Wright's romantic quip that the desert represents "where God is and man is not."[17] The term desert, Banham reminds us, is rooted in desertion and abandonment.[18] As human activity is integral to Morton's understanding of ecology, for Banham, people precede the desert.

And like Morton's ecology, Banham's desert is deeply weird. Each chapter in *Scenes in America Deserta* (1982) begins with a "Revelation" provoked by the desert's alien qualities. These range from strange atmospheric effects ("It was uncanny, as if the law of nature had been suspended.") to the appropriateness of the unusual ("Only the exotic or the outrageous in architecture tends to look at home…") to personal feelings of incongruity ("I kept my head down, and wondered if I seemed equally weird…").[19] At Mesa Verde and other "inscrutable" ancient sites, Banham feels alienated, as if he had "come up against a glass wall through which seeing was possible but comprehension was not."[20]

Yet with its alien forms, uncanny colors, and ethereal light, Banham finds the desert to be profoundly beautiful. Here again we find an eerie parallel with Morton. For Morton, the joy of ecognosis is akin to the experience of the immersive colored light in a James Turrell installation, in which "the environment at its purest seems to absorb me from all sides."[21] Banham finds a similarly ecstatic dissolution outside Las Vegas:

> The towers of lights and the changing skysigns were...wavering dizzily and fractured into flickering filaments and ripples of pink and electric blue and gold, floating above a reflecting pool of mirage in the purple air. ...the effect was...like a dream city dissolving in its own ecstasy.[22]

Like Morton, Banham finds traditional aesthetic terminology inadequate to understanding such beauty. "The desert," he observed, "is not strictly "beautiful" in the technical sense of the term as employed by eighteenth century philosophers of aesthetics."[23] Nor was Plato's discourse on beauty, "so good on solids...disappointing on color and...dull on light," up to the task.[24] Rather, in a distinct premonition of one of Morton's favorite phrases, Banham finally admits that the desert "just is" beautiful.[25]

Even so, the desert's beauty appears to have to do with a Kantian sense of displaced causality: "Something in my long-term uneasiness and fascination with the desert derives from my never having found a suitable disguise or function with which to designate my relationship to the landscape I love."[26] This insight leads Banham to reassess his own subjectivity:

> The desert has made me ask questions about myself that I would never otherwise have asked. And since I have no convincing answers to those questions...I have not done what one is supposed to do in the desert ever since the time of Moses—I have not "found myself." If anything I have lost myself, in the sense that I now feel that I understand myself less than before.
>
> What I have truly found, however, is something that I value, in some ways, more than myself.[27]

Thus, Banham arrives at a place Morton would discover three decades later, a place where we humans might learn to shed at least some of the persistent anthropocentrism we have inherited, to relinquish our claim to stand at the center of the universe, and to face up to the role we have played in making and unmaking the world around us. Whether we trace the twisting braids of Morton's dark ecology or set out along more scenic routes in the desert with Banham, we will discover an environment bereft of its mythological trappings and stripped bare of its supposedly "natural" purity, a landscape "stained and trampled, franchised and fenced, burned, flooded, grazed, mined, exploited, and laid waste."[28] This place is weird, alien, and uncanny, coiled into strange loops by persistent ironies and paradox. "We need to learn to live with situations like that," Banham reminds us, "to take pleasure and reward from the good we can extract from the results of our actions, as well as responsibility for our often unforeseeable consequences."[29]

Pleasure and responsibility. In place of the stark choice between (apparently extraneous) form and (supposedly productive) function with which we began, a last strange loop, this one between an end effect of beauty and a root cause of justice. Linked through language in shared affinities to the word "fair," the two concepts are analogous; beauty motivates the slackening of self-interest from which justice springs.[30] It should come as no surprise that aesthetics would figure so strongly in projecting viable futures in the Anthropocene.

NOTES

1. Elaine Scarry, *On Beauty and Being Just* (Princeton, NJ: Princeton University Press, 1999): 112.
2. Reyner Banham, "A Home Is Not a House," *Art in America* 53:5 (1965): 75.
3. See Todd Gannon, *Reyner Banham and the Paradoxes of High Tech* (Los Angeles: Getty Research Institute, 2017).
4. Positive feedback loops amplify changes in a system and often produce damaging ecological consequences, as when fertilizer is added to soil to increase its fecundity and eventually results in the degradation of that soil. Negative feedback loops mitigate change, as when increasing heat generated by a furnace signals a thermostat to break the circuit that powers the furnace. For a discussion, see Timothy Morton, *Dark Ecology: For a Logic of Future Coexistence* (New York: Columbia University Press, 2016): 7.
5. See Douglas Hofstadter, *Gödel, Escher, Bach: An Eternal Golden Braid* (New York: Basic Books, 1979).
6. Morton, *Dark Ecology*, 8.
7. For a more substantial discussion of OOO in the context of architecture see Todd Gannon, Graham Harman, David Ruy, and Tom Wiscombe, "The Object Turn: A Conversation," 200–25 in this volume. Mark Foster Gage's "Killing Simplicity, Object-Oriented Philosophy in Architecture, *Log* 33 (Winter/Spring 2015): 95–106 is also apropos.
8. Morton, *Dark Ecology*, 16. Morton develops the point in greater detail in *Realist Magic: Objects, Ontology, Causality* (Ann Arbor, Mich.: Open Humanities Press, 2013).
9. Graham Harman, *The Quadruple Object* (Winchester, UK: Zero Books, 2011).
10. Morton, *Dark Ecology*, 17. Also see Harman, *The Quadruple Object*, 69–81.
11. Morton's thinking, and the thrust of OOO more generally, starkly contrasts theories of direct causation (often referred to as "naïve realism"), which hold that objects in the world interact directly, and that that interaction is available, unimpeded, to our consciousness. References to the long history of philosophical assaults on naïve realism, as well to recent advances in theoretical physics and quantum mechanics that further strain its credibility, pepper the literature of OOO.
12. Causality was baked into Immanuel Kant's famous characterization of a beautiful object as involving purposiveness without purpose just as it was in Horatio Greenough's definition of beauty as "the promise of function." Notice in both cases that the cause of beauty, its purpose, is displaced in space and time. Kant relegates purpose to an ambiguous elsewhere (purpose is absent), while Greenough puts it off until later (function is in the future). See Immanuel Kant, *Critique of Judgment* [1790] (New York: Hafner Press, 1951): 56; and Horatio Greenough, "Relative and Independent Beauty" [1852], in idem., *Form and Function: Remarks on Art, Design, and Architecture* (Berkeley: University of California Press, 1947): 71.
13. Morton, *Dark Ecology*, 149–50.
14. It also answers objections that aesthetic effects are produced solely in the mind of the perceiving

subject, that beauty is in the eye of the beholder. Beauty, for Morton and other proponents of OOO, is very much in the world.

15. Morton, *Dark Ecology*, 153–58.
16. Banham, "The Man-Mauled Desert," in Richard Misrach, *Desert Cantos* (Albuquerque: University of New Mexico Press, 1987): 1–6. On the ubiquity of shell casings on the desert floor, see Banham, *Scenes in America Deserta* (Salt Lake City: Gibbs M. Smith, 1982): 170.
17. See Frank Lloyd Wright, *An Autobiography* (New York: Longmans, Green and Co., 1932): 304, where Wright attributes the phrase to Victor Hugo. Banham discusses Wright's activities in the desert in *Scenes in America Deserta*, 69–89.
18. Banham, *Scenes in America Deserta*, 205.
19. Ibid., 20, 68, 110.
20. Ibid., 120.
21. Morton, *Dark Ecology*, 158.
22. Banham, *Scenes in America Deserta*, 208.
23. Ibid., 17.
24. Ibid., 224.
25. Ibid., 221.
26. Ibid., 227.
27. Ibid., 228.
28. Banham, "The Man-Mauled Desert," 1. These are just some of the traces of the twelve-thousand-year history of "agrilogistics" that Morton outlines in *Dark Ecology*.
29. Banham, "The Man-Mauled Desert," 6.
30. Scarry, *On Beauty and Being Just*, 86–93.

What's Wrong with Making Federal Buildings Beautiful Again

2020

Fig. 13.1 Benjamin Latrobe, et al., United States Capitol (Washington, D.C., 1800–1960).

This past week, a frenzied debate erupted in response to "Making Federal Buildings Beautiful Again," a draft executive order that, if adopted, would effectively mandate "the classical architectural style" for US federal buildings.

Assembled by the National Civic Art Society, a little-known organization dedicated to the promotion of classical architecture and design, the order proposes to rewrite the US General Services Administration's "Guiding Principles for Federal Architecture," a three-point policy document written in 1962 by the late Senator Daniel Patrick Moynihan, then special assistant to the Secretary of Labor, to focus the architectural ambitions of the GSA.

Moynihan's first and third directives aim squarely at design, insisting that federal buildings "reflect the dignity, enterprise, vigor, and stability of the American National Government" and that careful consideration be given to the building site and the layout of adjacent streets, public spaces, and landscape. His second speaks more generally to matters of architectural style:

> The development of an official style must be avoided. Design must flow from the architectural profession to the Government. And not vice versa. ...The advice of distinguished architects ought to, as a rule, be sought prior to the award of important design contracts.

The crux of MFBBA's argument is that Moynihan's second principle precludes his first. By granting authority on matters of style to architects, it claims, the guiding principles supplant the preferences of the American people with "the architectural profession's reigning orthodoxy." This, it continues, "implicitly discouraged classical and other designs known for their beauty," and sanctioned instead modernist, brutalist, and deconstructivist buildings which "have little aesthetic appeal," citing work by Marcel Breuer, Mack Scogin Merrill Elam Architects, Morphosis, and others as examples. In so doing, the order claims, "the Federal government has largely stopped building beautiful buildings that the American people want to look at or work in."

To encourage the design of buildings that inspire "admiration" instead of "public derision," the order proposes that "in the National Capital [*sic*] Region and for all Federal courthouses, the classical architectural style shall be the preferred and default style absent special extenuating factors necessitating another style."

While this technically leaves open the possibility of non-traditional design, MFBBA sets an extremely high bar for its approval. Brutalism, deconstructivism, and their derivatives (specified by extremely problematic, open-ended definitions) are excluded outright. Other non-traditional buildings would be permitted to move forward only with approval from the president, who must first be provided with a detailed explanation of "whether such design is as beautiful...as alternative designs of comparable cost in a traditional architectural style."

The term *beauty*, or one of its derivatives, appears twelve times in MFBBA's seven pages. Though it is not included in the document's list of definitions, it is used throughout to signify those qualities that give pleasure to the senses and the intellect. At its core, then, this debate is about more than just architectural style. It is about publicly funded pleasure.

The art critic Dave Hickey similarly locates the essence of beauty in pleasure. In his 2009 essay, "American Beauty," he finds it primarily in the "pleasant surprises" one encounters in everyday life. Such pleasure, whether derived from monumental architecture, a clear blue sky, or a perfectly executed jump shot, often leads people—Americans in particular—to dialog. "Beautiful!" someone exclaims, moved by an arresting object or experience. Others respond, sometimes in agreement, sometimes in dissent. Chatter ensues, occasionally moving toward the consensus from which societies are built. "American beauty is inextricable from its optimal social consequence,"

Hickey writes, "our membership in a happy coalition of citizens who agree on what is beautiful, valuable, and just."

In American society, beauty, value, and justice are determined similarly—through the often-contentious debates we conduct in Congress, in court, in the press, in the marketplace, at school, at home, and out in the street. Given the complexity of these collective conversations (and the difficulty of surprising oneself), we often turn to trained experts—elected representatives, lawyers, cultural critics, brokers, artists, architects, and others—to generate possibilities and look after our interests. Though it often seeks guidance in expert opinion, American society is not based on timeless values, religious doctrine, or ancient edicts. It is based on mutual agreement.

With the Declaration of Independence, Americans mutually agreed to their collective right to pursue "pleasant surprises" and other forms of happiness, and to tentatively ascribe power to the government to secure that right. This is where it gets complicated. As Hickey points out, every pleasant surprise is an occasion for change, an opportunity to renegotiate our collective agreement regarding what we hold to be beautiful, valuable, and just. Such activity always threatens the status quo, which is why authoritarian societies often attempt to neutralize such threats by outlawing idiosyncrasy and mandating familiarity.

MFBBA adopts exactly this authoritarian posture, though its authors undoubtedly would point to their populist invocations of "the public" and to their proposal that all GSA architectural competitions convene public panels that exclude design and construction professionals as evidence of their efforts to foster exactly the sort of open debate I am advocating. Such arguments would ring false. With their thumb firmly on the scale from the outset, MFBBA's authors decide in advance the outcome of public deliberation on federal buildings. Their message is clear: when it comes to the most hallowed spaces of our democracy, the American debate on beauty—and by extension, on value and justice—is settled.

The authors of "Making Federal Buildings Beautiful Again" thus work entirely on the side of entrenched authority, and rightly recognize the federal buildings of Breuer, Morphosis, Scogin, Elam, and others as subtly subversive. These works signal that the brilliance of American democracy issues from its accommodation of periodic reinvention, from our collective agreement that what we held to be beautiful, valuable, and just yesterday may not align with what we will hold to be so tomorrow.

This is not to say that progressive architecture best represents our union, or that classically derived designs can no longer embody American values. It is merely to recognize, as Daniel Moynihan did, that we would do well to continue to draw on "the finest contemporary American architectural thought" to help us determine the best way forward, and to remember that the "dignity, enterprise, vigor, and stability" of the American government obtains from the right of its citizens to perpetually renegotiate the terms by which we are governed, to reimagine the values we wish to uphold, and to freely pursue the subversive pleasures of beauty.

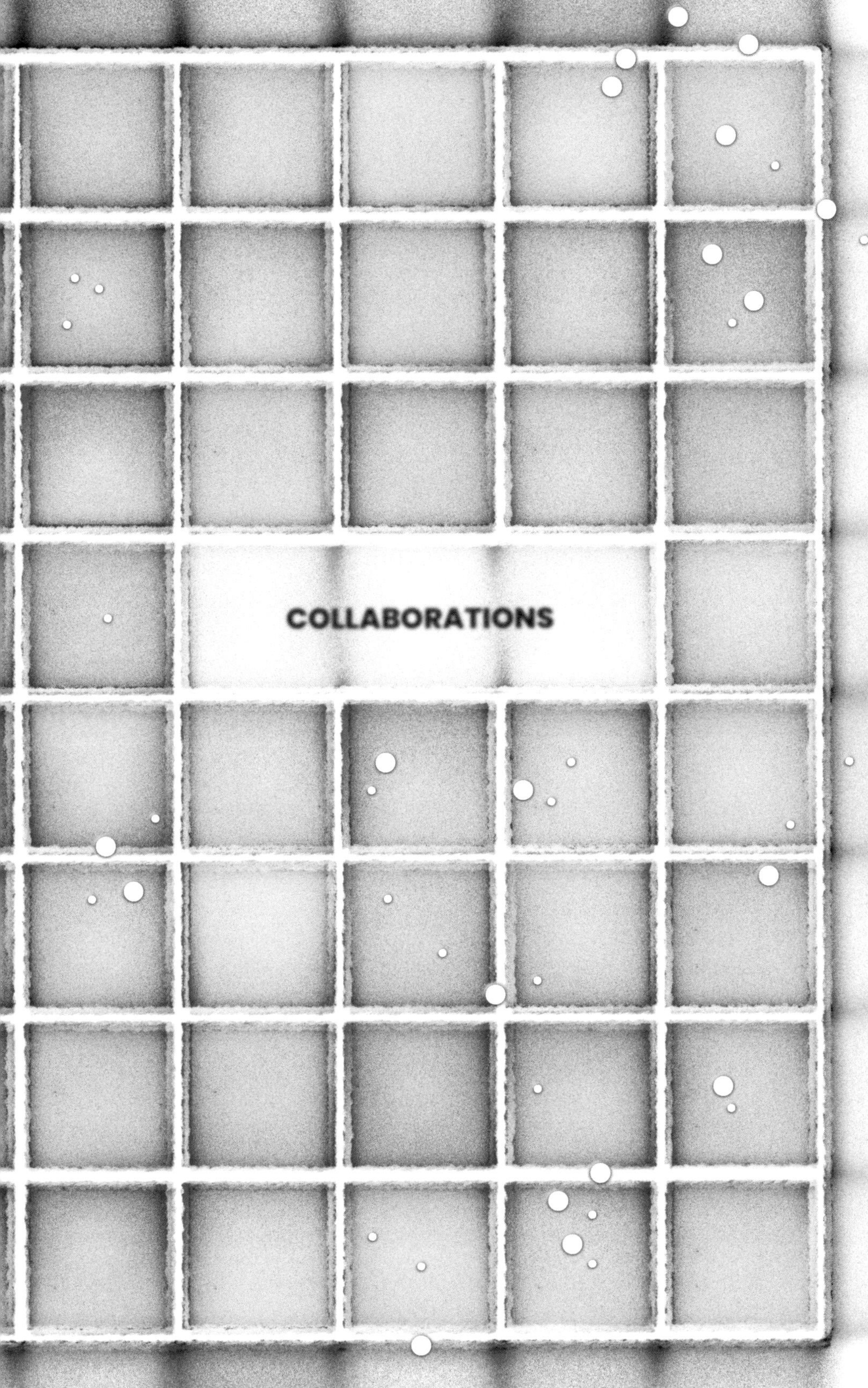
COLLABORATIONS

Mood Swings: The Aesthetics of Ambient Emergence

with N. Katherine Hayles, 2007

Fig. 14.1 servo, *Dark Places* (Santa Monica, 2006).

On or about August 1995, postmodernism died. Or at least one version did—the one characterized by shock, disorientation, and hyperbole at the meteoric rise of the information age. The demise was heralded by the IPO of Netscape, the first commercial web browser to be both robust and user-friendly. As the World Wide Web exploded at exponential rates, experiences of virtuality ceased to be confined to high-tech research laboratories funded by military grants and became part of everyday life in developed regions across the globe, including North America, Japan, Europe, and India, among others. Fredric Jameson's idea that space, mirroring the inconceivable complexities of the infosphere, had become fractally complex was not so much proved wrong as displaced by the increasingly banal activity of surfing the web;[1] Jean-François Lyotard's assertion that the contemporary period is marked by an "incredulity towards metanarratives" was absorbed into the cultural mainstream, only to come smack against a return to fundamentalism and simplistic global explanations emanating alike from evangelical Christians and Islamic extremists;[2] Jean Baudrillard's titillating suggestion that reality had "imploded" into hyperreality ceased to function as a transgressive theoretical conceit, displaced by the everydayness of navigating virtual spaces that somehow left no one in doubt reality was as "real" as ever.[3] With late capitalism showing no signs of giving way to a successor regime, the adjective began to appear less like a description and more like wishful thinking. As Bruno Latour already observed a couple of years ago, critique as it was practiced in the heyday of high theory, epitomized by the difficult productive obscurities of deconstructive rhetoric, has seemed to have run out of steam, with current practitioners sounding more nostalgic than cutting-edge.[4]

The shift from one period to another, or as Raymond Williams put it, one structure of feeling to another, is signaled less by successful solutions than by changing foci of attention. The problems the previous era found compelling have not so much been solved as they have ceased to be interesting. The new sensibility can aptly be characterized as a change of feeling, a shift in the mode of address, a new focus of attention. Let us call it a mood swing.[5] We are less interested in coining a clever new term to denote it than in describing its characteristics. Our target areas to assess its manifestations are literature and architecture, fields in which the two of us respectively have major investments. One of us is a literary critic with significant interdisciplinary interests, and the other a practicing architect and student of architectural and cultural theory. The two fields in which we count ourselves among the stakeholders have more in common than may at first appear. Literary studies was one of the major vectors through which postmodernism and deconstruction entered the North American scene, and architecture was foremost among the applied fields in which interpretations of deconstruction reached material instantiation.

Postmodernism in architecture was inaugurated when Charles Jencks declared the end of modern architecture to be 15 July 1972, 3:32pm, the moment Minoru Yamasaki's Pruitt-Igoe housing project (1952–55) was imploded. Standing for less than twenty years, the work symbolized for Jencks all that was wrong with the architecture of the modern period: sterile, inhumane, anonymous, and most importantly for Jencks, insufficiently equipped legibly to transmit information. Jencks brought the term postmodernism into architectural parlance and became its most enthusiastic proponent, with the many editions of his *Language of Post-Modern Architecture* functioning as a serialized chronicle of the movement. Borrowing from the semiotics of Umberto

Eco, Jencks championed an architecture of legible, multivalent meaning. From this point on, the practice of "reading" buildings, shorthand for the rigorous interpretation of architectural configuration previously practiced in a few vanguard institutions, became commonplace in architectural schools around the globe. Following Jencks and borrowing heavily from critical theory in other disciplines, intellectual architects devised robust techniques for writing cultural critique in architectural form. During the same period, Peter Eisenman drove advanced architecture further into a linguistic frame of mind. Influenced by the writings of Saussure, Chomsky, and later Derrida, Eisenman introduced a difficult indexicality to the cutting edge of architecture that paralleled deconstructive rhetoric in literary studies. Simultaneously, architectural publications mushroomed in number and intensity, as practicing architects and critics alike produced project monographs, critical essays, and theoretical texts at an unprecedented rate. By 2000, however, the major vehicles of critical writing in architecture launched during the period—*Assemblage, Oppositions,* and *ANY*—were all defunct.

Like contemporary literary studies, architecture has turned away from postmodernism and ventured into new structures of feeling. A broad set of thematics, perhaps more readily apparent at the intersections of literature and architecture than in either field alone, characterizes the shift. In both disciplines, we see a renewed emphasis on the materiality of surfaces, an effect closely related, we will argue, to the deep penetration of digital technologies into the practices of architecture and the conditions of production for contemporary electronic and print literature. Entwined with this attention to the materiality of surfaces is *intermediation,* a term that implies both mediation and intervention. As we use the term, it refers to the complex dynamics between old and new media, specifically digital and print media. As computers penetrate and inform everyday practices in virtually all areas of society and culture, performance acquires a more active role in the production of texts as well as buildings than was previously the case with print media, creating possibilities for dynamic physical and textual environments that change in response to user intervention and real-time data flows. The increased flexibility that digital technologies allow in creating ambient effects has also led to experiments in the limits of legibility for literature, and for architecture, a turn away from the tendency to "read" structures to an emphasis on the changing environmental inflections of ambient surfaces, along with renewed interest in the relation of architecture and affect. Enhancing the power and flexibility of design practices in literature and architecture, digital media have also reinforced and extended the ways in which human intelligence is enfolded together with machine cognition. This entwining has been accompanied by a sharper, deeper realization that agency is distributed across an entire complex system that contains both human and nonhuman actors, so that compositional practices for both literature and architecture are now, more than ever, not simply the enactment of pre-existing ideas but rather fluid transformative processes influenced both by the capabilities of intelligent machines and the creative intuitions and rational plans of human participants.

In richly diverse ways, then, these emphases connect with the spread of networked and programmable media. To rehearse only a few of the factors at work, we note that in architecture, computers have all but replaced the drawing board; 3D modeling, digital fabrication, and cinematic pre-visualizations are commonplace.[6] As Michael Speaks has pointed out, significant design theorization now takes place through the processes of design as well as fabrication, so that computation pervades architectural thinking on preconscious as well as conscious levels.[7] In literary studies, the advent of electronic literature as a significant component of the twenty-first-century canon has transformed reading and writing practices, introducing strong performative aspects and expanding the sensory range of texts not only into visual but also into kinesthetic, haptic, and proprioceptive realms. Moreover, even print texts have been transformed as contemporary printing technologies incorporate computers and digitally driven machines into every aspect of the design, production, and marketing of books. As a result, the legacy systems of speech and writing now dynamically interact with code as a language system addressed both to humans and intelligent machines, a situation that manifests itself in transformations of linguistic surfaces in both print and digital literature.

Just as postmodernism as an aesthetic did not emerge in isolation but rather as part of a constellation of forces that converged as the economy shifted from an industrial Fordist regime to what David Harvey has called the postmodern "regime of accumulation," so the mood shift we trace has complex connections with the emergence of network culture and what Manuel Castells has called "informationalism."[8] After delineating the characteristics of the shift, we will return briefly to discuss this entanglement. Let us turn now to a detailed exposition of materiality and intermediation, with glances at the other factors involved. In the analysis that follows, our two voices will together weave the story of the mood swing toward what we call the aesthetics of ambient emergence.

MATERIALITY IN ARCHITECTURE: LIGHT CONSTRUCTION

In September 1995, swift on the heels of Netscape's launch, the Museum of Modern Art in New York opened *Light Construction*, an international survey of projects that marked what curator Terence Riley dubbed a "shift in sensibility."[9] As he states in the exhibition catalog, this new sensibility "not only reflects the distance of our culture from the machine aesthetic of the early twentieth century but marks a fundamental shift in emphasis after three decades when debate in architecture focused on issues of form. In projects notable for artistic and technical innovation, contemporary designers are investigating the nature and potential of architectural surfaces."[10]

An important ingredient in this new sensibility was a keen attention to material effects, chiefly to those produced by glass. Though a key material in the theoretical conceptions of modernism, glass as *Light Construction* saw it had less to do with the idealized transparency espoused in the early twentieth century than with an array of materially contingent reflections, obscurities, opacities, and translucencies.[11] These effects, difficult to discern in traditional architectural representations, are not a function of architecture's abstract configuration but rather emerge from the interplay of that configuration with its brute physicality. Turning the tables on half a century of formalist compositional criticism, *Light Construction* celebrated the visual noise produced by fleeting reflections on glass surfaces, that troublesome feedback disdained in the work of Walter Gropius and ignored in the work of Le Corbusier by Colin Rowe and Robert Slutzky in their famous analysis of the former's Bauhaus in Dessau and the latter's Villa Stein at Garches.[12] The exhibition's attention to materiality highlighted the shortcomings of formalist interpretations that bracket individual works as autonomous objects and pointed to the necessity of considering the complex dynamics between architectural form, its specific material instantiation, and the particularities of its environmental context.

Light Construction traced a shift in attention away from projects such as Peter Eisenman's DAAP in Cincinnati [**Fig. 14.2**] to projects like Herzog and de Meuron's Signal Box auf dem Wolf in Basel [**Fig. 14.3**]. From his early work in the 1970s to the present, Eisenman has drawn extensively on literary and linguistic theory, even collaborating with Jacques Derrida on a design for the Parc de la Villette in Paris.[13] Throughout Eisenman's oeuvre, these theoretical influences are developed through relentless elaboration of architectural representations such as floor plans and sections as well as more abstract configurational diagrams. Like many practitioners through the 1970s, poor economic conditions offered Eisenman few opportunities to

Fig. 14.2 Peter Eisenman, Aronoff Center for Design and Art (Cincinnati, 1996).

Fig. 14.3 Herzog and de Meuron, Signal Box auf dem Wolf (Basel, Switzerland, 1995).

build his radical ideas, and the majority of his projects of the period remain unbuilt, their lasting influence a function of the extensive publication of his elaborate drawings and models. The few built projects of the 1970s, like the DAAP in Cincinnati and much of his later work, tend to be clad in cheap, neutral materials that primarily operate as notational signifiers. Of primary importance is the ability to read individual compositional components (signaled in Cincinnati by variously coloured EIFS, an inexpensive synthetic plaster[14]) as legible signs affiliated with one or another formal system. For Eisenman, drawings, texts, and completed buildings carried equal weight within the overall architectural project.

Herzog and de Meuron, on the other hand, eschewed overt theoretical references, complex plans, and fragmentary geometries, advancing instead simple cubic volumes clad in seductive skins of copper, patterned glass, natural stone, and other exquisite materials. HdM's floor plans, distilled to minimal, expedient solutions of functional needs, offer little formal interest. For the buildings' complexity, one must turn away from these abstract representations of the building form to the material instantiation of the building surface. In the Basel Signal Boxes, simple Cartesian volumes are uniformly clad in continuous copper bands. In certain areas, these bands are subtly twisted to reveal faint hints of mysterious windows beyond. Whereas Eisenman's complex assemblage of overlapping grids and layered geometries produce multivalent formal relationships, each compositional element is delineated as materially unequivocal and distinct. HdM in contrast treats the entire building as a single entity and employs material and lighting effects to modulate the illusion of depth across a continuous surface. In short, Eisenman suppressed materiality to underscore formal effects, while HdM suppressed form to foreground materiality.

This comparison of a programmatically complex architecture school and an effectively uninhabited container of electrical switching equipment is perhaps a bit unfair. Both projects represent extreme cases of the architects' respective ambitions, and in the ten years since the exhibition, the work of Eisenman and HdM has approached each other in many ways, with the former experimenting much more aggressively with material effects and the latter producing increasingly complex formal configurations. But the contrast between these two seminal works of the 1990s, particularly the role of representational drawings and theoretical content in each, clearly illustrates some of the tell-tale symptoms of the mood swing that swept through the discipline in the 1990s.

Though *Light Construction* championed a formal pluralism and included an array of diversely configured projects, Riley's show at the Museum of Modern Art was often characterized as dismissing "blobs," projects that explored increasingly complex geometries, in favor of "boxes," projects in which formal configuration took a back seat to material and perceptual concerns.[15] Structured as such, the debate was confined to purely formal terms and missed the broader implications of the exhibited works' renewed attention to materiality. The exhibition paralleled the rise of computers in the design studio; as programs became more robust and practitioners more facile, the formal debate between blobs and boxes was not so much decided as rendered irrelevant. To a computer, a blob and a box are fundamentally identical—each reducible to a distribution of a fixed number of pixels on a screen, and each described by equally complex program algorithms, binary codes, and fluctuating voltages.[16]

Whether aligned more closely to the configurationally complex "blobs" or to the geometrically restrained "boxes," practitioners of all stripes, spurred on by the computational horsepower of the computer, tended toward increased attention to material effects. Digital technologies allowed an expanded ability to measure and draw complex configurations, while structural forces in even maddeningly complex forms could be accurately calculated. With CAD/CAM technology,[17] these intricate shapes, at first confined to the virtual space of digital representation, have become increasingly cost effective to fabricate. In addition, powerful rendering packages allowed for the economical and realistic study of materials and lighting effects in the virtual space of the computer. These convincing simulations enabled increasingly subtle studies of material effects on even the simplest forms. Material conditions that previously could be represented only through painstaking and often prohibitively expensive analog techniques were now easily produced and effortlessly manipulated. Combined with the robust economy of the dot com boom, these technologies produced the ability to move the paper experiments of the 1970s and '80s into the physical world, and the profits these technologies generated launched a generation of clients and patrons eager to underwrite an avant-garde architecture of the information age.

LITERARY/LITERAL MATERIALITY

For literature, the emphasis on materiality in the 1990s and beyond has been catalyzed by the deep penetration of digital technologies into literary arenas. For electronic literature, materiality implies exploring the medium through which the works are created and performed; for print literature, a complex recursive dynamic has emerged in which the centuries-old print tradition becomes entwined with the new capabilities for print afforded by digital technologies in the composition, typesetting, and production of books. Moreover, since print and electronic texts are in continuous conversation with each other, second-order effects (i.e., effects in which the changes in one medium stimulate related changes in another) further complicate and enrich explorations of materiality in both print and electronic media.

Since literature is, unlike architecture, primarily a semiotic practice, a definition of materiality applicable to this context is in order. Materiality should not be confused with physicality. Whereas the physical aspects of any object are potentially infinite and neutral in themselves, materiality is intimately bound up with the quest for meaning. (As Jerome McGann has eloquently pointed out, meaning is not something that literary texts produce but rather the thing for which they search.[18]) To emphasize the distinction between physicality and materiality, we have elsewhere defined materiality as those physical aspects mobilized by a work's signifying strategies to create meaning.[19] The definition implies materiality is not pre-given and cannot be specified in advance; rather, it is an emergent property, subject to debates about whether a given physical characteristic is or is not important to a work's meaning. One of the distinctive characteristics that digital media have introduced into the production of literary texts is the use of code to generate the screen's flickering signifiers. Increasingly, writers who work in networked and programmable media insist that their work should be understood to consist not only of the screenic display but also the underlying code, and as Loss Pequeño Glazier among others has noted, writers in digital media are creating a wide variety of strategies to ensure their works cannot be fully understood without taking the code into account.[20] The strategies evident in print texts are more indirect, but there too interactions between the linguistic surface of the printed page and the code that produced it are mobilized to create a variety of material effects.

John Cayley's work exemplifies the mood swing in which information technology is engaged not for its shock value but for its penetration into cultural arenas, especially poetics and aesthetic theory. Cayley practices what he calls "literal art," a phrase that punningly invokes letters as well as the materiality of writing surfaces.[21] He creates works that explore the analogy between the discreteness of alphabetic language (where twenty-six elements can be combined into an infinitude of different words) and binary code. Because both letters and code are discrete rather than continuous, they share a pragmatics and aesthetics of fragmentation and recombination. Cayley's practice emphasizes the complexity of writing surfaces, particularly their construction as sites for negotiation between linguistic texts and the computer algorithms generating them.[22] He points to this interpenetration with a key question: "Is the display really a monitor of the programmaton's symbolic processing, or is it a window on computing's attempts to match and then exceed...the illusionistic simulations of film and television?"[23] To pose the question is already to suggest the answer, for the query implies that the screen can function in both roles simultaneously (perhaps with a slight sneer at "illusionistic simulations"). In Cayley's work, the screen is used to create a legible textual surface that simultaneously functions as a dark window onto the code creating the display. Two related works illustrate the dynamic; both use an algorithmic substitution of letters that cycles between different languages and/or different states of legibility. In *Translation,* text on the right is complemented on the left by a visual display of glyphs, the changes of which indicate how the algorithm is proceeding, a process also enacted by textual transformations as words cycle between different languages and states of legibility, as well as by the work's ambient music. Cayley suggests that if users stare at the mutating glyphs long enough, they can gain an intuitive understanding of how the algorithm works (similarly, perhaps, to the video game player who through much practice can anticipate the computer's moves). In *Overboard,* the text (taken from an account of the Mayflower crossing in Governor Bradford's *Of Plymouth Plantation*) describes a man who fell overboard and, clinging to a rope, was dragged along under the water until he could finally be pulled on board again. The text presents various stages of legibility, figured by Cayley as surfacing, floating, and sinking (or drowning).[24] Here reading becomes unavoidably algorithmic, less a practice of re-creating an imaginative world than of participating in a rhythmic dance of letters and glyphs reflecting algorithmic transformations wrought by the computer.

The complexity of a writing surface created by code is further explored by Giselle Beiguelman in "Code Movie 1," a collaboration with Helga Stein who created the soundtrack. In this clever and amusing work, dancing symbols morph into various patterns in time with the music; the symbols are not words, however, but hexadecimal codes extracted from jpg images and reworked in Flash. Thus the surface reflexively references the codes that produce it, conceptually performing what Douglas Hofstader calls the "eternal golden braid," whereby the apparatus producing the representation becomes itself part of the representation.[25] Similar dynamics are enacted by writers identified with "codework," including MEZ (aka Mary-Anne Breeze) in such works as *_][ad][Dressed In a Skin C.ode_*, Talan Memmott in *Lexia to Perplexia*, and Ted Warnell and collaborators in the collection *SyntacticalError*.[26]

Even when the writing surface is the print page, digitality leaves its mark on design and layout, especially the innovative graphics and increased visuality characteristic of many contemporary experimental novels. Frequently, digital code also appears in the represented worlds of these texts, creating the possibility for the kind of reflexive play noted above for digital works. Salvador Plascencia's *The People of Paper* is a good example of how the traditional dynamics of print novels are becoming entwined with digital representations.

The narrative's initiating act is the creation of a woman literally made of paper by Antonio, an "origami surgeon" gifted with the magical power to fashion living organs and entire organisms out of paper. Merced de Papel, as she is later christened, is the first instance of the novel's push toward literality in performances that entangle the represented world with the material surfaces on which the linguistic signifiers are inscribed. The literalization extends to encompass the conceptual hierarchy that distinguishes between author, narrator, and character in a descending scale of ontological dependence (that is, the author creates the narrator, the narrator creates the characters, etc.). The putative author enters the narrative as a character first called Saturn and then "Salvador Plascencia." Reflecting his ontological priority, he resides in a room whose floor is the sky of the characters. The central conflict revolves around the resentment that one of the characters, Federico de la Fe, feels toward Saturn's penetrating gaze, a surveillance he interprets as an intrusion of his privacy and limitation of his freedom as an autonomous subject.

This arrangement is exploited not so much for metafictional ends as for an exploration of the entangled materialities of the inscribed page and the represented world created by the inscriptions. For example, Merced de Papel's many abandoned lovers recognize one another by the paper cuts they sport on lips and tongues from having oral sex with her; one deliberately inflicts a fresh cut when he nostalgically licks the edges of the pages on which she appears as a character. In another instance of entangled materiality, Saturn, whose rejection by his lover is echoed in the sense of loss pervading the world he surveils, cuts his rival's name from the narrative, an act within the represented world that leaves an actual die-cut hole in the page surface. This and other visual/material effects are economically feasible for a mass market book, of course, only because digital technologies offer unparalleled flexibility in the printing process.

Code explicitly enters the text as a linguistic signifier in the interior monologue of a mechanical tortoise, represented as a block of ones and zeros. The mechanical tortoises, who stand in for intelligent machines capable of cognition and agency, are hunted and killed so that Federico de la Fe and his colleagues can use the tortoises' lead shells to shield themselves from Saturn's gaze. Read as metonyms for the code generating the textual surface, the tortoises' shells (and by implication, the tortoises themselves as intelligent machines) are used to disrupt the ontological hierarchy that positions the putative author above the characters, suggesting that the assumptions characteristic of a print novel are morphing as digital technologies reconfigure, literally and materially, the print page.

INTERMEDIATION AND SUBLIME BANALITY

As a term, *intermediation* has a rich history. Used extensively in the financial world to indicate mediators for financial transactions, it has also been appropriated to describe various kinds of software and software applications and even used as the name of a German art group. Denoting both mediation and intervention, intermediation has elsewhere been parsed by us by means of three related but distinct analytical cuts through the complex dynamics characteristic of the contemporary entanglement of print and digital media: interactions between language and code, electronic textuality and print media, and analog and digital modes of representation.[27]

One site where intermediation is at work is in algorithmic text generation. Although algorithmic text generation preceded digital computers by centuries, as Florian Cramer points out in his history of the topic,[28] computers greatly facilitated the process. They also created the possibility of mutable text that constantly changes, either in response to the user's actions or through random or timed sequences. There are several senses in which algorithmic text generation enacted by digital computers displays intermediation. Frequently the databases from which text generators draw consist of pre-scripted phrases taken from print media or alluding to printed works. Slicing and dicing phrases that in their "natural language" state were coherent, the text generators produce neologisms and nonsense phrases, as well as surprising juxtapositions that can be eerily insightful or hilarious. The disruption and strange familiarity characteristic of such works bespeak the interpenetration of language by code, as well as the interaction of electronic textuality with the print tradition. Moreover, such work manifests a hybrid ancestry of human intelligence and machine cognition, a point Brian Kim Stefans underscores when, in extensive annotations to his computer poem "Stops and Rebels," published in his print book *Fashionable Noise,* he refers to the program creating the poem as the "Demon."[29]

In digital literature, algorithmic text generation has become a pervasive technique, used in works as diverse as Stuart Moulthrop's *Reagan Library,* Loss Pequeño Glazier's *white faced bromeliads on 20 hectares,* Jim Andrews and collaborators' *Stir Fry Texts,* John Cayley's *Overboard* and *Translation* (discussed earlier), and a host of others. Millie Ness's "Sundays in the Park," one of six components of the collection "Oulipoems" co-authored with Martha Deed, shows intermediation at work. Referencing the constraint-driven practices of the French OuLiPo writers, the "text machine" displays phrases that the user can cycle through by clicking on them, with two to six different permutations for each phrase group. The phrases in a group are related to one another through punning homophonic variations, relationships accentuated by two female voices reading, in a gentle cacophony, different versions of the text. For example, "start war in bag dead" becomes, when clicked, "is tart warren baghdad;" "know wee puns of master ruction" becomes "no weapons of mass destruction;" "know won reeds fill awe sophies" becomes "no one reeds philosophies" and so on. Sliding in and out of legibility, the phrases create a kind of verbal wallpaper against which patterns emerge, giving a sense of political content while at the same time suggesting the phenomenon of floating signifiers that are impossible to pin down to exact denotations.

The sense of patterns emerging from an ambient background and then dissolving back into noise is a pervasive trope in contemporary digital works. Although the L=A=N=G=U=A=G=E poets used similar techniques (a heritage acknowledged by many of the writers noted above), digital media allows the transformation of durable inscriptions into mobile text, activating in the process the complex dynamics of intermediation. For example, in William Poundstone's *3 Proposals for Bottle Imps,* a Flash work that combines animated text with animation proper, extensive citation and intermediation allows idiosyncratic connections to emerge between the Cartesian devil and the Cartesian subject, a methodology modeled after Raymond Roussel's idiosyncratic connections in *Locus Solus* (1914). The Cartesian devil, known since the renaissance, refers to a toy device that consisted of a tube of water in which was placed a tiny folded figure made of special materials.[30] When the water was heated, the figure would rise, expand and unfold; when the water was cooled, the figure would shrink back to its original size and sink. In *Locus Solus,* Roussel's narrator imagines a further elaboration in which a "subtle mechanism" would generate a motto "written in fine bubbles of air laid out calligraphically;" this fictional account provides the inspiration for the calligraphic text Poundstone writes to accompany his animations. The Cartesian devil, connected to the Cartesian subject by a shared adjective as well as Poundstone's narrative, suggests a process whereby a mind whose existence provides the one surety in a world of doubt is transformed into a mutable subjectivity whose continuous morphing occurs in conjunction with the ambient conditions of an enveloping environment.

"An Allegory of Genius," one of the bottle imp proposals, performs as well as relates the kind of epistemology suited to this mutable subjectivity. The text, accompanied by a looping soundtrack that accentuates the theme of ambient emergence, is putatively taken from a story by Vasari that tells of an Italian renaissance painter, Piero di Cosimo, who was fascinated by all manner of freaks and monsters. Piero was especially attracted to a wall on which the "sick of the city aimed their spittle," perceiving in the bubbling mucus dancing patterns that he used as inspirations for his paintings. One day he discerned on the wall a sea monster, the epitome of all that was "gross and appalling in nature." Capturing the form in a painting, he presented it to Giuliano de Medici, who found it so repulsive he promptly covered it with a green cloth and consigned it to a closet. When Catherine de Medici inherited it, she whimsically returned it to the wall, whereupon the rabble spat upon it, so that it gradually sank back into the randomness from which it emerged. The narrative then continues by providing examples of bottle imps, a linguistic construction that is also visually performed by the animations showing the imps expanding, rising, shrinking, and falling.

3 Proposals for Bottle Imps suggestively illuminates why the aesthetics of ambient emergence should be characteristic of the contemporary moment. As the internet and World Wide Web are increasingly integrated into everyday routines in developed regions of the globe, they provide a vast and continuously changing landscape within which contemporary subject formation takes place. Moreover, this is a landscape defined by the dynamics of intermediation. Although most Web content remains text, increasingly graphics, images, animation, and sound combine with it to create complex surfaces whose behaviors perform and enact the interpenetration of language and code, electronic textuality and print, analog and digital representations. As digital effects cycle back into print, their aesthetic influences older media such as print novels as well, producing a range of second-order effects that in turn cycle back to digital media, thus creating feedback loops that provide ever-changing backgrounds against which mutable patterns emerge.

In Mark Z. Danielewski's *House of Leaves* (2000), the difference between the postmodern era and the contemporary emphasis on ambience manifests itself as successive layering, presenting a kind of textual archaeology in which various strata testify to different kinds of aesthetic concerns. The centrality of intermediation is immediately evident in this print novel's determination to include within its leaves an astonishing variety of media, including film, video, photography, telegraphy, painting, collage, and graphics, among others. The novel's implicit rivalry with the digital computer's ability to represent all other media with its binary code came close to the surface in Danielewski's long interview with Larry McCaffrey and Sinda Gregory. Asked if the computer was important for the composition of this unusually designed text, Danielewski replied:

> I didn't write *House of Leaves* on a word processor. In fact, I wrote out the entire thing in pencil! And what's most ironic, I'm still convinced that it's a great deal easier to write something out by hand than on a computer. You hear a lot of people talking about how computers make writing so much easier because they offer the writer so many choices, whereas in fact pencil and paper allow you a much greater freedom. You can do anything in pencil!

When McCaffrey pressed him on the issue, however, Danielewski admitted the necessity of digital technologies for the book's production:

> There's no doubt computers, new software, and other technologies play a big role in getting any book ready for production these days. They also make it easier for a publisher to consider releasing a book like mine that previously would have been considered too complicated and expensive to typeset by hand. Yet despite all the technological advantages currently available, the latter stages of getting *House of Leaves* ready for production involved such a great deal of work that Pantheon began to wonder if they were going to be able to publish it the way I wanted. So I wound up having to do the typesetting myself.[31]

Digital technology functions here like the Derridean *supplement;* alleged to be outside and extraneous to the text proper, it is somehow also necessary. The construction suggests that at issue is the text's ability to posit its origin without digital technology; conversely, including digital technology would alter the text's fundamental view of its own ontology.

These suggestions become explicit in the text's consideration of how other media have been threatened, and implicitly transformed, by the interpenetration of digitality. Divided between Zampanò's critical commentary on the film *The Navidson Record* and Johnny Truant's footnotes on Zampanò's manuscript, the layers include footnotes on Johnny's footnotes as well as interjections by the Editors, not to mention some two hundred pages of Exhibits, Appendices, and Index. Particularly revealing is Zampanò's discussion of digital photography. Distinguishing between documentaries and films representing fictional stories, Zampanò notes that documentaries "rely on interviews, inferior equipment, and virtually no effects to document real events. Audiences are not allowed the safety net of disbelief and so must turn to more challenging mechanisms of interpretation which, as is sometimes the case, may lead to denial and aversion."[32] The film at the book's center, *The Navidson Record,* purports to be a documentary, but the main object of its representation, the house on Ash Tree Lane into which Will Navidson moves with his partner Karen Green and their two children in an attempt to shore up the couple's shaky relationship, turns out to be an impossible object whose inside is bigger than its outside. At first the surreal excess measures a mere quarter of an inch but then stretches into distances greater than the diameter of the earth and older than the solar system. With its shifting walls, ashen surfaces, and labyrinthine complexities, the house's interior is not only impossible to map but also impossible to inhabit, for it destroys any artifact left within it. Combining an unrepresentable topography with an uninhabitable space, the house confronts those who enter its mysterious interior with the threat of nothingness that, far from being mere absence, has a terrible ferocious agency, figured by the beast-like growls Will and others think they perceive issuing from its interior. Moreover, even the film that putatively records this impossible object has an indeterminate status, for as Johnny Truant informs us in his introduction, *The Navidson Record* probably does not exist—which does not, however, prevent Zampanò from writing some five hundred pages interpreting it and the hundreds of critics (some fictional, some real) that he cites from putatively writing thousands of pages of exegesis about it.

Lurking at the center of the text, as at the center of the house, is a nothingness so intense and unrepresentable that it goes beyond nihilism and paradoxically becomes a catalyst for the graphomania that the text both performs and cites. We may see in this configuration the staging of a central insight of deconstruction, the inability of language to posit its own origin—an insight that, far from leading to silence, catalyzed the production of thousands of books and articles, as prolific a stimulus in the real world as the house is in its fictional realm. For *House of Leaves*, the result of the graphomania is the creation of a structure in which nothingness, allegorized in the beast that may or may not inhabit the labyrinth at the house's center, is surrounded by layer after layer of interpretation, exegesis, commentary, and analysis. Moreover, this material is punctured with so many holes and rife with so much ambiguity that the exegetical process could clearly go on forever, as critical articles are written about the critical articles contained in *House of Leaves*, functioning at once as a print novel and a material manifestation of the house it fictionalizes (a conflation evident even before the book is open in the cover design of a black-on-black embossed labyrinth).

Read as an allegory for our contemporary situation (a reading that all novels directly or indirectly invite), *House of Leaves* suggests that postmodernism has not so much disappeared as been swallowed up—or better, engulfed—by the flood of data, associations, information, and cross-references unleashed by the World Wide Web. The effect of an information landscape so vast and unruly has been to shift the focus for interpretive analysis to discerning patterns among its chaotic and unpredictable juxtapositions. The aesthetics of ambient emergence is a function, then, not only of the Web's incorporation into daily life but also of the sheer incomprehensibility of its vastness, a combination producing a condition that might be called sublime banality.

As if competing with this flood of information, *House of Leaves* inundates its readers with a roaring cascade of data, narrations, connections, and complexities. Although as a print book *House of Leaves* cannot literally animate the text to create ambient effects, Danielewski employs a number of techniques to intensify the complex materiality of the textual surfaces. Adapting the techniques of Concrete poetry, the author often treats the page as an omnidirectional writing plane on which text can go in many different directions. As if enacting what it names, Chapter IX (titled "The Labyrinth" in an appendix) displays text written upside down, backward, horizontal, and other unusual orientations. Footnotes are nested within other footnotes and appear not only at page bottoms but in the middle or upper portions as well. In addition, the text creates elaborate echoes between the represented world and the page's materiality. The notorious footnote 144 (pp. 119–45), for example, purports to list everything that is not in the house's mysterious interior, a quixotic endeavor since there is nothing in the house. Although the list begins by listing house-like objects—heating and cooling systems, vents, wiring—it soon expands to include items like Christmas trees, thus making clear that the list could potentially go on forever. And go on it does, for pages and pages. Even that involves a twist, however, for when the footnote continues onto the verso, the text appears not as a linear continuation of the recto but as the backward-reading version of preceding page. It thus vivifies, by performing the opposite, a property of print books we take so for granted we cease to see it, namely that pages are (normally) opaque rather than transparent. Acting as a window, the footnote reminds us through inversion that there are no windows through which one can look into or out of the house's interiority and thus no way to gain an objective perspective that would stabilize the house's (and the text's) changing shapes and fluctuating meanings.

The blue color outlining the footnote's textual blocks also is significant, since in the so-called "blue" edition, the word house (and its equivalents in foreign languages) always appears in blue, suggesting either a hypertext link or the blue screen used in films as a replaceable backdrop that can later be filled in with whatever background is desired. The footnote's blue outline suggests that the list is less an objective catalog than a representation reflecting the writer's and/or reader's desires, acting in this respect not as a window but a mirror. Moreover, even when the words end the footnote continues, for it appears as a black block surrounded by a blue outline, an image that could signify either the absence of words or words so densely overwritten they have become a solid block of black ink. The play between presence and absence continues on the next page, where the footnote has apparently disappeared but nevertheless lingers as a block of negative white space defined by the surrounding words. This entanglement of the page's material properties with the nothingness that haunts the house and text is typical of the ways in which the book's surfaces ceases to be neutral containers for words and spaces and instead become active agents capable of signifying practices.

Further intensifying the page surfaces are the ways in which the text re-defines itself as a collection of leaves, all of which are capable of signification. Rather than performing as a conventional narrative that begins with the story's first word and ends with the last word, this text insists that it consists of *every* surface the book contains as a material artefact, including the front and back covers, the author and title pages, the copyright pages, the spine and colophon, the index, and the final acknowledgments. For example, at the bottom of the copyright page that conventionally follows the title page there appears "A Note on This Edition," which tells us that in the "Full Color" edition, "The only struck line in Chapter XXI appears in purple." This seemingly innocuous note, which most readers would normally skip in their eagerness to begin the narrative, becomes crucially important to the interpretation of the final chapter of Johnny Truant's narration and thus to the story as a whole. The struck phrase, which comes immediately before the story of the deformed child that ends Chapter XXI, is a narrative interpolation: "~~what I'm remembering now~~."[33] In all the first editions the phrase appears in black, and only those readers who recall the note on the copyright page (now some five hundred pages distant) will make the connection and imagine the line in purple.[34] Throughout purple is associated with Pelafina, Johnny's mad mother who was confined to a mental institution and committed suicide several years before the manuscript was putatively compiled. Her presence is directly manifested in the text only through the appendix that contains her letters. Readers who follow the editors' advice (on p. 72) and skip ahead to Pelafina's letters will recognize, however, that many details from those letters eerily echo through the main narrative about Will and Karen Navidson. The echoes suggest that in addition to Zampanò and Johnny Truant, either of whom might have made up the other, another contender for the one who is "actually" writing the text is Pelafina. Although this idea defies conventional logic, the struck phrase reinforces her claim to be the narrator telling the entire story, including those texts supposedly written by Johnny Truant and Zampanò. Reading the text from this perspective obviously forces a reinterpretation of all that has come before, so that precisely when the narrative should be winding down, it instead opens up in a way that throws everything up for grabs. That this startling reversal was set up by prefatory material most readers ignore indicates the intensity that the text imparts to even its most humble surfaces.

Other examples are the ninety-eight index entries followed by the letters "DNE," evidently an acronym for "Does Not Exist." The strangeness of listings words that do not appear in the text carries the play between presence and absence into the index. Further enhancing this weirdness is a strategy that slowly reveals itself as a self-reflexive ploy. The DNE entries do indeed appear but in ways that separate them from the text proper, often in the textual apparatuses that Gérard Genette has called paratexts.[35] The paratextual index thus references not only the text but also its fellow paratexts, whose shadowy presences are both acknowledged and erased in the DNE appellation. Some of the DNE entries, for example, appear in bits of texts incorporated into the collages collected in "Appendix III: Contrary Evidence." Perhaps the most insidious is the entry "house (black)...DNE." The phrase functions as a visual oxymoron, for here as elsewhere in the text (of the blue edition), "house" is in blue. The astute reader, however, can find the elusive black "house" in the acknowledgments that appear on the book's penultimate page, where the reprint notice references "Vintage Books, a division of Random **House**, Inc." As a result of these kinds of strategies, readers are re-conditioned to regard the text as the *entire* material object—an object, moreover, that constantly subverts its status as an object by performing as an active agent capable of affecting the world around it.

Within the text, the house's agency occupies an indeterminate status figured by the beast whose presence (and absence) seems to haunt the house's interior. Never actually seen, the beast can be inferred from the deep claw marks that Johnny Truant finds beside Zampanò's body, the seeming growls recorded on *The Navidson Record*, and the "fingers of blackness [that] slash across the lighted wall and consume Holloway." Everywhere the beast is mentioned, the text wavers between representing it as an actually existing creature and a consensual hallucination created by the characters. Typical is the passage where Johnny reproduces in the edited manuscript the unexplained burn holes that pepper Zampanò's notes, creating a play between the letters actually inscribed on the page and the absences signified by square brackets. "It seems erroneous to assert," Zampanò argues, "that this creat[ ]e had actual teeth and claws of b[ ]e (which myth for some reason [ ] requires). [ ]t d[]d have claws, they were made of shadow and if it did have te[]th, they were made of darkness. Yet even as such the [ ] still stalked Holl[] way at every corner until at last it did strike, devouring him, even roaring, the last thing heard, the sound []f Holloway ripped out of existence."[36] Even as we reconstruct the noisy message for ourselves by supplying the missing letters, the brackets puncturing the text evoke the nothingness that the beast paradoxically signifies in its very presence.

This play between the absence of presence and the presence of absence is intimately related to the house's ambiguous agency. Perhaps it acts on its own, or perhaps, as the fictional critic Ruby Dahl cited by Zampanò claims, the house merely reflects the personalities of those who venture inside it.[37] Significantly, immediately after the beast consumes Holloway's body, the house goes crazy and eats Will's brother Tom, as if infected by the psychosis that drove Holloway to hunt his comrades, murder one and wound another, and then commit suicide.

Following Mark B. N. Hansen's key insight that there is a deep connection between the house and digital technologies, we arrive at a somewhat different explanation for its operation.[38] Increasingly human attention occupies only the tiny top of a huge pyramid of machine-to-machine communication, including cell phones, networked computers, ATMs, and RFID (Radio Frequency Identification) tags that give every indication of spreading faster than mold in New Orleans. Often these digital machines, ranging from the obvious to the nano-scaled, are coupled with sensors and actuators that carry out actions, from something as mundane as raising a garage door to the world-shaking launch of a nuclear missile. In the field of artificial life, for example, programs have been constructed that produce species capable of mutating and evolving in unpredictable ways. Genetic algorithms go further in evolving not just the output of the programs but the programs themselves. Programmable gate arrays go further yet in evolving the hardware, changing the patterns of the logic gates to arrive at the most efficient way to solve certain problems.[39] We would perhaps like to think that actions require humans to initiate them, but human agency is increasingly dependent on intelligent machines to carry out actions and, more alarmingly, to provide the data on which the human decisions are based in the first place. *House of Leaves* reflects these ambiguities in attributing the house's actions both to the humans who enter it and the beast that can seemingly act on its own, a non-human creature whose agency is completely enmeshed with that of the characters, the author, and the reader.

For digital technologies, the initiation of action ultimately translates into binary code. From the brute simplicity of ones and zeros, the successive layers of code build up constructions of enormous complexity, from genetic algorithms that produce advanced circuit designs[40] to the digital typesetting programs that produced *House of Leaves* as a material artifact. Although humans originally created the computer code, the complexity of many contemporary programs is such that no single person understands them in their entirety. In this sense our understanding of how computers can get from simple binary code to sophisticated acts of cognition is approaching the gap that yawns between our understanding of the mechanics of human consciousness—the neural structures, chemical transmitters, networked cells, and molecular interactions from which consciousness must emerge—and the apparent autonomy and freedom of human thought. The parallel with computers is striking. As Brian Cantwell

Smith observes, the emergence of complexity within computers may provide crucial clues to "how a structured lump of clay can sit up and think."[41]

Yet human cognition is unlike machine cognition in being mediated through emotions and the complexities of bodily processing. Despite similarities in the layered architectures of neural nets and coding languages, huge differences remain between human thought and machine processing. In particular, humans seek meaning while computers execute commands. Although research in such fields as artificial life, emotional computing, and artificial intelligence is ongoing to create computers that can achieve some sense of meaning, it remains to be seen whether an intelligent machine capable of sentience can ever be built. The nothingness with which the house—and the beast—are consistently associated in *House of Leaves* functions to provide a figure for the absence at the core of the text's multiple layers and acts of inscription—an absence that draws into the question the very possibility of meaning and, at the same time, paradoxically provokes a riotous excess of meaning-making.

As the litmus test separating human and machine cognition, meaning in *House of Leaves* may be recovered through the multiple layers of remediation that this print novel creates (as we have argued elsewhere),[42] and linked to embodied human reading (as Mark Hansen argues). Yet another implication lurks in the layered complexities of this print novel. An ambiguous agent, the beast both threatens and mimics the agency of the human characters. Above all else, the characters in the text, like the humans who read the text, are meaning-seeking animals. Nevertheless, they (and we) cannot determine the meaning of the beast's actions, or even if it exists. Its elusive presence that takes only a slight shift in perspective to transform into absence stands in for the digital technologies that, ignorant of meaning, nevertheless initiate actions that often have consequences for humans across the globe.

Like the nothingness infecting the text's signifiers, a similar nothingness would confront us if we could take an impossible journey and zoom into a computer's interior while it is running code. We would find that there is no there there, only alternating voltages that nevertheless produce meaning through a layered architecture correlating ones and zeros with human language. From the nothingness of alternating voltages emerges the complexities of digital culture, including effects that shift us away from postmodernism and toward ambient emergence. In this sense *House of Leaves* performs within its fictional world the banal miracle that produced it as a material artifact and that also produces us as readers of the complex surfaces of contemporary literature.

PAPER TO PIXELS TO PLASTIC: INTERMEDIATION THROUGH ANALOG REPRESENTATION, DIGITAL FABRICATION, AND VIRTUAL INTEGRATION

Architects do not usually make buildings. Architects make instruction manuals that guide the construction of buildings by others. Configured as such, the discipline has always been pervaded by techniques of intermediation, and for much of its history, architects have developed ideas through representations on paper and in scale models and only later translated these concepts to wood, stone, and steel. But this disciplinary structure is of relatively recent vintage. In the Middle Ages, architectural innovation took place primarily in the field. The great cathedrals of the period were made possible in large part through tectonic advances in masonry construction. But as vaulting grew increasingly complex, complicated intersections were solved less by trial-and-error stonecutting and more through the use of projective drawings. The development of stereotomy in sixteenth-century France, an arcane method for accurately delineating geometrically complex three-dimensional stone shapes, opened the way for a boom of innovative structural solutions in stone vaults.[43] During the renaissance, linear perspective was developed by practitioners invested heavily in both painting and architecture; advances made in one field quickly came to bear on the other. In the intervening centuries, the increasing availability of paper and architecture's slow migration from the craft guilds to the academy widened architects' remove from the physical instantiation of their projects and intensified their dependence on techniques of intermediation.

Through the 1970s and '80s, architectural drawing remained the primary vehicle of advanced research in the field. Influential practitioners of the period, Eisenman, Bernard Tschumi, Daniel Libeskind, and others, resistant to capitulation with the machinations of advanced capitalism, produced dizzyingly complex drawings and collages, painstakingly hand-crafted and often accompanied by dense theoretical texts, giving rise to the phenomenon known as "paper architecture."[44] Some of the most important work in the field was being produced with no intention of being physically constructed.[45] As the computer entered into the design studio through the late 1980s and early '90s, its initial effects were felt in advancing the geometrical complexities of these theoretical investigations. But as the decade progressed, a constellation of conditions converged to radically transform the opportunities and ambitions of the paper generation.

The formidable graphic techniques developed through the 1970s by these architects helped them win prestigious competitions for built work as world economies rebounded, as evidenced by Eisenman's Wexner Center for the Arts in Columbus, Ohio (competition 1983, project completed 1989), Tschumi's Parc de la Villette in Paris (competition 1983, project completed 1993), and Libeskind's Jewish Museum in Berlin (competition 1989, project completed 1999). As they were awarded additional commissions through the 1990s, these firms integrated digital technologies into their studios to assist in the conceptualization and documentation of their complex designs. Soon a younger generation, many of whom had worked as project assistants on these commissions, emerged from the shadow of their analog mentors. Armed with a first-hand knowledge of computer technologies, close affiliations with computer-savvy fabricators and consultants, and unencumbered by the hallmark suspicions of capitalism that haunted the previous generation, practices such as Greg Lynn Form, UN Studio, servo, and others radically transformed the state of advanced architectural research as well as the organization of the practices conducting it.[46]

Servo, an international design collaborative with its four principals based in different cities throughout the world, stands as a new kind of networked practice made possible by digital technologies.[47] Founded in 1999, the firm focuses on the transformations of both architectural space and the practice of design these technologies have brought about. As is now commonplace in even the most conservative architectural practices, servo employs the latest modeling and animation software throughout the design process, but rather than employ these technologies simply to streamline traditional practice, servo aims to exploit unforeseen potential at all stages of design, practice, and construction. Depending on the internet to collapse the distance between its four principals, servo exhibits a nimble flexibility difficult to achieve in larger, less technologically advanced firms. With their capabilities distributed across geographical borders and time zones, the firm has the ability to work normal hours around the clock, to draw on a vast pool of collaborators and fabricators around the globe, and to easily shift resources from one location to another as opportunities and interests dictate. In contrast to the stereotypical figure of the lone architect hunched over a drafting table, servo exists as a constantly fluctuating constellation of collaborators and consultants, a loose band of affiliated practitioners working in an array of production media and made to cohere not through physical proximity but rather through technological immersion.

Unlike the paper practitioners of the 1970s, servo's ambitions were from the start resolutely directed at translating their designs into physical space with the aid of computer-controlled fabrication technologies. Further, the firm incorporates an array of digital projections, real-time data sensors, and interactive control terminals within their built projects, greatly expanding their work's repertoire of effects. Intermediation pervades their design process and designed projects with equal intensity, producing architectural interventions that inhabit an ambiguous zone between physical instantiation and virtual simulation.

Many of servo's projects have been commissioned by galleries and other cultural institutions, the relatively small scale of these commissions affording them the opportunity to maintain a central role in project fabrication as well as design. Rather than provide paper construction documents to a contractor, servo seamlessly integrates physical production with their design process, producing preliminary studies and final building components on the same machine. As pointed out by Michael Speaks, such rapid prototyping constitutes a new form of "design intelligence" in which digital technologies, dramatically increasing the rate at which iterations and alternatives can be produced, ushers in a wholesale re-conception of the design process.[48] With advanced modeling and rendering software, the effects of even the most subtle adjustments to configuration, lighting, materiality, and other variables within project that once required time-intensive analog labor can be instantly assessed in virtual simulations and alternative versions quickly produced with computer-controlled fabrication devices such as CNC milling machines, laser cutters, and 3D printers. These machines are much more than expedient tools used to translate a preconceived idea from the mind of the designer to the material world. Instead, unexpected solutions emerge from the complex feedback loops between human designers and increasingly intelligent machines. The design process is no longer one of representational speculation, but rather of materially specific iteration, and agency in the system is no longer lodged in the individual designer but rather distributed through a dynamic network of human actors and digital devices.

All of these technologies were employed in the completion of *Dark Places* (2006), servo's design for a digitised survey of contemporary art and architecture curated by Joshua Decter at the Santa Monica Museum of Art [**Fig. 14.1**]. From conception to completion, digital technologies and intermediation deeply pervade the project. Decter solicited submissions from seventy-six artists and architects from the United States and abroad. Some completed original work specifically for the exhibition, while others submitted previously existing materials. With the ambition to "reanimate relationships among art, architecture, media, and technological design," Decter re-presented each work, regardless of its initial medium, as a digitized video clip emanating from eight video projectors mounted within a glowing, sculptural armature designed by servo and suspended in the gallery.[49]

Servo's armature, like the practice itself, embodies many of the symptoms of the contemporary mood swing this essay elucidates. Constructed in translucent vacuum-formed plastic, the project's material effects are amplified by internal fiber-optic lighting that imparts an otherworldly glow. These lights are connected to real-time data sensors that cause light intensities and patterns to fluctuate based on the presence and ambulation of museum visitors. Decter's video clips are displayed using both front- and rear-projection systems, causing the featured artworks to inhabit the surfaces of the armature itself as well as the adjacent gallery walls. Interactive computer terminals mounted within servo's construct allow visitors to browse the collected works in any combination. The work is not a fixed object designed by a single creator but instead a set of complex feedback loops between content and context. These feedback loops shift attention from the specific properties of individual works to an immersive atmospheric ensemble that promiscuously mingles the real with the virtual

These shifts in focus—from element to ensemble, from close attention to distracted immersion, from autonomous objects and stable subjects to a complex dance between physical and virtual instantiations of each—signal the significant distance between today's most advanced practitioners and their postmodern predecessors. Rather than resist physical construction in order to develop theoretical arguments in abstract representations, servo, like many of their contemporaries,[50] aggressively employs digital technologies directly to engage the physical. Their ambitions are not critique and resistance, those postmodern aims that direct attention backward, either suspiciously to an object of critique or nostalgically to some (often imagined) lost past. Rather, these architects reject the cynical "impossibility of architecture"[51] and instead strive to innovate and project alternatives. Equipped with a formidable kit of new digital tools and techniques, today's most innovative designers exude a forward-looking optimism unthinkable under the skeptical regime of postmodernism. Though the discipline still maintains internal debates that parse the relative criticality of various camps within the field,[52] the marked transformations that have taken place over the last fifteen years have rendered these arguments increasingly irrelevant. Spurred by the increasing contamination of architecture by dynamic intermediations rather than critical theory, today's most innovative practitioners are moving the field away from the legible representation and negative critique. Unlike the deeply referential drawing projects produced by their counterparts in the 1970s, works like *Dark Places* do not solicit sustained close attention either to their representational content or to the formal specificities of the container. Instead, both content and construction are combined into a single entity that gives rise to powerful and dynamic atmospheric and performative effects. Though the appellation of this new condition is still up for grabs,[53] its effects, products of a renewed attention to materials and to the dynamic intermediations made possible by digital technologies, have insinuated themselves throughout contemporary architecture and literature to usher in a new, optimistic, and distinctly contemporary mood.

THE AESTHETICS OF AMBIENT EMERGENCE

We conclude with a few remarks about ambient emergence, our suggested name for the new aesthetic, and its connections with network culture and informationalism. Both words in the phrase have multiple connotations in this context. *Ambient*, usually understood to mean "surrounding" or "encircling," refers first to the play of surfaces characteristic of the attention to materiality in architecture and to the play of shifting letters and words in digital literary works. For example, servo's construction of an architectural setting responsive to the location and number of viewers in the gallery creates transforming patterns as environmental conditions change; John Cayley's *Overboard* and *Translation*, which allow limited user interaction to shift the screen display between various modes of legibility, provide examples from electronic literature. Although print novels obviously have durable inscriptions and so cannot participate in changing environmental conditions, they too show the influence of the shift. Immersive fiction is often said to create a "world," but in fact the evocation of an atmosphere typically occupies only a small portion of the text; most of the focus is on the characters' perceptions and actions as they engage in the conflicts and resolutions that give plots their characteristic Aristotelian shape. Many contemporary novels are turning away from this traditional mode of discourse and instead attempting to create something like an ambient environment that does not so much serve as background for plot development as displace plot altogether. Examples include (among others) Joseph McElroy's *Plus*, William Gaddis's *The Recognitions*, David Markson's *Wittgenstein's Mistress*, and Kazuo Ishiguro's *Never Let Me Go*. Falling somewhere between conventional plot and evocation of ambience, Salvador

Plascencia's *The People of Paper* shows the dynamics of intermediation at work. The traditional narrative structure is satirized as Federico de la Fe and his colleague realize they are being forced into an escalating series of plot developments. They rebel against the formula first by attempting to think nothing at all while under Saturn's surveillance, and then, when that doesn't work, by everyone thinking different thoughts. The chapters follow various formatting schemes, one of which is a series of parallel vertical columns, with each column representing the thoughts of a character. As the characters rebel, the ordered columns break into a visual cacophony, overrunning the usual margins and breaking the rigid symmetry that previously defined the page space. The breakup can be read as an allegory about the shift from focused world to enveloping environment, from plot to ambience.

The shift in contemporary architectural and literary productions is deeply related, as we have shown, to the changed conditions that digital media have brought about, especially the advent of the World Wide Web. As computers move out of the desktop and into the environment through such technologies as RFID tags, sensors linked with real-time data flows, and "smart" devices in which nanodevices are embedded in everything from clothing to surfactants, the reach of digital technologies both expands and sinks into obscurity, increasingly becoming part of the environment we take for granted. Thomas Whalen has called this expanding sphere of networked and programmable media the "cognisphere," a term that emphasizes its ability to carry out independent cognitions and initiate actions beyond the awareness (and sometimes even the control) of humans.[54] In this larger context, ambient denotes not only the environmental emphasis evident in contemporary architecture and literature but also the sense that we are surrounding ourselves with new kinds of environments in which human and machine cognitions are deeply entwined.

Emergence, the other term in play here, typically denotes the appearance of unpredictable complex patterns at a global level that result from interactions between local elements governed by relatively simple rule sets. Emergence has a rich scientific and philosophical history, linked with important research in a wide variety of fields, including neurophysiology, artificial life, scientific simulations, game theory, biology, and cognitive science, among others. One of the key ideas in theories of emergence is dynamical hierarchies, in which sites at many different interlinked levels interact with one another via feedback loops that operate between and among levels, creating continuously circulating interactions up and down the hierarchical chains. These kinds of structures are found everywhere complex systems operate, from the emergence of life from proteins and amino acids to the emergence of consciousness from individual neurons.

Nicholas Gessler, a researcher in human complex systems, has used the term *intermediation* to analyze how emergent structures arise, arguing that a key move in building a dynamical hierarchy is capturing an emergent pattern at a low level and re-representing it in a different medium as a primitive (or elemental component) at a higher level of organization, which in turn results in a different emergent pattern at that level.[55] For example, atoms interact to form molecules, which create new patterns that are the emergent result of atomic interactions. Molecules in turn create proteins, the emergent result of molecular interactions, which in turn create cells, and so forth. In this way, each higher level piggybacks on a lower level by incorporating its results in a transformative process that makes what was an emergent pattern at the lower level into a component that, interacting with other components in a different context, leads to yet more emergences, which in turn are used by higher levels as they build contexts out of which new emergent structures will arise.[56] In Gessler's view, the shift in medium is crucial, since it is the re-representation of a lower level pattern in a new medium that allows its re-contextualization as a primitive rather than a global result. In understanding how dynamical hierarchies work, we should keep in mind that such structures are never static, and that the patterns at each level are always in dynamic interaction with all the other levels. Atoms do not cease to move when they are incorporated into molecules, and molecules continually transform as they become proteins, just as proteins change and morph when they participate in the process of DNA replication. This framework, in recursive fashion, gives us a way now to re-contextualize our own argument. The complex dynamics of intermediation between print and digital media create feedback cycles in which the re-representation of emergent patterns leads to yet more emergences at different levels in the hierarchy, each interacting with and contributing to the overall emergences of the cognisphere, which in turn participates in interactions all the way up and down the dynamic hierarchies that produce it.

Perhaps the most typical way to understand these multi-causal, multi-agent interactions is through networks, the formal properties of which are analyzed using graph theory. Graph theory, a form of mathematical analysis that considers networks to be comprised of nodes and edges, has been applied in a wide variety of contexts, including biological, technological, and sociological systems. As Eugene Thacker and Alexander Galloway point out in *The Exploit: A Theory of Networks* (2007), the disadvantage of graph theory is that it does not sufficiently account for the dynamical transformative aspect of networks; this deficiency is mitigated if we keep in mind the close connection between networks and dynamical hierarchies. While network models yield ways to understand complex interconnections between multiple components and linking patterns, dynamical hierarchies explore the circumstances in which these connections can lead to emergent phenomenon and transformative dynamics.

In *The Exploit*, Galloway and Thacker ambitiously attempt to show that network modelling provides new perspectives on everything from transnational economics to contemporary subjectivity. In a political context, the importance of networks arises not only from network culture as such; more generally, it derives from a shift away from centralized power centers toward networks as a means of political control and resistance. Galloway and Thacker argue that "in recent decades the processes of globalization have mutated from a system of control housed in a relatively small number of power hubs to a system of control infused in the material fabric of distributed networks."[57] Networks in themselves, they point out, are neither repressive nor liberatory; rather, they represent new ways to exercise and resist power. For example, as terrorist organizations have shifted toward semi-autonomous cells loosely connected in a global network, the National Security Agency has adopted a mirroring strategy of using the immense telecommunication networks to identify potential terrorist plots. Regardless of whether one sees the terrorists as freedom fighters or nefarious agents of evil, and NSA surveillance as protecting or eroding the freedom of American citizens, the point is that both groups seek to implement and disrupt power through a network model. The applicable domains for this kind of analysis have dramatically increased in scope and range, including not only the usual references to the internet and World Wide Web but also such diverse phenomena as epidemiological vectors of contagious diseases, artificial intelligence implemented through neural networks, and the U.S. Army's plans to move from warfare strategies based on such traditional platforms as tanks, ships, and planes to "swarms" that flexibly respond and reconfigure themselves using high-bandwidth communication networks. In brief, networks have become the new playing field for the exercise of power and the analysis of its dynamics.

Going along with this emphasis on networks is an increased attention to topology, mediation, materiality, and nonhuman agency, all of which are necessary, as Galloway and Thacker point out, to understand fully how networks function. Although the complexities of how these factors contribute to network functioning are beyond the scope of this essay to explore, they suggest the expanded contexts in which the aesthetics of ambient emergence, with its emphasis on surface, materiality, intermediation, and nonhuman agency should be understood not as an isolated effect but part of the world-wide transformations that information technologies and globalization are co-producing. To position the mood swing as an aesthetic is to point specifically to the cultural and artistic manifestations of the complex dynamics of networks and dynamical hierarchies. The larger contexts, however, remain inextricably involved in these interactions, as both cause and result of the inconceivably vast number of feedback loops dynamically operating throughout the entire complex system of the networked cognisphere.

What stands out in the mood swing as we have delineated it is the sense of expanded possibilities for artistic and aesthetic creation and expression. While none of the practitioners we have discussed are ignorant of the dangers of network culture and the inimical effects of globalization, they are generally more interested in building than in critique, more oriented to discovery and innovation than to paranoia and suspicion. For them and others like them, the mood swing is not so much a change of attitude for its own sake as it is an attempt to embrace the constantly transforming sphere of interlinked networks and dynamical hierarchies, which are at once immeasurably beyond human ken and part of our everyday ordinary experience. Like consciousness and life itself, these interactions are the banal miracles that we take for granted even as they awesomely exceed what we can understand.[58]

NOTES

1. Fredric Jameson in *Postmodernism, or the Cultural Logic of Late Capitalism* (Durham: Duke University Press, 1991): 54, calls for "an aesthetic of cognitive mapping: a pedagogical political culture which seeks to endow the individual subject with some new heightened sense of its place in the global system."
2. Jean-Francois Lyotard, *The Postmodern Condition: A Report on Knowledge, Theory, and History of Literature, Vol. 10* (Minneapolis: Univ. of Minnesota Press, 1984): xxiv.
3. Jean Baudrillard, *Simulacra and Simulation* (Ann Arbor: Univ. of Michigan Press, 1995): 1–3.
4. Bruno Latour, "Why Has Critique Run Out of Steam," *Critical Inquiry* 30:2 (Winter 2004): 225–48.
5. In recent years, the term mood has been appearing in architectural discourse with increasing frequency, due in large part to the writings of Jeffrey Kipnis, who used the term as a curatorial device in *Mood River,* his 2002 exhibition at the Wexner Center of the Arts, and Sylvia Lavin. See Kipnis, "On Those Who Step in the Same River...," in *Mood River* (Columbus, Ohio: Wexner Center for the Arts, 2002): 34–45; and Lavin, "The Three Faces of Tel Aviv," *Competition for the New Building, Tel Aviv Museum,* exhibition catalog: *A+U* (June 2004): 88–113.

6. For a cogent treatment on the transformative potential of architectural pre-visualization films, see Tali Krakowsky "Algorithmic Anthologies," *34 Magazine* 8 (2006): 207–15.
7. Michael Speaks, "Design Intelligence, Part 1: Introduction," *A+U* 12: 387 (2002): 10–18.
8. David Harvey, *The Postmodern Condition: An Enquiry into the Origins of Cultural Change* (London: Blackwell, 1991): 121–29; and Manuel Castells, *The Rise of Network Society,* 2nd ed. (London: Blackwell, 2000): 77, 100, 162, 164.
9. Terence Riley, *Light Construction* (New York: Museum of Modern Art, 1995): 9. Significantly, Riley did not attempt to elucidate the features of a distinct style, as had been the habit of MoMA curators since its inception. In particular, the specific determination of style manifest in Philip Johnson and Henry-Russell Hitchcock's influential 1932 exhibition, *Modern Architecture: International Exhibition,* stands as an important foil to Riley's *Light Construction.* See the exhibition catalog, *Modern Architecture: International Exhibition* (New York: Museum of Modern Art, 1932), as well as Johnson and Hitchcock's influential work, The *International Style: Architecture Since 1922* (New York: W.W. Norton, 1932), which expanded upon the themes of the exhibition and effectively defined the terms of Modern Architecture as practiced through the remainder of the twentieth century.
10. Riley, *Light Construction,* 9.
11. For an expansion of the theoretical underpinnings of the exhibition, see *The Light Construction Reader,* ed. Todd Gannon (New York: Monacelli, 2002).
12. Colin Rowe and Robert Slutzky, "Transparency: Literal and Phenomenal," *Perspecta* 8 (1964): 45–54. See also the sequel, "Transparency: Literal and Phenomenal, Part II," *Perspecta* 13/14 (1971): 287–301, in which formal effects are further elaborated as emerging from complex two-dimensional patterns.
13. For a particularly lucid treatment of Eisenman's literary affiliations, see Rosalind Krauss, "Death of the Hermeneutic Phantom," in Peter Eisenman, *Houses of Cards* (New York: Oxford University Press, 1987): 166–84. For more on Eisenman's collaboration with Derrida, see Derrida and Eisenman, *Chora L Works* (New York: Monacelli, 1997).
14. Critic Jeffrey Kipnis has described this notoriously inexpressive material as "the architectural equivalent of food coloring and gruel." See "P-Tr's Progress," in *Eleven Authors in Search of a Building,* ed. Cynthia Davidson (New York: Monacelli, 1996): 178, in which he further elaborates on the suppression of material effects in Eisenman's work.
15. Terence Riley, "Afterword," in *The Light Construction Reader,* 437.
16. The influences of computer code on the conceptualization of work inflect architecture and literature with equal intensity. See N. Katherine Hayles, *My Mother Was a Computer* (Chicago: Univ. of Chicago Press, 2005).
17. The acronym stands for computer-aided design/computer-aided manufacturing, a process that seamlessly integrates digital design software with computer-controlled fabrication equipment.
18. Jerome McGann, *Radiant Textuality: Literature after the World Wide Web* (New York: Palgrave MacMillan, 2001): 111.
19. Hayles, *My Mother Was a Computer,* 103.
20. Loss Pequeño Glazier, *Digital Poetics: The Making of E-Poetics* (Tuscaloosa: University of Alabama Press, 2001).
21. John Cayley, "Literal Art," *Electronic Book Review* (2004).
22. John Cayley, "Writing on Complex Surfaces," *dichtung-digital* 35.2 (2005).
23. John Cayley, "LENS: The Practice and Poetics of Writing in Immersive VR: A Case Study with Maquette," *Leonardo Electronic Almanac: New Media Poetry and Poetics* 14:5–6 (2006): 6.

24. The piece is available for download on John Cayley's website, www.shadoof.net/in. He describes it in "Overboard: An Example of Ambient Time-Based Poetics in Digital Art," *dichtung-digital* 32 (2004).
25. See Douglas Hofstader, *Gödel, Escher, Bach: An Eternal Golden Braid* (New York: Basic Books, 1999).
26. Though produced through analog means, certain strains of postmodern architecture strangely prefigure this conflation or process and product. In particular, Peter Eisenman's extensive elaboration of design process in his early houses should be noted. See his "Cardboard Architecture: House I" and "Cardboard Architecture: House II" in *Five Architects* (New York: Oxford University Press, 1972): 15–24.
27. Hayles, *My Mother Was a Computer*, 15–38.
28. Florian Cramer, *Words Made Flesh: Culture Codes, Imagination* (Rotterdam: Piet Zwart Institute, 2005).
29. Brian Kim Stefans, *Fashionable Noise: On Digital Poetics* (Berkeley: Atelos, 2003).
30. Raffaello Maggioti mentions the device in a 1648 pamphlet, *Renitenza certissima dell'acqua alla compressione.*
31. Larry McCaffrey and Sinda Gregory, "Haunted House: An Interview with Mark Z. Danielewski," *Critique: Studies in Contemporary Fiction* 44:2 (2003): 117–18.
32. Mark Z. Danielewski, *House of Leaves* (New York: Pantheon: 2000): 139.
33. Ibid., 518.
34. Prior to the "remastered" edition, which appeared in May 2006, the blue edition showed "house" in blue but the struck Minotaur passages in black. The red edition showed "house" in gray and the struck Minotaur passages in red. The black-and-white edition, most commonly sold in Europe, had neither the blue "house" nor the red Minotaur passages. The "remastered" full color edition has "house" in blue and the Minotaur passages in red, along with the struck line in Chapter XXI in purple. We surmise that the full color edition was what the author wanted all along, but economic considerations limited the main text to only one additional color until sales justified the "remastered" version.
35. Genette says this about paratexts: "The paratext is what enables a text to become a book and to be offered as such to its readers and, more generally, to the public. More than a boundary or a sealed border, the paratext is, rather, a threshold, or...a 'vestibule' that offers the world at large the possibility of either steeping inside or turning back. It is an 'undefined zone' between the inside and the outside, a zone without any hard and fast boundary on either the inward side (turned toward the text) or the outward side (turned toward the world's discourse about the text), an edge, or as Phillippe Lejeune put it, 'a fringe of the printed text which in reality controls one's whole reading of the text'" in *Paratexts: Thresholds of Interpretation* (Cambridge: Cambridge University Press, 1997): 1–2.
36. Danielewski, *House of Leaves*, 338.
37. Ibid., 165.
38. Mark B. N. Hansen, "The Digital Topography of Mark Z. Danielewski's *House of Leaves*," *Contemporary Literature* 45.4 (2004): 597–636.
39. For an account of these fields, see Hayles, *How We Became Posthuman*, 222–46.
40. The process of creating genetic programs that can design circuits is described in John Koza, et al., *Genetic Programming IV: Routine Human-Computer Machine Intelligence* (New York: Springs, 2005).
41. Brian Cantwell Smith, "The Foundations of Computing," in *Computationalism: New Directions*, ed. Matthias Scheutz (Cambridge: MIT Press, 2002): 76.
42. N. Katherine Hayles, "Saving the Subject: Remediation in *House of Leaves*," *American Literature* 74 (2002): 779–806.
43. For extended discussions of stereotomy and the innovations it made possible both in stone and on paper, see Alberto Pérez-Gómez, *Architecture and the Crisis of Modern Science* (Cambridge: MIT Press, 1985): 203–36, and Robin Evans, *The Projective Cast* (Cambridge: MIT Press, 2000): 179–239.

44. Some of the more influential drawings of this period were exhibited at the Wexner Center for the Arts in the 2001 exhibition, *Perfect Acts of Architecture*. See Jeffrey Kipnis, *Perfect Acts of Architecture* (New York: Museum of Modern Art, 2001).
45. Throughout history, from Piranesi and Boullée to Finsterlin and Taut, architecture's vanguard has periodically turned its attention to theoretical speculations through the elaboration of unbuildable projects.
46. For a discussion of Lynn and other of Peter Eisenman's well-known protégés, see Todd Gannon, "The Shape of Things to Come," 36–42 in this volume.
47. The four partners, David Erdman, Marcelyn Gow, Ulrika Karlsson, and Chris Perry, are based in Los Angeles, Zurich, Stockholm, and New York respectively.
48. Speaks, "Design Intelligence," 16.
49. See the exhibition catalog, Joshua Decter, *Dark Places* (Santa Monica: Santa Monica Museum of Art, 2006).
50. Similar tendencies can be seen across architecture's younger generation. Emergent (led by Tom Wiscombe), Gnuform (Heather Roberge and Jason Payne), and Xefirotarch (Hernán Díaz Alonso) are just a few of the firms led by designers in their thirties that share servo's digitally-driven material and atmospheric ambitions.
51. Cf. Manfredo Tafuri: "there can never be an aesthetics, art or architecture of class, but only a class critique of aesthetics, art, architecture and the city." See his "Towards a Critique of Architectural Ideology," *Architecture Theory since 1968*, ed. K. Michael Hays (Cambridge: MIT Press, 2000): 32–33. Tafuri later revised and elaborated this text as *Architecture and Utopia: Design and Capitalist Development* (Cambridge: MIT Press, 1979).
52. These conversations were succinctly traced over three issues of *Harvard Design Magazine* in 2004 and 2005. See Allen et al., "Stocktaking 2004: Nine Questions About the Present and Future of Design" *Harvard Design Magazine* 20 (2004): 4–52; George Baird, "'Criticality' and its Discontents" *Harvard Design Magazine* 21 (2005): 16–21; and Reinhold Martin, "Critical of What?" *Harvard Design Magazine* 22 (2005): 104–9.
53. In architecture, R. E. Somol and Sarah Whiting have advanced "the projective," while in other fields, the terms "post-critical" and "posthuman" have both been appearing with increasing frequency. See Somol and Whiting, "Notes Around the Doppler Effect and Other Moods of Modernism," *Perspecta* 33 (2002): 72–77; and N. Katherine Hayles, *How We Became Posthuman.*
54. Thomas Whalen, "Data Navigation, Architectures of Knowledge," Banff Summit on Living Architectures: Designing for Immersion and Interaction. Banff New Media Institute. Banff, 23 Sept 2000.
55. Nicolas Gessler, "Evolving Cultural Things-That-Think," in *Computational Synthesis: From Basic Building Blocks To Higher Level Functionality*, Hod Lipson, Erik Antonsson, and John R. Koza, eds. (Palo Alto: AAAI Press, 2003).
56. For a wide-ranging analysis of how the process works on a cosmic and global scale in the natural world, see Harold Morowitz, *The Emergence of Everything: How the World Become Complex* (New York: Oxford University Press, 2004).
57. Alexander Galloway and Eugene Thacker, *The Exploit: A Theory of Networks* (Minneapolis: University of Minnesota Press, 2007): 3.
58. We are grateful to Alan Liu for thoughtful comments that were helpful in re-thinking the larger contexts for our argument and for other insights.

Virtual Architecture, Actual Media

with N. Katherine Hayles, 2011

Fig. 15.1 Diller + Scofidio, Blur Building (Yverdon-le-Bains, Switzerland, 2002).

Architectural studies boasts a wealth of material that examines the role of print, paper, and other analog media in forming and transforming architectural practice.[1] While numerous titles on the significance of digital media exist that explore their impact on architectural production, no definitive analysis has yet emerged.[2] Indeed, given the rapid pace of change and the development of new digital devices and applications, a definitive work on this topic may never be possible. We offer this chapter as a gathering of resources and a framework within which analyses may proceed. The work done on print media's effects clearly shows that medial effects go beyond architectural practice into such issues as the spread of architectural ideas, the dissemination of architectural writing, and the formation of an architectural canon of forms, styles, and components.[3] Even this, however, is not a complete inventory. Media effects can be explored in four distinct but interrelated areas: effects on how buildings are conceptualized, effects on how buildings are constructed, effects on the subjectivities of those who envision buildings, and effects on those presumed to inhabit the structures. Given limitations of space, we will focus our analysis on the last two areas—subjectivities of practitioners and assumptions about what constitutes the human, with glances at environmental, spatial, technological, and cultural forces that most deeply affect the transformations.

First, some ground clearing on our central terms. Virtuality currently has two central clusters of meanings, one deriving from virtual reality technologies, the other from the influential Deleuzian concept of the virtual as that which is in dynamic tension with the actual.[4] Both these senses are relevant to our discussion. We begin by offering the hypothesis that all architecture, built or unbuilt, is virtual in the Deleuzian sense. Architecture, we propose, is not building, nor is it some privileged subset of building. Rather, we posit architecture as an emergent property of building. It is that which makes building meaningful to an ongoing tradition. Not building itself, but, as the dictionary tells us, a particular "art," "science," or "manner" of building; as Reyner Banham put it, "what distinguishes architecture is not *what* is done...but *how* it is done."[5] Further, we posit that architecture is a function of embodied discourse, that is, discourse instantiated in speech or, more typically, written or graphical documents. *Document*, as the term is used in textual studies, is distinct from *text* or *work* because it implies the existence of a physical (or digital) object.

Just as all buildings hold within them the potential of becoming architecture, so the documents that precede, surround, and follow buildings are constitutive players in imagining, planning, and implementing architectural practices and thus also participate in creating architecture. Embodied buildings and embodied documents are physical objects witnessing to architectural acts, but architecture can never be reduced to these objects. Rather, architecture partakes fundamentally of the virtual in the Deleuzian sense, a nimbus of potentialities in dynamic interaction with the actuality of buildings and documents. Both the virtuality of architecture and the physicality of documents and buildings are real, but whereas documents and buildings are location-specific, comprising myriad individual instances, architecture is malleable, dispersed, always in flux. As a totality, architecture is ineffable, for as soon as it is written or built, it moves from the virtual to the actual. The collective labor of the discipline acts as midwife to architecture, moving from the raw materials of architectural actual media (whether buildings, construction documents, or philosophical writings) and guiding the emergence of architecture's virtuality into the actuality of things we can read, touch, and traverse.

An important implication that follows from this view is the impact of media on architecture. Like love, the term *media* evokes universal recognition, yet there is a surprising lack of consensual definitions. For a field such as communication studies, media mean communication technologies such as television, radio, and the internet; for Marshall McLuhan, media were famously configured as "extensions of man," a definition that cast telegraphy into the same bin as roads. For our purposes, we regard media as materio-semiotic systems that enact the circulation of signs. A neologism coined by Donna Haraway (among others), "materio-semiotic" connotes objects that partake both of signifying practices and physical instantiation. An earthy example is provided by the rural Midwest landscape one of us (NKH) knew as a child, a time when indoor plumbing was ubiquitous but not quite universal. In that landscape, one occasionally encountered outdoor privies, and not infrequently, visits to them revealed, in the form of a Sears catalog, the spirit of thriftiness that indelibly marked those who lived through the Great Depression. A materio-semiotic object, the catalog served a dual purpose: as one lingered while waiting for certain biological processes to occur, it provided casual reading material; later, its material properties (the tearability of the relatively cheap paper, etc.) came to the foreground.

Media, as material systems conveying signs, have two principal strategies at their disposal: circulating signs through people, and circulating people through signs. Typically, documents are identified with the first strategy and buildings with the second. Library books circulate among people, for example, while Gothic cathedrals functioned as sign systems through which people circulated as they performed liturgical rituals. The history of books and buildings shows many other possible combinations of strategies. Medieval codices were often chained to podiums, so that it was the people who moved while the books were stationary. Conversely, as Robert Venturi and Denise Scott Brown taught us,[6] buildings may be designed to be seen from moving cars, so from a relativistic perspective that takes the viewer's position as constant, the buildings circulate while the person remains seated.

Considering both documents and buildings as media—that is, as materio-semiotic systems—has multiple advantages. Defamiliarizing the usual categories that parse buildings as durable architectural entities and documents as ephemera, the medial perspective articulated above encourages interpretations that link semiotic functions to material actualities, so that buildings and books are neither reduced only to discursive entities nor to material objects. Another advantage inheres in the new configurations that emerge when the usual dichotomy between built and paper architecture is broken down and replaced by more flexible and dynamic interactions between virtuality and actuality. As media change—for example, from print-based documents to digital files—the dynamic between architecture's virtuality and the medium's actuality changes accordingly, often with dramatic effects. Virtual architecture, those unbuilt or unbuildable digital constructions of the contemporary generation, becomes not a pseudo-architecture suffering from a lack of physicality but rather an essential architecture unencumbered by physicality. Virtual architecture does not operate outside the pale of the discipline in a lesser realm of the unbuilt (the design equivalent of the undead), as many detractors have insisted. Rather, architecture, by virtue of its dynamic interaction with actual media, infuses the physicality of the written and the built with the infinite potential of the virtual. Inhering at the very heart of the discipline, architecture's ineffability, unspeakable as such, is the reservoir that renews the discipline and makes innovation possible.

VIRTUALITY AND MEDIUM SPECIFICITY

One cannot develop a critical theory of new media if one begins from the assumption that they are somehow immaterial.
– Mark Poster[7]

The rise of the virtual, stimulating a renewed consideration of material specificity, has catalyzed new interpretations of materiality. Matthew Kirschenbaum, for example, has distinguished between forensic and formal materiality.[8] Materiality, referring to the artifactual nature of an object, should not be confused with physicality. As we have argued elsewhere,[9] an object has a potentially infinite array of physical attributes. One could, for example, refer to the chemical composition of ink when discussing print technology, and beyond that to the molecular components, their energy states, etc. Physicality alone, then, is insufficient to specify an object. Rather, certain physical attributes are typically of interest in a given circumstance—say, the colors associated with the chemicals in ink. Materiality expresses this conjunction of attention and attributes, focus and physicality. Attention shifts, focus changes, and materiality transforms. Always embedded in an overt or implied context, materiality, far from being given by an object's physicality, is an emergent event.

Kirschenbaum's formulation of formal and forensic materiality builds on this idea and carries it further by distinguishing between the material substrate of computer technologies (forensic materiality) and the formal sign systems that constitute computer codes (formal materiality). Reconfiguring the usual dichotomy of hardware and software by incorporating their material properties into the definitions, Kirschenbaum draws attention to issues of scale and contingency. Just as any artifact can be parsed in an infinite number of ways, so any two apparently identical artifacts can be seen to differ if the scale of observation is small enough. Two boards, for example, may be judged the same size, but drop to a smaller scale—millimeters rather than inches, nanometers rather than millimeters—and differences previously undetectable become observable. Kirschenbaum illustrates the point by taking a CD-ROM to a nanotechnology laboratory, where a scanning tunneling microscope reveals very slight irregularities in the bit patterns. Although we are accustomed to say that information is infinitely and exactly reproducible, this is only true within given tolerances. Along with a context of attention, materiality implicitly references a context of measurement from which observations are generated. Consequently, materiality has borderlands in which it can be transformed, either by a shift of attention or a shift of scale. Like the coastline of Britain in Benoit Mandelbrot's well-known example,[10] materiality cannot be specified in advance and without reference to context, for social, cultural, and psychological aspects interact with technical specifications.

Complementing and complicating this idea of forensic materiality is formal materiality, which in Kirschenbaum's formulation consists of the processes or behaviors in which a computational object engages. Just as one bit is not identical to another bit when the scale of observation is small enough, so the codes that the computer executes may have idiosyncrasies that testify to their origin's historical circumstances, as Kirschenbaum demonstrates by finding the kernel of an older computer game embedded within the code of a newer one.[11] As with forensic materiality, formal materiality has social, cultural, and psychological dimensions as well as technical ones. Thus both formal and forensic materialities are inherently emergent; in Bruno Latour's terms, they are nature/culture hybrids.[12] As emergent entities, they are path-dependent; they have histories, and these histories mark their materiality in ways that break open simple categories such as one and zero bits or executable and not executable code. The material entities become individuals capable of revealing their stories when interrogated with the proper (i.e., forensic) techniques.

What changes when we move from hardware and software to formal and forensic materiality? From the outset the emergent nature of forensic and formal materiality makes clear that multiple recursive feedback loops cycle between physicality and sociality, media as technical objects and social processes. Adrian Mackenzie has convincingly argued that software construction is an intensely social process.[13] The framework sketched above broadens this insight to include the technical functioning, social practices, and media representations of architectural work. Researchers may understandably choose to focus on a particular aspect of a multiple recursive cycle (as for example Friedrich Kittler does in his emphasis on hardware in such essays as "There is No Software" and "Protected Mode,"[14] but in our view it is a mistake to fetishize any one component as if it alone could explain the dynamics of a complex system. As Donald M. Lowe shows, social, economic, and technological factors work together to form "the body" in late-capitalist USA.[15] Take, as another example, our claim above that attention is a co-specifying factor in the emergent dynamics shaping which aspects of physicality become materiality. This might seem to privilege attention as the determining component. Attention itself, however, has historical and culturally specific dimensions that spring from the effects of media and other technologies, as numerous studies have shown. Jonathan Crary's *Suspensions of Perception* (2001) traces the emergence of attention as a medical and industrial concern and explores the complex dynamic between its creation and dissolution; Wolfgang Schivelbush's *The Railway Journey* (1986) demonstrated the effects of rail travel on modes of attention in the late nineteenth and early twentieth centuries; and Steven Johnson and we have argued for the effects on attention of contemporary media.[16] To engage a richer sense of the complex dynamics that co-determine media specificity, interactions throughout the system should be understood as entwined with and mutually affecting one another.

Media specificity has been a minority interest in the humanities for most of the twentieth century, with the long dominance of print inducing a kind of somnolence in this regard. (An important exception is textual studies, which has typically engaged with what Jerome McGann has called "bibliographic codes," that is, the material aspects of texts.[17]) All this changed, however, with the rapid development of networked and programmable media in the later twentieth century. Signs of crisis are now everywhere apparent as the humanities struggle to come to terms with the importance of media specificity in composition, publishing, credentialing, and a host of other areas. Architecture has been significantly in advance of other areas of the human sciences in investigating interactions between architecture and the objects, subjects, contexts, and media that conspire to produce it. A convenient example can be found in Robin Evans's widely read 1986 essay, "Translations from Drawing to Building."[18]

Fig. 15.2 Philibert de l'Orme, Royal Chapel at Anet (near Dreux, France, 1547–52).

Evans's text relates a simple tale: the constructed dome of the Royal Chapel at Anet (1547–52) by Philibert de l'Orme [**Fig. 15.2**] does not match the drawing of it inscribed in the pavement below nor does their relationship match de l'Orme's description of it in his *Premier tome de l'architecture* (1567). For Evans, these differences do not signal a deficiency in the work, a failure on the part of the architect to translate precisely an architectural concept from one medium to another; rather, the case reveals the differences between the various media (drawings, books, and buildings) that were deployed to produce the architecture in question, as well as the way in which those differences condition and inflect it.

De l'Orme's work hinges on a consonance between the two-dimensional, three-dimensional, and textual instantiations of a complex geometrical pattern, a consonance that Evans's analysis demonstrates to be incorrect geometrically. The work may *look like* a virtuoso feat of projective geometry (and in fact it is), but this feat was not executed as advertised. Constructing an alibi for de l'Orme, Evans surmises that the architect fudged the floor paving, cropping the aesthetically inferior portions at the projection's edges and scaling up the entire pattern to produce an effect that more closely resembled that of the dome above. De l'Orme's adjustments can be seen as an extension of the ancient Greek practices of visual correction (entasis, the modulation of column spacing, etc.), which likewise torqued, stretched, and adjusted elements to produce a more convincing appearance of their being parallel, perpendicular, evenly spaced, or plumb.[19] Evans demonstrates that de l'Orme's corrective adjustments extend into the *Premier tome* as well, which similarly values the effect of rigorous method over its actual application. We might append de l'Orme's triumphant finish, "forming by this means compartments that are plumb and perpendicular above the plan of the said chapel,"[20] with "but this didn't look quite right, so we cropped off the outer, ugly bits and made the whole thing bigger." The addition, while ruining the text's rhetorical effect, would nevertheless have the salutary effect, important for our argument, of revealing the transformational effects of translating between and among media.

In each mediated instantiation of the chapel—the constructed dome, the patterned floor, du Cerceau's engraved drawings, de l'Orme's printed text, Evans's diagrams and photographs—the architectural effect of dizzying geometrical precision was crafted and modulated according to the specific media through which that effect was produced. In the end, we understand that these effects at Anet issue not from a single source but rather from the dynamic interaction of the building's materiality with its myriad mediated representations, as well as with the architect(s) that produces it and the perceiving subjects that engage it.[21] Like writing, each of the media involved made possible and also precluded specific inflections of the thoughts they embody. In many cases, media deployed by architects give rise to ideas that are thinkable only through those media; recall, for instance, Peter Eisenman's cunning redrawing of Le Corbusier's Maison Dom-ino. Originally published by the Swiss-French architect as a two-point perspective [**Fig. 20.3**], the image was re-drawn by Eisenman as a series of axonometric diagrams [**Fig. 20.13**].[22] This translation of an iconic drawing from one style of projection to another opened the simple form to a host of new interpretations.

Another avenue along which this line of thinking might develop is architectural photography. Migrating built form to the printed page through the lens of the camera, with its cultural affiliations with truthful representation, made possible modes of architectural thinking unavailable to drawing or writing. Truth travels in step with fiction, producing productive slippages between assumed facts and media representations. As pointed out by Beatriz Colomina, photography and its attendant body of techniques can manipulate reality as much as reflect it. "Rather than *represent* reality, it *produces* a new reality."[23] Colomina goes on to demonstrate in her interpretation of Le Corbusier's serial redrawing of postcards that these new realities signify not as a function of single images but rather through their accumulation and relation to other media: "a photograph does not have specific meaning in itself but rather in its relationship to other photographs, the caption, the writing, and the layout of the page."[24]

As photography is multiplied in film and made infinitely malleable with digital technologies, these potential "new realities" are likewise multiplied, and with them their available interactions with other media and their potential to produce new forms of architectural thinking. Let us return for a moment to Eisenman's representations of the Maison Dom-ino. Here, Eisenman uses an abstract drawing technique to produce a series of spare interpretations of Corbusier's already stripped-down original. Taken together, Eisenman's drawings produce an effect of teleological development, an implied history of a primitive form's articulation over time. This effect is particularly effective rendered as an axonometric, which imposes a three-dimensional framework revealing spatial relations while retaining dimensional congruence. The argument instantiated in Corbusier's more realistic perspective would occlude much of the essential information.[25] Over a series of projects through the 1970s and into the present, Eisenman developed this technique further in analyses of the work of Giuseppe Terragni as well as in his own work, producing a series of projects that adopted a narrative syntax to produce the effect of the serial elaboration of primitive forms over time.[26] With the advent of 3D computer modeling and animation software in the 1990s, such serial elaborations were possible not only in far greater degrees of complexity but also with much higher frame refresh rates. From Le Corbusier's single iconic image to Eisenman's step-by-step transformations to Greg Lynn's fluid animations, we see the persistent development through various media of architecture as a specific narrative discourse, the articulation of which is only possible through the specific media that produce it. Coupling these digital animations with soundtracks, live actors, and cinematic techniques, firms operating outside the discipline of architecture such as Imaginary Forces push this discourse still further in their development of architectural pre-visualizations and what has been called "experience design."[27] The perceivable effects of this discourse do not inhere solely within the objects produced, regardless of whether those objects take the form of buildings, drawings, computer animations, or texts. Rather, these effects obtain from the dynamic interactions that arise in the virtual space between the various media that embody them and the perceiving subjects that engage them.

NEW MEDIA AS ARCHITECTURE

Over the past twenty years, digital technologies have perpetrated a fundamental transformation not only of architectural working methods, but also of the kind of work architects produce and the manner in which that work is interpreted and discussed. Shifts in attention from form to surface, from objects to atmosphere, from meaning to mood, and from critical to post-critical (or projective) practice have been advanced by critics and historians from all camps as symptoms of a more general move away from a discursive paradigm centered upon stable objects and legible meaning to one concerned primarily with fluid environments, ephemeral effects, and ambiguous moods.[28] While others, such as Robert Venturi, have attempted to situate new technologies within old regimes of signification and iconography, we eschew his tendency to cast architecture and media as opposing forces.[29] While architecture might emerge from the interaction of iconography and electronics with generic buildings in the work of Venturi and others, in our view, more interesting work is being done by firms committed not to a conceptual separation of digital media and built form but rather to their seamless integration.

The New York office of Diller, Scofidio, and Renfro has long been at the forefront of integrating technology and virtuality in architecture as well as in extending architectural practice into neighboring disciplines such as gallery art, theater, and film. The firm's precocious facility with virtual effects as well as the trademark elements of their work may be attributed to their long history of collaboration with the theater and stage production. In contrast to the earnest monumentality of architectural form, the theater deals unapologetically in artifice, regularly deploying actual construction and virtual projection to construct its illusions. DS+R operates in a similar fashion, and recurrent elements in their projects recall standard theatrical elements and tropes. Their famous mechanical apparatuses, for example, evoke the ad hoc mechanical tackle of the theater fly-space. Their aggressive use of architectural drawing conventions (plan and section projections, linear perspective, etc.) to manipulate spatial perception corresponds to the intermingling of architectural technique and theatrical illusion described in early treatises ranging from Vitruvius to Alberti and illustrated in mannerist examples such as Palladio's Teatro Olimpico in Vicenza or Scamozzi's Teatro di Sabionetta. In theater as in the work of DS+R, mechanical and projective devices, from illusionistically painted sets to the split and distorted perspectival recessions of the *scena per angolo* to Diller and Scofidio's early deployment of angled mirrors,[30] come together to produce a range of virtual effects that confound the distinctions between the actual and the virtual and in recent works have become the primary locus of their architectural experimentation.

Fig. 15.3 Diller + Scofidio, *The Rotary Notary and His Hot Plate*, multimedia theater work (Philadelphia, 1987).

This tendency is apparent in such hallmark projects as their production design for "The Rotary Notary and His Hot Plate" of 1987 [**Fig. 15.3**]. Drawing inspiration from Marcel Duchamp, Diller and Scofidio devised an apparatus composed of an opaque screen that divided the stage parallel to the proscenium and a mirror fixed at forty-five degrees that revealed a plan view of the concealed space to the audience.[31] Viewed head-on (and in the most commonly published photographs), the apparatus effectively flattens into a single plane akin to an elevation drawing, reproducing the gendered separation of bride's and bachelor's domains of Duchamp's *Grande Verre* while producing a multiplication of the performance space that unleashes a panoply of illusory potential. Moving into the concealed area of the stage displaces the actor's bodies into the virtual space of the mirror apparatus where they are rendered weightless, fragmented, and dismembered. Diller and Scofidio honed their techniques and expanded their repertoire to include video projections in a series of theatrical productions through the 1990s,[32] as well as in installations such as Para-Site at the Museum of Modern Art in New York (1989), Loop-hole at the Second Artillery Armory of Chicago (1992), and in projects such as the Slow House on Long Island (unfinished, 1992) and the Brasserie at the Seagram Building in New York (2000). In each case, carefully positioned cameras and video monitors displaying both real-time and time-delayed imagery produced on-site as well as remotely, displace and multiply architectural spaces, producing jarring spatial and temporal juxtapositions heightened by their architectural constructions but impossible to devise through strictly mechanical means. The firm also devised complex presentations of each work, from armatures that blurred distinctions between drawings, models, and the structures designed to support them in earlier works to clever combinations of analog and digital representational techniques in later presentations. The firm's work developed in scope and ambition through the 1990s and into this century alongside rapid advances in digital technologies, and the office remains at the forefront of experimentation with them that re-imagines the affective potential of architectural projects as well as the technical scope of architectural practice.

Perhaps the firm's most ambitious attempt at integrating digital technologies and physical construction is their Blur Building at Yverdon-les-Bains, Switzerland (2002) [**Fig. 15.1**]. To construct an artificial cloud on the grounds of Swiss Expo '02, the firm employed digital technologies in concert with analog techniques through all stages of conceptualization, design, construction, and operation. Their use of these techniques, from the fusions of analog and digital drawing methods in presentation materials to the integration of computer-controlled weather sensors to modulate the complex fog generation system on the project, is well known and widely published. The project's dissemination in other media, from extensive publication in the popular and scholarly press to the use of its imagery in contemporary products ranging from telephone cards to chocolate bars, has also been noted.[33] For the present discussion, the firm's eradication of the boundary between virtual and actual spatial environments through the integration of digital media is most pertinent.

In the indeterminate space of the Blur Building, familiar architectural depth cues were to be all but erased by the mist. To compensate for diminished visual stimuli, alternative modes of spatial orientation were to have been made available through digitally controlled sound and light effects. As the Blur Building developed, the firm and its many collaborators experimented with a number of integrated media components, from scrolling LED text displays to automated "braincoats" to interactive online controls, most of which were eliminated due to budget constraints from the final built work. We have noted previously the unfortunate lacunae their absence left in the experience of the built work,[34] but, as has been noted by Mark Hansen, "in addition to being a temporary built project in the world, the Blur Building exists as a work of embodied conceptual art preserved in the archive of traces that document its making and that include—as a central core of its drama—the media components."[35] While these unrealized media components did not inflect the constructed spectacle at Yverdon-les-Bains, they are essential to an understanding of the full architectural significance of the Blur Building and point to the burgeoning potential of architecture born out of the interpenetration of new and old media.

Offering much-needed protection from the cool mist of the pavilion, Diller and Scofidio's digitally enhanced braincoats open new avenues of social interaction and spatial organization. Upon arriving at the pavilion, visitors were to complete a simple questionnaire meant to divine specific personality traits, the answers to which were then uploaded to a central database and to the individual's braincoat. Sensors and transmitters embedded in the coats would communicate with each other as visitors moved through the space, causing visual, aural, and mechanical transformations to the coat based on proximity to other coats and the programmed information they carried. As a visitor wandering in the mist approached another visitor who had given similar answers to the questionnaire, the system would signal a potential affinity by shifting the color intensity of each coat toward green and increasing the frequency of audio pulses emitted by the coat. Contrasting answers would elicit an antipathetic response signaled by a red hue, and exact matches would trigger a vibrating sensation in the coat, "mimicking the tingle of excitement that comes with physical attraction."[36]

The results of this new spatial experiment remain unknown. Like-minded visitors might have attracted one another, causing a segregation of inhabitants based on personality that would have resulted in uniform clusters of glowing green coats and rapid aural pulses. Alternatively, visitors might have been turned off by the advances of their supposed matches, causing those with similar profiles to repel one another. This might have led to an ironic arrangement of mismatched personalities seeking the comfort of strangers in the closest proximity to one another. More likely, of course, would have been an oscillating swarm of rising and falling pulse tones and a full spectrum of glowing coats as individual visitors pursued individual agendas and entered and exited the system at varying rates—a field of peripatetic denizens blushing, beeping, and vibrating their way through an otherworldly milieu.

In another aborted embellishment, the pavilion was to be equipped with PTZ cameras capable of being controlled by virtual visitors experiencing the space through the internet. While these visitors would not have been able directly to enjoy the full range of physical sensations and alternative social opportunities offered by the braincoats, they would have been afforded a remote view of the spectacle as well as an opportunity to affect the content of the LED displays (and perhaps, by extension, the behavior of the visitors at Yverdon) through interaction with web-based interfaces. As such, the Blur Building would have inhabited the virtual space of the internet as it simultaneously occupied the physical space over Lake Neuchâtel, with its virtual and actual visitors likewise occupying multiple positions in the manifold virtual instantiations of the space projected around the globe by the Internet.

While budgetary constraints precluded the inclusion of these elements in Yverdon, other projects demonstrate the potential of active digital media on architectural design. Linking integrated sensors to computer-controlled lighting elements, Toyo Ito's 1986 Tower of Winds in Yokohama transformed contextual data into "environmental music" expressed in constantly changing light patterns.[37] Greg Lynn's Embryological House project (2000) invites clients to participate in the design process through an interactive website.[38] More recently, the D-Tower by Lars Spuybroek and artist Q. S. Serafin combines physical construction with web-based components to produce a hybrid, interactive work that colorfully maps the collective emotional state of a small Dutch town.[39] Younger practices such as Höweler + Yoon, servo, Xefirotarch, and others routinely combine digital technologies with physical construction to produce architectural works impossible to consider in a strictly analog terms. Far exceeding Venturi's call for a generic architecture adorned with electronic signage, these works (in all their varied instantiations) guide the emergence of an aggressively intermediated architecture that choreographs a complex, integrated ensemble of physical construction, virtual simulation, and pervasive interaction of human subjects and intelligent machines.

VIRTUALITY AND NOTIONS OF HUMAN SUBJECTIVITY

I am teaching a design studio at UCLA. A student has been working on a 3D model of a building and is walking me through the latest changes. It is an early summer afternoon in Southern California and the studios, designed with analog drafting in mind, are bathed in natural light. The sun's glare makes it difficult for me to see the image on the screen, so I ask the student to turn it toward me so that I might get a better view. A second later, without lifting a hand, she asked, "Is that better?" Flummoxed, I reply, "You didn't move anything." Her right wrist flicks the mouse almost imperceptibly, and the 3D image on the screen rotates about its vertical axis. "How about now?" I reach forward and turn the monitor myself.

Two generations peer at the screen, the older seeing the screen in space, the younger the screen as space. Such anecdotes pepper the literature surrounding the advent of digital technologies in design studios through the 1990s to the present. As more robust platforms and projects such as Second Life come online, these occurrences have become increasingly commonplace. While virtual spaces in built work are only beginning to alter the architectural environment, the virtual spaces in which work is produced have been fully assimilated into workplace practices and, increasingly, into leisure time as well. These professional and leisure practices have had dramatic effects not only on architects but also on artists, writers, and cultural critics. In the cultural imaginary, the virtual in architecture, in vibrant conversation with the actual media of networked and programmable machines, leaps ahead of present construction to envision a built world in which simulated overlays merge seamlessly with actual buildings to create mixed reality environments inhabited by augmented humans.

Such a world is given pride of place in Vernon Vinge's speculative fiction *Rainbows End* (2006), where it is imagined so vividly and pervasively that it almost qualifies as the novel's protagonist. In Vinge's near-future world, buildings are quite plain and even ugly, for they are not designed to be seen in themselves but rather to function as underpinnings onto which virtual overlays are projected.[40] They are in this sense malleable, mutating as the projections change; Juan, a student at Fairmont High School, notices that the "buildings were mostly three stories today. Their gray walls were like playing cards stacked in a rickety array."[41] There would indeed be little sense in creating elaborate exteriors when what the eye perceives comes not from the building but the computer. Programmable gear provides the projections, texturing, and detailing that transform surfaces into whatever the user has fashioned in his or her wearable. Visions are shared either through VR projections or directly as digital files. Users thus become instant collaborators with architects, creating custom visual effects that advertise their virtuosity in manipulating digital information.

The cumulative effects on human culture and subjectivity are profound. The novel's putative protagonist, Robert Gu, is an older man who had been a world-class poet before he descended into the deep twilight of Alzheimer's. Rescued from darkness by medical advances, he reawakens to a contemporary world in which most people around him are living in a mixed reality that he can enter only through arduous re-education. The plot foregrounds how class has been reconfigured; the emphasis is no longer on the haves and have-nots but on the digitally facile and digitally obtuse. Just as in former times one was required performatively to display a certain class, gender, and race to have access to a gentleman's club, so now the elite are defined by their skills in manipulating the wearables that create the environments to which other people respond.

The ornate surfaces created by VR projections cover over architectural infrastructures permeated by computational devices. In contrast to their unremarkable exteriors, buildings have remarkable functionalities that, invisible to casual inspection, bestow smart capabilities that make them something like intelligent entities in their own right. "Cryptic machines are everywhere nowadays," Gu thinks. "They lurked in walls, nestled in trees, even littered the lawns. They worked silently, almost invisibly, twenty-four hours a day. He began to wonder where it all ended."[42] Such is the retrofitted Geisel Library at the University of California at San Diego campus, whose infrastructure includes stabilizers enabling the building to absorb earthquake tremors by counter-movements that ensure continuing stability. A climax arrives when the digital stabilizers are hijacked by a mysterious hacker (who may be, the narrative hints, an emergent virtual entity produced spontaneously by the network's complexity). In answer to a challenge from a rival faction, the hacker literally makes the building walk by converting the stabilizers' countermeasures into coherent directionality. The scene underscores the complexity of agency when it is distributed among embodied individuals, non-human agents, and actual buildings and media.

The novel dramatizes effects documented in a host of non-fictional studies, including rapid technological change and the concomitant obsolescence;[43] global microsociality emerging from a combination of instantaneous transnational communication and the exigencies of local times and places;[44] crowdsourcing,[45] here envisioned as "affliances," short-term contracts establishing relationships between citizens and corporations for temporary cooperation on a project; government power at once centralized and exercised through distributed networks;[46] and conspiracies that thrive on asymmetric warfare.[47] Subjectivity is not about interiority expressed through verbal constructions (metaphorized in the poet protagonist, who finds he has lost his gift to make words sing) but about manipulating information so that it forms a pervasive real-time interface with everyday life. Human intelligence has been so thoroughly integrated with intelligence augmentation technologies that "media," properly conceived, are no longer external affordances but integrated systems rippling across multiple artifactual and biological interfaces.[48]

This near-future scenario lies on a trajectory that stretches back at least as far as the early years of the twentieth century. Writing on the influence of media, particularly film and photography, on Le Corbusier's architecture, Beatriz Colomina notes that "to inhabit" means "to inhabit the camera. But the camera is not a traditional place, it is a system of classification, a kind of filing cabinet. 'To inhabit' means to employ that system."[49] Similarly, "to inhabit" the structures in *Rainbows End* means to occupy the systems of classification and protocols that enable information to flow smoothly along the networks. Working from the extensive materials in Le Corbusier's archives, Colomina shows that "the traditional humanist figure, the inhabitant of the house, is made incidental to the camera eye; it comes and goes, it is merely a visitor." Architectural elements, particularly windows, are consistently superimposed with contemporary media: "Telephone, cable, radios...machines for abolishing time and space. Control is now in these media." Colomina argues that "the window in the age of mass communication provides us with one more flat image. The window is a screen."[50] Further along the trajectory, the screen in *Rainbows End* leaps out of the frame and projects directly onto ambient surfaces, dynamically engaging with and indeed co-creating environments. The novel performs a world consonant with Anthony Vidler's observation that "contemporary subject identity, if it is optical at all, finds its subject in screens, in clouded surfaces, in the indeterminacy of non-perspectival structure."[51]

What, then, of contemporary subjectivity? Writing about the earlier twentieth century, Colomina concludes that "a dematerialization" follows from "the emerging media. The organizing geometry of architecture skips from the perspectival cone of vision, from the humanist eye, to the camera angle. It is precisely in this slippage that modern architecture becomes modern by engaging with the media."[52] Architecture in the present and near future, however, does more than displace the "traditional humanist figure." Rather, it incorporates the individual (or as Deleuze says, the "dividual") as a node in a global network of interconnectivity that promiscuously mingles human with non-human agency, local embodiments with global communication flows, virtual overlays with actual buildings and media.

HOW TO FASHION A PRO-HUMAN POSTHUMANISM

If there is to be a new urbanism it will not be based on the twin fantasies of order and omnipotence, it will be the staging of uncertainty, it will no longer be concerned with the arrangement of more or less permanent objects but with the irrigation of territories with potential; it will no longer aim for stable configurations but for the creation of enabling fields that accommodate processes that refuse to be crystallized into definitive form...it will no longer be obsessed with the city but with the manipulation of infrastructure for endless intensifications and diversifications, shortcuts and redistributions—the reinvention of psychological space.
– Rem Koolhaas [53]

As we confront the issue of contemporary subjectivity, it is worth remembering that humans have been co-evolving with technology almost from the beginning of the species. This complex co-evolutionary spiral has aptly been called *technogenesis*,[54] producing and produced by the complex feedback loops whereby the production of new tools creates new visions of human being, which leads to new environments, which puts selective pressure on some features and enhances others, which leads to different practices and related ontogenic changes, which in turn stimulates the creation of yet more tools. As Deleuze has remarked, the pertinent question ought not to be whether the present era is better or worse than what came before (a question impossible to answer comprehensively).[55] Rather, we might better ask what opportunities for constructive interventions are presented to us by our information-intensive environments. One way into the question is to take seriously objections raised to our posthuman condition and consider carefully how undesirable effects can be mitigated and salutary effects enhanced.

The traditional humanist subject was seen as having a body, but (at least in the philosophical tradition) that body was reductively viewed as a support system for the all-important rational mind, as has been shown, among others, by Elizabeth Grosz in *Volatile Bodies* (1994) and George Lakoff and Mark Johnson in *Philosophy in the Flesh* (1999).[56] With the advent of cyberspace, enthusiasts made extravagant claims for leaving the body behind, and transhumanists such as Ray Kurzweil confidently looked forward to the near future when the body could either be extensively re-engineered for radical life extension or, in Hans Moravec's visions, dispensed with altogether by uploading consciousness into a computer.[57] In light of such fantasies, we can sympathize with Francis Fukuyama's warning that there is a human nature and we mess with it at our peril,[58] or Arie Graafland's important comment that we have "finally lost all ground." "What gets lost here," Graafland continues, "is corporeality in a threefold way: three bodies are lost at the same time, the territorial body of the planet and ecology, and social body or socius, and our human body."[59] Graafland is correct but only in theory—that is, in reference to theories that erase the enduring biological inheritance we call the body and all the richly sedimented behaviors, inclinations, and proclivities it encodes, chief among them the desire to socialize with other humans, the origin of socius.

Graafland and others who want to resist contemporary erasures of the body may ironically participate in the very movements they would contest, for they accept as given problematic claims from which they extrapolate a dire state of affairs. For example, in arriving at the above conclusion, Graafland cites Christine Boyer to the effect that "in the Cartesian world of computers there is no longer any reference to the body."[60] This statement is both true and false—true if one focuses only on logic gates, bit patterns, and so forth, but false if one considers the full range of affordances in networked and programmable machines, which include multiple body interfaces from the GUI to the mouse and extensive software packages designed specifically with human perceptual systems in mind, for example PET scans and functional magnetic resonance images. Moreover, computers themselves have bodies in the sense of being instantiated entities. As we saw earlier with forensic materiality, these bodies bear the marks of specific histories that place them within social, economic, and political contestations. As Kirschenbaum remarks, "[computers] are material machines dedicated to propagating a behavioral illusion, or call it a working model, of immateriality."[61] We should not, however, be seduced into taking this illusion for reality. Materiality introduces difference, and difference opens the way for the contingent, the unexpected, the aleatory.

This is the crucial missing point in Boyer's later argument in "The Body in the City: A Discourse on Cyberscience," which gives a solid account of first- and second-order cybernetics but in its conclusion accepts ideal abstractions as reality. Discussing artificial life and emergence, she argues that "this model ushers in by the back door via its bio-social episteme a totalizing desire for omnipotence as a post-humanist fabricator of artificial life or generic cites. Followed to the extreme, signs in this second cybernetics engender the capacity of complex systems to alter, modify, and develop their own programs controlling life and death decisions. This is what 'second-order' emergence is all about."[62] Such a conclusion erases an important aspect of emergence: once evolutionary processes are given a chance to work, they may well produce something no one expected, including those who engineered the evolutionary programs. As materio-semiotic actors, artificial life programs can and do exploit small differences in materialities to enact path-dependent trajectories entirely different from those their creators imagined.

What one makes of these unexpected events is an open-ended question that cannot be answered by referring solely to the technology; the emergent result is radically under-determined with respect to the technology and therefore susceptible to a wide range of interpretations and interventions. John Cage, for example, sought in "chance operations" (his version of emergence) a release from the limits of the ego and an opening out of human consciousness to the inconceivable diversity that lies all around us, if only we have the mindsets and orientations to perceive it. Gregory Bateson (whom Boyer does not mention) saw in second-order cybernetics possibilities for new alignments between human consciousness and the recursive processes that connect us with our environment.[63] Our point is not that claims by second-order cyberneticians or researchers in artificial life should be taken at face value, or that we should credit the much more problematic fantasies of the transhumanists. Rather, we want to underscore the importance of interventions that emphasize the positive ways in which current technological trends can open opportunities for progressive actions and empowering practices.

Although limitations of space prevent us from discussing such opportunities in detail, we will point to four areas that seem to us especially promising. The first group is characterized by *theoretical emphases on embodiment and its potentialities*. Richly diverse, these approaches seek to use our present lack of ground as an opportunity to re-envision the relationship between embodied perception, digital media, and artistic and architectural practices. If the body is one important component of our ground, as Graafland argues, perhaps "losing our ground" is not such a bad thing if it means sluffing off outmoded conceptions of the body that are the residue from a liberal tradition saturated with universalist assumptions about the superiority of the white race, the male gender, and the rational mind. Once we have moved on from this ground, new conceptions of embodiment can coalesce around a number of important sites. Research in brain functioning and imaging technologies, for example, is interpreted in light of art traditions in Barbara Stafford's *Echo Objects* (2007).[64] Gerald Edelman's work,[65] which draws in part on imaging technologies, has stimulated a number of responses from the humanities and arts communities, including those by Joseph Tabbi's *Cognitive Fictions* (2002) and Warren Neidich's "Resistance is Futile: The Neurobiopolitics of Consciousness" (2006).[66]

Mark B. N. Hansen in *New Philosophy for New Media* (2006) sees in the lack of ground instantiated in digital media positive opportunities for digital artists to foreground embodied responses as the stabilizing component necessary to make sense of artistic digital productions.[67] Bernadette Wegenstein in *Getting Under the Skin* (2006) goes further by conceptualizing the body itself as a form of media, a move also made by Eugene Thacker in *Biomedia* (2004).[68] After recapitulating much of the recent research on the body, Wegenstein remarks, "We still do not know what the body really is."[69] Working from a similar idea of enlightened ignorance, Arakawa and Madeleine Gins treat it as an empowering premise, for it enables them to start with the primacy of embodiment (not from the body, which is always already a social, cultural, and technological construction) and devise architectural structures designed to short-circuit customary perceptions and open onto new sensory experiences and embodied orientations.[70]

A second kind of positive intervention takes the form of *recognizing the irreducible social and cultural complexities of contexts* in which perceptions of embodiment (and the body) are embedded. The celebratory rhetoric surrounding the advent of cyberspace and globalization is contextualized by David Harvey's *A Brief History of Neolibralism* (2007) as part of a transnational movement by the upper classes to recuperate the economic ground lost in the inflationary periods of the 1970s.[71] Harvey convincingly shows that neoliberalism, although taking different forms in the United States, Chile, England, and China, nevertheless represents class warfare by other means. His richly textured analyses provide salutary examples of how underlying patterns can be discerned without treating reductively the social and cultural complexities in which they are embedded. On the negative side, we might think of transhumanist rhetoric as it appears in such prominent spokespeople for the movement as Max Moore. Focused on the transcendent possibilities for individuals, transhumanist rhetoric almost entirely ignores the complex issues that would arise from even modest life extension, including generational conflict, scarcity of resources, and the just allocation of resources when the world population explodes uncontrollably.

A third kind of positive intervention comes in *recognizing new modes of organization that digital media require* and developing theoretical approaches that take their specificities into account. In *Protocol* (2005), Galloway makes an important contribution in developing what he calls a "protocological" approach, focusing on the regimens that allow information to flow through the networks or, conversely, that prevent the release of high-value informational assets to unauthorized users.[72] In *The Exploit* (2007), Galloway and co-author Thacker work from the theoretical models of Delueze and the sweeping historical panorama of Hardt and Negri's *Empire* (2000) to theorize the network as a ground for political action, showing for example that the networks can be integrated into centralized bureaucracy as well as into asymmetric warfare.[73] Other important contributions have been made by Friedrich A. Kittler. Wittily observing that "the entertainment industry is, in any conceivable sense of the word, an abuse of army equipment,"[74] Kittler traces the technological lineages that resulted in the contemporary configuration of the military-industrial-entertainment complex. Although his methodology is anti-humanistic, in that it refuses the primacy of the human as an adequate explanation for technological development, his approach nevertheless recognizes the importance of social and cultural presuppositions as they are entwined with technological issues of data storage, transmission, and manipulation.

Last but hardly least are theoretical approaches, artistic creations, and architectural practices that *emphasize the importance of recursive feedback loops between embodied practices, social constructions, and the specificities of digital media.* The videographer Paul Ryan, for example, has focused on the tendency of complex systems, particularly turbulent flow, to produce chaotic patterns that endure over time without ever repeating themselves exactly.[75] Collaborating with Ryan, Stephanie Strickland and Cynthia Lawson Jaramillo created *slippingglimpse*, a digital art work of considerable beauty and theoretical sophistication.[76] Our own contribution in this area develops the concept of intermediation as a framework within which digital literature, art, and architecture may be understood.[77]

Returning again to Graafland's comment on the loss of ground, we note that complex systems in general lack a ground in the sense that they defy formalization through explicit equations, precisely because every factor interacts with, influences, and is influenced by every other factor. Complex systems do not, however, lack order; rather they instantiate a particularly complex kind of order capable of demonstrating emergent properties. Seeking a ground has historically been represented through such monumental enterprises as the Russell and Whitehead's *Principia Mathematica* (1911), which sought to axiomatize mathematics.[78] This grand enterprise was driven by the hope that mathematics could be made logically consistent and formally complete; it would then, so the reasoning went, provide a solid ground upon which all the other sciences (and perhaps the social sciences and even the arts) would build. When the enterprise was proven impossible by Gödel's theorem and related developments such as the Church-Turing proof, the lack of ground became the catalyst for important artistic explorations typified by M. C. Escher and, later in the twentieth century, the reading and writing protocols associated with deconstruction.

The lack of ground need not mean the end of agency, the loss of order, or the utter transformation of the human into some post-biological version that would be more machine than biological entity. Rather, viewed as an opportunity for constructive interventions, the recognition that complex systems are how the natural world mostly operates opens onto a number of important realizations: that agency is always distributed; that cognition is a much broader function than consciousness and includes many embodied capacities outside the central nervous systems; that action always takes place within embedded and recursive systems that can unpredictably amplify the consequences of our actions; and that ethical considerations should therefore always be a component of our considerations. Architecture, deeply entwined with digital media and necessarily attentive to social and cultural constructions, constitutes an ideal site from which to explore and intervene in the recursive feedback loops co-constitutive of materiality, contemporary subjectivity, and digital media.

NOTES

1. Pertinent studies include Beatriz Colomina, *Privacy and Publicity: Modern Architecture as Mass Media* (Cambridge: MIT Press, 1996); Mario Carpo, *Architecture in the Age of Printing: Orality, Writing, Typography, and Printed Images in the History of Architectural Theory* (Cambridge: MIT Press, 2001); and compilations including *Architectureproduction*, ed. Beatriz Colomina (New York: Princeton Architectural Press, 1988); *Paper Palaces: The Rise of the Renaissance Architecutural Treatise*, ed. Vaughan Hart (New Haven: Yale University Press, 1988); and *This is not Architecture*, ed. Kester Rattenbury (London: Routledge, 2002), among others.
2. See *The Virtual Dimension*, ed. John Beckman (New York: Princeton Architectural Press, 1998); Michael Benedikt, *Cyberspace: First Steps* (Cambridge: MIT Press, 1992); *Collective Intelligence in Design*, eds. Chris Perry and Christopher Hight (London: Academy Editions, 2006); Mark Poster, *Information Please: Culture and Politics in the Age of Digital Machines* (Durham: Duke University Press, 2006); and Edward Castronova, *Exodus to the Virtual World: How Online Fun is Changing Reality* (New York: Palgrave Macmillan, 2007).
3. See Colomina, *Privacy and Publicity*; and Carpo, *Architecture in the Age of Printing.*
4. Gilles Deleuze, *Difference and Repetition* (New York: Continuum, 2005).
5. Reyner Banham, "A Black Box: The Secret Profession of Architecture," in *A Critic Writes: Essays by Reyner Banham*, ed. Mary Banham (Berkeley: University of California Press, 1996): 294. Emphasis in original.
6. Robert Venturi, Denise Scott Brown, and Steven Izenour, *Learning from Las Vegas* (Cambridge: MIT Press, 1972).
7. Mark Poster, *Information Please: Culture and Politics in the Age of Digital Machines* (Durham: Duke Uni-

versity Press, 2006): 56.

8. Matthew Kirschenbaum, *Mechanisms: New Media and the Forensic Imagination* (Cambridge: MIT Press, 2008).
9. N. Katherine Hayles, *My Mother Was a Computer: Digital Subjects and Literary Texts* (Chicago: University of Chicago Press, 2005).
10. Benoit Mandelbrot, *The Fractal Geometry of Nature* (New York: W.H. Freeman, 1983).
11. Kirschenbaum, *Mechanisms*, 114–32.
12. Bruno Latour, *We Have Never Been Modern* (Cambridge: MIT Press, [1993] 2007).
13. Adrian Mackenzie, *Cutting Code: Software and Sociality* (New York: Peter Lang, 2006).
14. Friedrich Kittler, "There is No Software," and "Protected Mode," in *Literature, Media, Information Systems* (London: Routledge, 1997): 147–55 and 156–68.
15. Donald M. Lowe, *The Body in Late-Capitalist USA* (Durham: Duke University Press, 1995).
16. Jonathan Crary, *Suspensions of Perception: Attention, Spectacle, and Modern Culture* (Cambridge: MIT Press, 1999); Wolfgang Schivelbush, *The Railway Journey: The Industrialization and Perception of Time and Space in the Nineteenth Century* (Berkeley: University of California Press, 1986); Steven Johnson, *Everything Bad is Good for You* (New York: Riverhead Trade, 2006); and N. Katherine Hayles, "Hyper and Deep Attention: A Generational Shift in Cognitive Modes," *Profession* (2007): 187–99.
17. Jerome McGann, *Radiant Textuality: Literature After the World Wide Web* (New York: Palgrave Macmillan, 2001).
18. Robin Evans, "Translations from Drawing to Building," in *Translations from Drawing to Building and Other Essays* (Cambridge: MIT Press, 1997): 153–94.
19. For a discussion of visual correction in ancient Greek architecture, see J. J. Coulton, *Ancient Greek Architects at Work* (Ithaca: Cornell University Press, 1977).
20. De l'Orme, *Le premier tome de l'architecture* (Paris, 1567): 112, quoted by Evans, "Translations from Drawing to Building," 191.
21. It is interesting to note that Evans produced his analysis of the Royal Chapel without having visited the building and relied only on mediated representations to develop his argument. Further, his subsequent visit to the chapel compelled him to add a postscript in which he slightly altered his findings, based as much on his visit as on additional photographs he took while there. See Evans, "Translations from Drawing to Building," 188.
22. Peter Eisenman, "Aspects of Modernism: Maison Domino and the Self-Referential Sign," in *Eisenman Inside Out: Selected Writings, 1963–1988* (New Haven: Yale University Press, 2004): 111–20.
23. Colomina, *Privacy and Publicity*, 80. Emphasis in the original.
24. Ibid., 93–100.
25. This observation was often pointed out in graduate seminars led by R. E. Somol at both Ohio State and UCLA, but we know of no published essay in which these thoughts are recorded.
26. Peter Eisenman, *Diagram Diaries* (New York: Universe, 1999); and Peter Eisenman, *Giuseppe Terragni: Transformations, Decompositions, Critiques* (New York: Monacelli, 2003).
27. Tali Krakowsky, "Algorithmic Anthologies," *34 Magazine* 8 (2007): 207–15.
28. The literature on this pervasive phenomenon is vast. For a sampling of the most influential works on the subject, see Terence Riley, *Light Construction* (New York: Museum of Modern Art, 1995); Jeffrey Kipnis, "On Those Who Step in the Same River…," in *Mood River* (Columbus: Wexner Center for the Arts, 2002): 34–45; R. E. Somol and Sarah Whiting, "Notes on the Doppler Effect and Other Moods of Modernism," *Perspecta* 33 (2002): 72–77; Michael Speaks, "Design Intelligence and the New Economy," *Architectural Record* ((Jan 2002): 72–79; Sylvia Lavin, "Three Faces of Tel Aviv," *A+U* (June 2004): 88–113; and George

Baird, "Criticality and Its Discontents," *Harvard Design Magazine* (Fall/Winter 2004): 16–21. Our own contribution focuses on the role digital design technologies play in these shifts in focus. See Gannon and Hayles, "Mood Swings: The Aesthetics of Ambient Emergence," 140–73 in this volume.

29. Venturi's position regarding the role of symbolic form was famously advanced in *Learning from Las Vegas* (1972) and has been developed to incorporate electronic display technologies in *Iconography and Electronics on a Generic Architecture: A View from the Drafting Room* (Cambridge: MIT Press, 1996).
30. For a discussion of the importation of these illusionistic techniques into historical architecture, see Werner Oechslin, "Between Painting and Architecture: The Artificiality and Autonomy of Scenography," *Diadolos* 14 (1984): 21–35. We are indebted to Sylvia Lavin for fruitful discussions on the theater, architecture, and Diller and Scofidio as well as for directing our attention to Oechslin's essay.
31. The project, and Liz Diller's 1987 discussion of it at the Architectural Association in London, is reproduced in Elizabeth Diller and Ricardo Scofidio, *Flesh: Architectural Probes* (New York: Princeton Architectural Press, 1994): 103–34.
32. For a documentation of these projects and an illuminating essay, see Rosalee Goldberg, "Dancing about Architecture," in *Scanning: The Aberrant Architectures of Diller + Scofidio* (New York: Whitney Museum of Art, 2003): 44–60.
33. Elizabeth Diller and Ricardo Scofidio, Blur: *The Making of Nothing* (New York: Abrams, 2002).
34. Todd Gannon, "The Light Construction Reader," lecture delivered at The Ohio State University, 2 Oct. 2002.
35. Mark B. N. Hansen, *Bodies in Code: Interfaces with Digital Media* (London: Routledge, 2006): 180.
36. Diller and Scofidio, *Blur*, 217.
37. See Riley, *Light Construction*, 132–33.
38. The project was exhibited at the 7th Venice Biennale of Architecture in 2000 and can be accessed at www.embryologicalhouse.com.
39. See www.d-toren.nl.
40. In many ways, Vinge's fiction follows Venturi's lead toward generic buildings adorned with electronic iconography. But as we will see below, his projection of Venturi's ideas into a dystopian near future gives rise to consequences well beyond the intentions of Venturi's graphic urbanism.
41. Vernon Vinge, *Rainbows End* (New York: Tom Doherty Associates, 2006): 50.
42. Ibid., 75.
43. See Bruce Sterling, *Shaping Things* (Cambridge: MIT Press, 2005); and David Harvey, *The Condition of Postmodernity: An Enquiry into the Origins of Cultural Change* (New York: Wiley-Blackwell, 1992).
44. Karin Knorr Cetina and Urs Bruegger, "Global Microstructures: The Virtual Societies of Financial Markets," *American Journal of Sociology* 107:4 (2002): 905–50.
45. Jeff Howe, "The Rise of Crowdsourcing," *Wired* 14:6 (2006).
46. Alexander Galloway and Eugene Thacker, *The Exploit: A Theory of Networks* (Minneapolis: University of Minnesota Press, 2007).
47. James Der Derian, *Virtuous War: Mapping the Military-Industrial-Media-Entertainment Network* (Boulder: Westview Press, 2001).
48. Eugene Thacker, *Biomedia* (Minneapolis: University of Minnesota Press, 2004).
49. Colomina, *Privacy and Publicity*, 323.
50. Ibid., 329–34.
51. Anthony Vidler, "The b-b-b-Body: Block, Blob, Blur," in *The Body in Architecture*, ed. Deborah Hauptmann (Rotterdam: 010 Publishers, 130–37.
52. Colomina, *Privacy and Publicity*, 334.

53. Rem Koolhaas, "What Ever Happened to Urbanism?" in *S,M,L,XL* (Rotterdam: 010, 1995): 969.
54. Mark B. N. Hansen, *New Philosophy for New Media* (Cambridge: MIT Press, 2006); and Bernard Steigler, *Technics and Time, 1: The Fault of Epimethus* (Stanford: Stanford University Press, 1998).
55. Gilles Deleuze, "Postscript on Control Societies," in *Negotiations, 1972–1990* (New York: Columbia University Press, 1995): 178.
56. Elizabeth Grosz, *Volatile Bodies: Toward a Corporeal Feminism* (Bloomington: Indiana University Press, 1994); and George Lakoff and Mark Johnson, *Philosophy in the Flesh: The Embodied Mind and its Challenge to Western Philosophy* (New York: Harper Collins, 1999).
57. Ray Kurzweil, *The Singularity is Near: When Humans Transcend Biology* (New York: Penguin, 2006); and Hans Moravec, *Mind Children: The Future of Robot and Human Intelligence* (Cambridge: Harvard University Press, 1990) and *Robot: Mere Machine to Transcendent Mind* (New York: Oxford University Press, 2000).
58. Francis Fukuyama, *The End of History and the Last Man* (New York: Free Press, 2006).
59. Arie Graafland, "Looking into the Folds," in *The Body in Architecture*, 156.
60. M. Christine Boyer, *CyberCities* (New York: Princeton Architectural Press, 1996): 117.
61. Matthew Kirschenbaum, "Every Contact Leaves a Trace: Computer Forensics and Electronic Textuality," presentation at *The History of Material Texts*, University of Pennsylvania, 4 April 2005.
62. M. Christine Boyer, "The Body in the City: A Discourse on Cyberscience," in *The Body in Architecture*, 47.
63. Gregory Bateson, *Mind and Nature: A Necessary Unity* (New York: Bantam Books, 1980).
64. Barbara Stafford, *Echo Objects: The Cognitive Work of Images* (Chicago: University of Chicago Press, 2007).
65. Gerald Edelman, *The Remembered Present: A Biological Theory of Consciousness* (New York: Basic Books, 1989).
66. Joseph Tabbi, *Cognitive Fictions* (Minneapolis: University of Minnesota Press, 2002); and Warren Neidich, "Resistance is Futile: The Neurobiopolitics of Consciousness," in *The Body in Architecture*, 188–211.
67. Mark B. N. Hansen, *New Philosophy for New Media* (Cambridge: MIT Press, 2006).
68. Eugene Thacker, *Biomedia* (Minneapolis: University of Minnesota Press, 2004).
69. Bernadette Wegenstein, *Getting Under the Skin: Body and Media Theory* (Cambridge: MIT Press, 2006): 16.
70. Shusaku Arakawa and Madeline Gins, *The Mechanism of Meaning: Work in Progress, 1963–1971, 1978 based on the Method of Arakawa* (New York: Harry N. Abrams, 1979); and *The Architectural Body* (Tuscaloosa: University of Alabama Press, 2002).
71. David Harvey, *A Brief History of Neoliberalism* (London: Oxford University Press, 2007).
72. Alexander Galloway, *Protocol: How Control Exists after Decentralization* (Cambridge: MIT Press, 2005).
73. Alexander Galloway and Eugene Thacker, *The Exploit: A Theory of Networks* (Minneapolis: University of Minnesota Press, 2007); Michael Hardt and Antonio Negri, *Empire* (Cambridge: Harvard University Press, 2000).
74. Friedrich Kittler, *Gramophone, Film, Typewriter* (Stanford: Stanford University Press, 1999): 96–97.
75. Paul Ryan, "From Video Replay to the Relational Circuit of Threeing," *Leonardo* 39:3 (2006): 199–203.
76. Stephanie Strickland, Cynthia Lawson, and Paul Ryan, *slippingglimpse*. http://slippingglimpse.org (2007).
77. N. Katherine Hayles, *My Mother Was a Computer*; Hayles, *Electronic Literature: New Horizons for the Literary* (Notre Dame: Notre Dame University Press, 2008); and Gannon and Hayles, "Mood Swings."
78. Bertrand Russell and Alfred North Whitehead, *Principia Mathematica*, vol. 1 (Cambridge: Cambridge University Press, 1911).

The Object Turn: A Conversation

with Graham Harman, David Ruy, and Tom Wiscombe, 2015

Fig. 16.1 Tom Wiscombe Architecture, Kinmen Port Terminal (Taiwan, 2014). Competition proposal.

In recent years, a growing number of architects have taken an interest in the writing and thinking of theorists and philosophers including Graham Harman, Tristan Garcia, Tim Morton, Levi Bryant, Ian Bogost, and others loosely associated with the speculative realism movement in philosophy and the concept of object-oriented ontology (OOO). At the same time, several of these thinkers have begun specifically to engage architecture in their work. In August 2014, architects Todd Gannon, David Ruy, and Tom Wiscombe engaged in a running online conversation with Graham Harman to speculate on how this mutual interest might be made productive both for philosophy and for architecture. The following transcript of that interchange has been edited for length and clarity.

TODD GANNON: A constellation of factors motivated this conversation. We are all friends and colleagues with abiding interests in the discourses of both architecture and philosophy, and all of us were trained at a time when the writings of Gilles Deleuze and related thinkers held sway over our respective disciplines. Now, a few decades past that training, all of us feel a certain frustration with the discursive status quo in our fields and a desire to strike up new conversations. We also, I think, share a feeling that the Deleuzian thematics which have been so influential for the last several decades—and so influential on us—have raised significant questions that need to be addressed.

A big issue, indeed, one of the Os in OOO, is the role of objects in that discourse. As many thinkers associated with OOO have pointed out, so-called philosophies of becoming such as Deleuze's seem more interested in flows, intensities, and the processes operating beneath or beyond things than in the things themselves. In the 1990s architects developed similar interests in flows, continuities, and process, interests that were intensified by digital technologies. Of course, a lot of great work came out of this, and all of us have well-worn copies of *A Thousand Plateaus* lying around our studios.

Much of the issue, I think, can be encapsulated in the now-clichéd jury question asked of so many process-driven proposals: "How do you know when to stop?" In other words, at some point one has to reckon with the object itself, however productive the processes related to that object's becoming might be.

Of course, the problem extends beyond specifically "digital" factions in architecture. As David made clear in a recent essay,[1] architecture *qua* architecture also has a hard time in more mainstream conversations having to do with ecology, sustainability, and urban planning. Architectural objects, he argues, are often atomized into the flux of their environmental and political contexts, just as they were dispersed in the digital realm. In each case, we are left with no *there* there. If architecture is robbed of its objects, it is also robbed of all the wonder, mystery, surprise, and power they hold.

Graham makes a strong case for objects throughout his work—as well as for all the wonder, mystery, surprise, and power they hold—and his castigation of both reductionist *undermining* and relational *overmining* of objects resonates with David's, Tom's, and other writings that attempt to place objects at the center of the conversation.[2]

Another important issue has to do with how we understand the coherence of an architectural object. By what means do its parts constitute a whole? How do we define the boundary or limit of a project, both in terms of its aesthetics, which is Tom's primary concern, and its ideological implications, to which David attends? This, I think, is why the idea of *flat ontology*, which has been developed by a number of thinkers with ties to speculative realism, has become so interesting to architects.[3]

To get things moving, I'll offer this recklessly oversimplified historical gloss. Architecture has had a long and often unfortunate relationship with established power. Typically, it was hegemonic political power that put up all the architecture, and much of architecture's point was to reinforce that power. The hierarchical, often symmetrical, and proportionally rigorous part-to-whole relationships of classical, and many non-Western, architectural systems established idealized conventions that, in their compositional rigor, became models for—or were modeled after—political and social hierarchies:

the king on top, everybody else arrayed by class status below. Architecture worked this way for a long time.

First romanticism and then modernity introduced ways to reimagine these hierarchies. "Smashing the idols" or attacking "the Man" are among the more well-known approaches. Such attitudes fired innovation throughout the arts, and new forms of coherence were introduced, oftentimes conceived in direct opposition to classical integration. Of course, there was a lot of interaction between architecture and philosophy throughout the twentieth century, and for most of that century both fields often found it necessary to set up a stable object to attack in order to do their work, as Sylvia Lavin has demonstrated probably better than anyone.[4] In short, if Nietzsche and Jacques Derrida taught architects how to smash the idols into fragments and destabilize power from within, then Deleuze and his followers showed us how to pulp those fragments into atomized flows.

But, as Jeffrey Kipnis has argued in recent lectures, it seems like all that idol-smashing and fragment-pulping has largely run its course. Though it's important to make sure old idols aren't bandaged back together, our job today has more to do with inventing new ways of making than with rehearsing old tactics of undoing. Unfortunately, critical demolition is the only training a lot of us ever got.

Flat ontology offers a hint as to how we might think about these new forms of coherence. Rather than part-to-whole hierarchies, or their critical dismantling, flat ontology privileges part-to-part relationships. There is still coherence, but it's not the kind of coherence we've seen before. If classical composition ultimately led to hierarchical, static objects and criticality attacking objects ultimately produced homogeneous rubble, the concept of flat ontology might prove useful in imagining new forms of coherence that both maintain objects and consecrate difference.

GRAHAM HARMAN: Two quick thoughts to begin. As for the question of architects and/or philosophers serving power, this isn't a problem in quite the same way in philosophy, since unlike in architecture, one does not need massive amounts of capital to bring projects to fruition. Indeed, the philosopher does not need much cooperation from anyone else at all. As long as an individual philosopher has a sustainable income, original work can be done. It's also my understanding, in the few years that I've recently spent with architects, that the capital-intensive component may be overestimated in architecture given that unbuilt theoretical projects can still make major contributions to the field. And furthermore, I'm always skeptical in principle of focusing on who has the "power" in any given situation. People will rally to fresh ideas. Power is overrated as an intellectual theme, and too many people have overdetermined both themselves and others as "powerless." Domination is not the only thing that happens when people get together, and not even the most important thing that happens.

As for flat ontology, I have both positive and negative things to say about it. In positive terms, it means that any entity can potentially be taken seriously, rather than some privileged entity—the human subject comes to mind—sticking its nose under every tent and trying to constitute a full half of reality, as in most Western philosophy since Descartes. Think of how ridiculous it is that we set up a basic opposition in philosophy between the mind and "the world"—the latter is a pretty sloppy catch-all category, given the countless lizards, stars, bacteria, sand grains, black holes, and shrimp that are assembled on one side of the boxing ring with the human species alone on the other. Flat ontology should be praised for shaking up this stale modern scenario.

But there's a problem with flat ontology, and you can see this, for instance, in Bruno Latour's philosophy. His flat democratic acceptance of all entities on the same plane initially led him to say that everything is an entity in the same way: through each entity's force, through its effects on other entities. This means that Latour turns everything into relations, but has no robust conception of the *relata* behind the relations. Mystery and surprise are, in effect, evacuated from Latour's world, since his phrase "follow the actors" means "follow the effects." But much of what is real is what does not have an effect but just threatens to have an effect. In architectural terms, the parallel idea to combating Latour's rather brilliant relationism is to combat part of what Todd described: the notion that everything flows smoothly into everything else around it. Timothy Morton once referred comically to this kind of thinking as an "everything-is-everything-else Deleuzean Hinduism." That fashion is still in the air, but it needs to be replaced by the imperative to indicate how everything is *not* everything else. I would go so far as to call this the intellectual mission of our time in just about every field, since relationism has spread like a virus and become horribly stale without people realizing it.

TG: I agree. It's important to stress that while everything might be equal, everything is not everything else. This idea runs productively counter to some rumblings from the '60s, such as Hans Hollein's famous catchphrase *"Alles ist Architektur"* or Archigram's "It's all the same." Both statements, while they've found plenty of traction since they were uttered, are pretty dubious. If they were true, we'd be in a pretty sad place.

TOM WISCOMBE: The concept of a flat ontology is relatively new and untested in architecture. I find it useful because it reverses the trend of thinking of the world as one giant communication network, as a bundle of relations without barriers or enclosures. A flat ontology allows all things in the world to exist "equally but differently," as Ian Bogost puts it in *Alien Phenomenology*.[5] It avoids undermining specific instances with general categories such as systems, taxonomies, and genera. I think it is no coincidence that the time of Deleuze's rhizome and werewolf—the 1990s—was also the time of revolutions in both the internet and digital design techniques that allowed for the production of unprecedented conceptual and formal continuity. Today, the model of "world as open network" is no longer a matter of speculation. It has been consumed and reified—think of the moralizing super-unity of all things in James Cameron's *Avatar*. But the World Wide Web can no longer be described as a continuously differentiated field. Now it is more accurately defined in terms of niches and communities that are becoming more pronounced and vocal. Edges and boundaries are beginning to develop. Insides and outsides are appearing.

In architecture, a similar shift is underway. Formal experimentation based on smooth manifolds and continuous variation—both generalizing models despite claims to the contrary—seems exhausted as a project. Instead, an alternative is gaining traction, one focused on a world made of discrete, withdrawn entities, things that vex and exceed definition through relations alone. This impulse decenters the human-object or mind-world relation that weaves through architecture as phenomenology or other modes of direct human access, instead tapping into a strange sub-phenomenal world that we can't see or know but can try to imagine. It forces a reevaluation of the discourse of sensation and superficiality in architecture, opening up the possibility of crossing over between how things appear and their strange inner realities. In *Guerilla Metaphysics*, Graham talks about this crossing over in terms of *allure*, which could be understood as a combination of *allusion*—we can only allude to objects to which we have no direct access—and *alluring*, that is, powerfully seductive.[6] Reorienting toward objects also injects life back into the concept of difference in kind over difference in degree, which '90s architectural discourse promised but ultimately failed to deliver. Difference in kind is actually very difficult to achieve through continuous variation of form because this method begins by imposing a fundamental continuity of things rather than a fundamental difference between things.

After a long period of focus on fluidity and connectivity, a new formal lexicon is in order. Chunks, joints, gaps, parts, interstices, contour, near-figure, misalignment, patchiness, low-res, nesting, embedding, interiority, and above all, *mystery* are terms that resonate for me. I'm not interested in architecture that is always looking over its shoulder to processes or forces, but rather architecture that is irreducible and inexhaustible. I prefer the idea of buildings that produce new worlds to buildings as products of the world. To be clear, this is not a call for a return to previous forms of autonomy, with their explicit resistance to external forms of power, nor to deconstructivism, with its tortured breakages and linguistic indeterminacies, but rather for new models of coherence that allow for discreteness and intimacy of elements without fusion. In my recent work, I am attempting to produce this kind of coherence through near-figuration, where strong figures are established and then partially obscured via elastic enclosures. The mission in any case is to put an edge back into the all-too-familiar digital flow, creating stoppages and moments of partial recognition, in order to produce something more resistant to consumption and cliché.

Another route toward objects is through estrangement of the real. David, you are clearly working on that angle. Here too, figuration is back on the table in order to recoup abstraction, which has lost its efficacy after so many years of pulling points around in digital space. This "weird realist" approach taps into the specificity and strangeness of objects we encounter in the world, defamiliarizing them by teasing out their possible inner worlds, recontextualizing them, or mashing up several objects into something entirely new. It's an intriguing approach, which I think predates the Deleuzian era, and I'm hoping we can get into its specific architectural lineage during this discussion.

DAVID RUY: I think it's worth addressing the turn away from Deleuze and describing how this conversation evolved out of the conversations we were having in the late '90s.

First, two labels pop up in discussions: speculative realism and object-oriented ontology (OOO). Speculative realism is the larger umbrella term under which OOO (Graham's project) is located. At the 2007 meeting at Goldsmiths College where the term *speculative realism* was born, the target shared by Graham, Quentin Meillassoux, Ray Brassier, and Iain Hamilton Grant was Kant. They all wanted to question the centrality of the human being in philosophy—the ever-present correlation of mind with world (*correlationism*). Because all four wanted to overturn the mind-world correlate, they can be loosely categorized as belonging to a general posthuman philosophical interest today, but I don't think they share a common project anymore.

Meillassoux was highly influenced by Alain Badiou, and Brassier by François Laruelle. Both Badiou and Laruelle were for a long time the lesser-known rivals of Deleuze in the hothouse that was French philosophy following May '68. So it is unsurprising that from the beginning speculative realism had some bias against Deleuze. It is also striking that so many of the philosophers we have cared about in architecture were from University of Paris VIII and University of Paris X Nanterre, the two schools so intimately bound to May '68. Relative to this context, it is important to note that Graham comes to us from an entirely different genealogy. In fact, he once worked as a sports reporter in Chicago.

As a student at Columbia University while Bernard Tschumi was dean, I was quite familiar with Derrida and Deleuze, as was everyone else there at the time. Though Columbia in the '90s is typically thought of as the place where digital experimentation first happened, I think the more important discourse during that time revolved around the implications of Derrida's work and then of Deleuze's, which seemed to be a distant aftershock of May '68. The way in which computers were being recontextualized and estranged as a different kind of machine was, I think, an offshoot of that larger movement. With regard to this historical context, speculative realism, for Meillassoux and Brassier, is still related to this specific continental tradition even though they run counter to some of the other philosophers we had previously read. In contrast, with Graham we're connecting to a different genealogy that echoes other concerns.

When I accidentally reconnected with Graham a few years ago I was very surprised to learn from him about these other important lines of thought that continued to develop in the shadows of these famous personalities. I was immediately struck by the originality of these authors, but even more so by how foreign and strange the ideas at first seemed. What I thought was a philosophical landscape of a few giant trees started looking more like a field of many strange flowers.

TW: Looking back, the extent to which our generation was nurtured on Deleuze in architecture school was quite extraordinary. While the dangers of applying philosophy directly to architecture were discussed openly—I remember Jeff Kipnis warning against it even in 1993—it resonated so strongly as an alternative to postmodern criticality that it was hard to resist. With OOO the situation is different. The shift away from relational ontologies in recent discourse is an independent development in architecture. Stumbling on Graham's writings was a shock for me—like glimpsing a parallel universe. The difference between Deleuzian concepts entering architecture and those of OOO is that the latter offers fewer operative terms, which I think is a good thing. Of course, we all remember the misreadings of Deleuze's *The Fold* and *Difference and Repetition*, which generated a torrent of literally folded single-surface and iterative-section projects. With OOO, however, we are talking about a more mysterious set of core concepts, from the cleaving of effects off of things, to speculation on the nature of interaction of autonomous objects, to vicarious causation, where things act on one another, but only indirectly and at a distance.

Because OOO makes no specific or obvious overture toward architecture, multiple niches and generations in contemporary architectural discourse, some with opposing agendas, seem to have affinities for it. I find this fascinating. For instance: the "new ancients" presented in *Log* 31, with their suspicion of perception and reengagement of the conceptual project through drawing; the neo-naturalists, presented in Frédéric Migayrou's ArchiLab 2013 exhibition, *Naturalizing Architecture*, and their hybridization of technology and biology; and a loose cadre of forty-something American formalists moving past the discourse of sensation laid out in *Log* 17, the so-called superficial issue, that is, shifting from an interest in things *for us* to things *in themselves* that cannot be fully known. It seems that this time there isn't a convergence between advances in digital tools, aesthetic sensibilities, and theory, although there are some common threads. For example, digital tools have become so powerful and ubiquitous and able to deliver sensual effects that there is an emerging desire to break or misuse them. We are seeing new interest in low-fidelity forms, the inexact, fake physics, narrative fictions, glitches, and a turn away from the naïve realism of so-called generative design and photo-realistic rendering. This reminds me of Graham's Heideggerian concept of *broken tools*—that is, the idea that things become present to us only when they malfunction. Ironically, breaking tools does not make them more present in architecture—rather, the opposite is true. Breaking and, more importantly, muting tools keeps architecture from accidentally being reduced to an index of its means of production and losing its durability and mystery as a thing in itself.

GH: I first read Deleuze—it was *Anti-Oedipus*—in my first semester of graduate school, in the fall of 1990. We also read Jean Baudrillard in that class, and though it's hard to remember now, in 1990 Deleuze and Baudrillard seemed roughly equivalent in stature: flashy irreverent French guys who weren't quite as central as Derrida and Michel Foucault. But starting from about 1994, perhaps a little earlier in Britain, Deleuze started to gain the stature in continental philosophy that we still see today: viewed as one of the giants, a master of the history of philosophy, mathematics, biology, etc.

As for the 2007 Speculative Realism workshop, we did package it initially as an anti-Kantian movement. But that angle on speculative realism began to fade as we realized that none of us meant the same thing by it. Meillassoux was primarily interested in getting rid of the finitude in Kant in order to make room for a renewed deduction of absolute and eternal truths. Obviously I couldn't follow him there, since I think the Kant/Heidegger insights into finitude are decisive and are merely trivialized by Hegel, Badiou, and Slavoj Žižek. For me, the problem with Kant was different: the way he made finitude nothing but a special burden of human beings. He should have seen that finitude does not result from any special limitation of human categories and pure human intuitions of time and space, but rather is characteristic of relations in general. When fire burns cotton, it is obstructed from exhaustive access to the cotton just as much as humans and insects are. Finitude is not a feature of humans and a few smart animals such as dolphins and monkeys, but of relations in general. This is the key principle of object-oriented philosophy.

DR: Graham, I think you touch on the very issue that has made your work, in particular, important for architectural discourse. Because Meillassoux and Brassier seem primarily concerned with the problematics of knowledge, I find their work less relevant to architecture, because architects are primarily dealing with problems of representation and performance—problems that evade epistemologies. In architectural history we can point to various moments where attempts were made to frame architecture as specific knowledge. But I think these moments are relatively minor, and such attempts to frame architecture as applied knowledge oftentimes resulted in disastrous buildings. In contrast, the masterpieces of the discipline are impossible to reduce to embodied knowledge. They are far stranger than that.

With regard to representational problems, I'd like to go back to Todd's comments about architecture's problematic history relative to the representation of power. Though I agree with Graham that it's never as adversarial as

Marxist critiques would state, there does remain an ever-present obligation for a building to represent the values of its given milieu. At some moments in architectural history, these values were monolithic and clear; at other moments, they were dispersed and ambiguous. Nonetheless, the representational obligations of architecture have never gone away. Though Graham's work does not eliminate the problem of representation, OOO reframes the problem in a very productive way for architecture. If the architectural object is "withdrawn" (like all objects in his discourse), the representational content of the architectural object is never essential. It can never be associated with some absolute truth nor completely disassociated from the real.

Because architecture's basic magic is in how representations are mistaken for the world itself, we should scrutinize how we construct representations far more than we do, as these representations make certain forms of power seem real. There remains in architectural practice a strange belief that there is a "real world" out there and that architects have to compromise with it. This implies that our senses provide us with direct access to the world as it really is, an idea philosophers call naïve realism. I think it's important to appreciate the philosophical critique of naïve realism, which has been available to us since the ancient Greeks.

Along these lines of thought, I think architecture's engagement with the real has less to do with what the world might be in an absolute sense and more to do with a problem of what we think the real should look like. In his essay "Art as Technique," Viktor Shklovsky develops his concept of *ostranenie*, usually translated as "defamiliarization" or "estrangement."[7] In the early twentieth century, the Russian formalists were already developing a principle of a "weird real." This isn't exactly the same idea Graham is setting out, but it is related. Graham proposes the surprising idea that the estrangement of objects is not a special feature of what an artist might do to the real, but the basic ontological problem between all *real objects*. I can't grasp all of the implications of this for architecture because I am limited by my particular relationship to the real as a human being. Though posthumanist thought has offered incredibly valuable insights, I don't see how the architectural discipline can ever go completely posthuman. Posthumanist critiques are not necessarily incorrect, but architecture might not be there anymore after humanism.

The posthumanist discourse might indicate what might be the final limitations of the architectural discipline. It seems to have productively undercut the notion that our particular relationship to the real, as human beings, is somehow privileged, and that the absolute is somehow disclosed through the genius of great architects. This insight, for me at least, seems to obligate architecture to jettison any remaining arguments about the transcendence of its expressions and to work harder, through architecture, to demonstrate just how weird the real might be.

With regard to the performative, I think the tension has always been between the measurable and the immeasurable performances of architecture. There is some concrete knowledge that can be applied to buildings: how to deal with trusses, HVAC, plumbing lines, elevators, etc. But none of this matters much when we're thinking about great architecture. How many people can move through a revolving door per minute might be an important problem to solve, but it is not part of disciplinary discourse. Most, if not all, performances that really matter have no metrics and are unverifiable in an absolute sense. To the degree that epistemologies are extensions of ontologies, it is interesting to observe how inadequate our epistemologies still are relative to problems that evade measure. Though traditional epistemologies and their underlying ontologies have been successful for the sciences, they have been pretty lame for other disciplines. Most architects probably haven't noticed an aspect of Graham's work that is likely disturbing to most contemporary philosophers: aesthetics becomes primary and replaces epistemology. I don't think the radicality of this is properly appreciated. Instead of using philosophy as a means of legitimizing new formal and compositional agendas, it would be much more productive to examine how these ideas make accessible a new set of values for the primacy of aesthetics in general.

TG: I would like to return to a theme we touched on earlier: if everything is not everything else, it should follow that architecture is not philosophy, nor vice versa. Nonetheless, there is a tendency in many fields to look to philosophy as a kind of master-discipline (read: infallible alibi). I remember a Dave Hickey piece in which he apologized for all the times he didn't dig deeply enough into some topic and instead just "footnoted Foucault and moved along."[8] Too many architects look to philosophy—or science, or the art world, or context, or the budget—for that kind of bottom-line infallibility. It's understandable, and I'm sure each of us has been guilty of it at some point, but I think it is a pitfall to keep in mind.

Since architects and philosophers are not the same thing, their interests and ambitions are not always going to be aligned. For instance, there is a lot in Graham's and other OOO writings that, while interesting as philosophy, probably has very little direct relevance to architecture. And most of what is relevant, I'm willing to bet, operates primarily at the level of metaphor. The main benefit of intellectual dalliances with other fields is that those extradisciplinary ideas become lenses through which to see your work a little differently, to keep feeding your own understanding with fresh metaphors. If nothing else, this sort of interchange is good for you, like broccoli or yoga, and it's probably necessary. But as soon as those energizing outside ideas start to become alibis, thinking starts to sound like incantation, discourse devolves into dogma, and metaphors get dressed up to look like Truth.

TW: I agree that it is very important that philosophy not be seen as an instruction manual for architecture and that we maintain and assert disciplinary boundaries. So far, though, I feel like we are attending very specifically to OOO in its own context, rather than in terms of how (or if) it has already been absorbed into architecture and what specifically has been achieved. While it is still early, I think it's possible to identify a few tendencies. An important one is a suspicion of physical context as a "generator" of architecture. In response to this suspicion, we are seeing hesitancy in how architecture meets the ground, and avoidance of any form of "mapping," which infers that architecture can be *drawn forth* from the world. Some strategies include balancing a building on a small footprint, indenting or squishing it into the ground, and deferring landing by constructing a new ground. Another approach I find intriguing is inverting the entrenched relational hierarchy of context-to-building by producing context from the resonance of the building itself. In this case, fictional reflections, shadows, and other sensual effects emanating from a building might be constructed as part of the architecture to create uncanny relations with the context.

In terms of massing strategies, there is interest in what Graham refers to in his book on H. P. Lovecraft as "the general outline," which has to do with the captivating charm of things that can only be described through allusion rather than through direct language.[9] Lovecraft knew that tapping into the unknown reserve of enigmatic things like monsters was best done obliquely; Ridley Scott's original *Alien* does this masterfully, creating dread through extremely limited direct appearances of the creature shrouded in darkness. Massing that appears simultaneously as single and multiple figures, avoiding resolution into a unified whole, is another example. These are by no means the only approaches, but what is important is the tendency toward withdrawn forms and away from semiotic legibility or other forms of direct access.

Use of black is another impulse, at least for now, along with mirror chrome, which is another form of black. Jason Payne's dark, mutant moons and disco balls [**Fig. 16.2**] and Andrew Atwood and Anna Neimark's projects evoking Malevich's *Black Square* create realities that lie somewhere at the limits of perception, not erasing the object but rather making it more present as a gap or hole. Like Kubrick's monolith in *2001: A Space Odyssey,* a black object defies access, but at the same time, seems to absorb and contain everything in the universe. This contemporary fascination with black has an important lineage in architecture, notably the mysterious autonomy it produces in Mies van der Rohe's National Gallery—the building's visual withdrawal from Berlin ironically produces deep engagement with the city—and Bahram Shirdel's concept of "black stuff" from the early 1990s, which proposed a muted, completely detached form of blackness.

Fig. 16.2 Hirsuta, Variations on the Disco Ball (2011).

The discourse of ornamentation and refinement is also taking a turn, in some cases, from extroverted surface intricacy toward more muted effects that almost slip off the architecture, effects produced through techniques such as oblique projections, patchy and glitchy textures, and form-independent figuration which I have referred to elsewhere as "tattoos."[10] These moves tend to create strange scalar effects that release architecture from its deathmatch with tectonic expression in the form of panels and other little pieces of material that have been employed to "give architecture a human scale," as if that were architecture's inherent duty. Loosening surface effects from underlying objects and letting them drift is a relatively contemporary development, one that has interesting echoes in Graham's concept of real versus sensual objects.

New forms of interiority are also being considered, often in terms of independent or hidden spaces within. Like Russian dolls, there is always another world nested inside. Imagine opening a Russian doll and finding a galaxy—that would invert the conventional relationship of container and contained and imply a nonhierarchical relation of things and their insides, something Morton considers in *Hyperobjects.*[11] This leads to a new spatial realm where the relation between world and interior is broken. Such a realm might be vast, chunky, and filled with a surprising litany of objects in various orientations, objects normally encountered on the flat, extended plane of the city. Peter Trummer's aggregated cities, for example, point to a reconsideration of the extruded city as a spherical, self-contained entity, like Spartan city-states or planets.

TG: A lot of this resonates with Sylvia Lavin's concept of "twoness" in *Kissing Architecture.*[12] Many have misread that book as little more than a prescription to project images on buildings in order to make them less boring, but in fact it's a significant contribution to discussions about devising new forms of coherence. For me, a crucial passage is her reading of Paul Rudolph's Elman Apartment, in which she undoes the project's unity by understanding the interior as something other than the architecture. Having reimagined the project as two things, rather than one, those two things can come back together in a new kind of object-to-object relationship—that is, they can kiss. Lavin also makes an important critique of Latour's idea that there is no outside. Where Latour sees no boundaries, Lavin insists on them. The argument she makes in the name of difference is very relevant here.

TW: I like that Lavin's "kissing" allows for objects to "brush up"—I think that's Graham's term—against each other without full access or one becoming the other. Things can squish into or wrap around one another while still retaining their discreteness. One can imagine that at the moment of the kiss, qualities might slide from one object to another without compromising their independence. One of my favorite examples of this is Mike Kelley's *Deodorized Central Mass with Satellites* (1999), with its wild arrangement of plush toys pressed and nestled into one another in such a way that they produce a lumpy but distinguishable overall silhouette while retaining their individual features within the mass. That project reveals how part-to-part relations can produce a kind of weird coherence that doesn't depend on values of unity and balance from classical composition.

DR: I'd like to return to this interest in producing architectural objects that have a "broken" representational system. For example, Marcelo Spina and

Georgina Huljich produce mute icons through their interest in recuperating brutalist architecture. The absence of a projected political essence was never an explicit ambition of brutalism, but it is interesting to see it as an untapped potential of this denigrated moment in the discipline. Related to this is Michael Speaks's recent assertion that architecture needs to explore alternative strategies of iconicity and meaning in contemporary urbanism. To paraphrase, as a consequence of globalization, he says, there simply isn't any single representational system that can address the multiplicity of contemporary culture. Architects like Neil Denari and Jesse Reiser and Nanako Umemoto have been experimenting with an approach to iconicity through new kinds of architectural objects that avoid singular meanings, acknowledging the strangely indeterminate and often contradictory milieus of globalization.

Another example is Payne's interest in planetesimals and Albanian bunkers.[13] Planetesimals are objects difficult to observe. They are quite literally withdrawn from our access. The Albanian bunkers are objects that completely turn away from any presence as an architectural representation. Though they're everywhere in Albania, they have a strange mute presence and seem to defy every attempt to bring them into a relationship with other things in the context. Payne's investigations raise some important questions about the limits of architectural representation.

Is it possible to design a withdrawn object? Is it possible to design a building whose relations remain deferred? What would an object-oriented architecture look like? Designing something to look weird is not the answer, because it inevitably looks weird in a way we would expect the weird to look. Think of a monster movie that is not frightening but tragically hilarious. Most of our celebrated monsters are not monsters at all but familiar friends that make us laugh. This kind of monster is not about novelty or strangeness but familiarity. In contrast, some of the strangest encounters can be with an object we've seen every day for years. The weirdest moments occur when familiar objects have their relationships to other objects severed and rewired.

The moment of estrangement is also frustratingly fleeting. Once we recognize it and think something about it, it's already too late. It's instantly in a relationship. The moment you sit down to do some work in a space, or sleep on a bed, you're in a relationship. But as Graham points out, none of these possible relations constitute an essential relationship. The real object is inaccessible and remains withdrawn. This is true about every building, but also everything else, for that matter. However, what I find interesting about these initial experiments in nonrepresentational architecture is that they are attempts to destabilize what we think architecture should look like by deliberately compromising, or breaking, architecture's own representational structure.

TG: Isn't it the case that you can't *not* design a withdrawn object? If I'm reading Graham correctly, every object (at least every real object) is always already withdrawn. But here again is an instance of measuring an architectural effect against a philosophical concept—or manufacturing an architectural object in terms of one. Maybe a better way to ask the question is whether it's a good idea for architects to try to represent severed or frustrated relations. If the point is to make architecture a kind of paraphrase of philosophy, I don't think it's such a good idea, because it's tantamount to rehearsing all the same pitfalls of architecture's previous philosophical interactions that we have discussed. Also, I don't want to put so much stock in representation as architecture's *raison d'être.*

But to pursue an architecture that appears to be aloof or reluctant to enter into traditional relations, as Payne does, can be very interesting. His recent projects are great, but not because he's managed to architecturalize OOO ideas. They're irreducible to OOO, which is important. Although the planetesimals and bunkers might resonate with OOO in interesting ways, there is a lot more going on in those projects, and you need to have recourse to architectural ideas, not just philosophical ones, to unpack them. To see them as a mere paraphrase or rehearsal of OOO misses their point and underestimates their force as architecture. It also implies an unfortunate hierarchy between the two disciplines. There might be a metaphorical link (or relation) between these projects and OOO, but I don't think there is a causal or instrumental one.

GH: Philosophy absolutely must not try to be an instruction manual for architecture or for anything else. If someone does work in any field that literally embodies a given philosophy, then there's no reason to do the work; we can just read the philosophy. That's why I agree with Todd that if OOO holds any significance for architecture, it's on the metaphorical level. It was shown long ago—by José Ortega y Gasset on the continental side of philosophy, Max Black on the analytic side, and Cleanth Brooks in literary criticism—that a metaphor can never be paraphrased in literal terms. This means that I will never be able to look at an architectural project and say, "Aha! This is OOO transposed into architecture!" There will always be various degrees of resonance and different possible paths.

Here's another way of describing the heart of the object-oriented method. There are actually two major gaps in the world. The first is between the real, which withdraws and can only be detected indirectly, and the sensual realm that Husserl, Merleau-Ponty, and most other phenomenologists talk about. By insisting on this gap, we oppose the "everything is immanent, nothing is hidden" platitudes that in philosophy today are enforced by decadent, late-stage phenomenology, by the currently triumphant neo-German idealist approach of Žižek, Badiou, and my good friend Meillassoux, and in a different way by the Deleuzians. The second gap is between objects and their qualities. By insisting on this gap we are opposing Hume and the whole of empiricism, which holds that there's no such thing as an apple, just "bundles of qualities": red, sweet, round, juicy, and so forth. Though it is rarely recognized, this is what Husserl tore apart forever by saying that the object comes first and its qualities come second; he's usually just seen as another refuter of hidden things-in-themselves, which unfortunately he also is.

So what does most philosophy try to do? It tries to eliminate these two gaps. Philosophy usually tries to tell us that there's no object hidden behind its accessible qualities. As a result, philosophy becomes something Socrates never meant it to be: a claim to knowledge. There are three ways we can know a thing: we explain it in terms of its parts, its effects, or both. These three methods are what I call *undermining, overmining,* and *duomining,* all of which must be avoided. The object must not be replaced by knowledge! The object cannot be paraphrased, just as a metaphor cannot be paraphrased. What I love so much about architecture and the arts, and what I think some practitioners in these fields like about my work, is that in architecture and the arts you are most likely a *failure* if your productions can be adequately paraphrased in terms of some sort of knowledge. This is also why I have an instinctive distaste for blatantly "political" work in either field. The works that capture my interest have this one point in common: they somehow drive wedges both between the hidden object and its manifestations, and between the accessible object and its qualities. How that plays out in architecture is something I cannot legislate or even properly judge.

David earlier used the term *masterpieces* in reference to architecture, and this is a word that I think needs to be taken more seriously, even in philosophy. Whatever it is that constitutes a masterpiece in any field, though it may often involve elegance and economy, more likely there needs to be a certain strangeness, a weirdness. The weird is an object that cannot be adequately described, not just something deviant and eccentric. Harold Bloom discusses this in connection with literature. He tells us that he's read John Milton's *Paradise Lost* countless times, but the more he reads it, the stranger it becomes—like science fiction, even though it doesn't try to sound like science fiction.[14] A masterpiece has an inassimilable strangeness that makes us return to it repeatedly.

TW: What you are saying is extremely important at this moment, when architecture is constantly being misaligned with science rather than the humanities. There is a dual problem in architecture: technical and engineering issues, which are real but rarely surprising, on the one hand, and the reification of scientistic concepts in architectural design processes, on the other. Both of these are often used to present architecture as a type of knowledge. If you have the parameters, if you have the sun angles, if you have the material logics, you have a path to an architecture that will be intelligible. Often this work is referred to as "research," which is telling. This is the conundrum of architecture: while intelligibility is imperative in the practice of architecture, in the discipline the matter of intelligibility or legibility of various things is a productive battlefield. It constitutes discourse to a very large degree, whether we are talking about figuration (legibility of the figure), structural expressionism or sustainability (legibility of technology), criticality (legibility of politics), postmodernism (legibility of legibility), biomorphism (legibility of nature), camouflage (legibility of illegibility), and so on.

TG: The tension between abstraction and legibility is a crucial one. There has been a strange resurgence of overt, neo-postmodern legibility in recent years. Alejandro Zaera-Polo's discussion of the necessity of legibility in his "Hokusai Wave" essay a few years ago is a significant moment in that resurgence, as is the "radical post-modernism" put forward by the firm FAT in collaboration with Charles Jencks in a recent issue of *Architectural Design*.[15] We all remember the pointed and emphatically anti-representational responses to Zaera-Polo that came from Kipnis and Lavin, who rejected his appeal to legibility and pointed instead toward specific objects that evaded, or at least deferred, legibility.[16] Lavin liked the seductive meaninglessness of fishnet stockings and the Theme Building at LAX; Kipnis preferred mute figures, such as Jeff Koons's *Balloon Dog*, which seem to avoid both representation and abstraction. I think these ideas resonate with some of the ways that OOO is being picked up in architecture. Earlier we were talking about the problem of objects being overpowered by their relations. It seems to me that the parallel in architecture has to do with architectural objects being overpowered by representation, which of course can be construed as a relation between an object and what it "means." The Theme Building and *Balloon Dog* aren't meaningless, but they aren't exactly meaningful either, at least not in the representational sense. Yet, they don't easily align with the legacy of abstraction in architecture or art. Though they flirt with both labels, ultimately they're just too weird to be convincingly categorized as one or the other. As a result, they just seem to hang there, uncomfortably suspended between legibility and abstraction.

Payne's planetesimals and bunkers do something similar. He uses specific antecedents as points of departure, but by the time he's finished, the bunkers and planetoids are more or less beside the point. The actual objects he makes wrestle free of their representational affiliations and sort of revel in their autonomy, an autonomy that excludes even the formal sources that gave rise to them in the first place. Similarly, Tom's recent Kinmen Passenger Service Center [**Fig. 16.1**] project plays with the geometry of Taiwanese roof profiles, but the project could never be reduced to a recapitulation or representation of those forms. Unless he told you about them, it's unlikely you'd make the connection yourself. At the same time, the strange specificity of the massing makes the project difficult to categorize as an exercise in abstraction. It gives the impression that there's more going on than what you see, but the form is reluctant to give up exactly what that is. The suggestion that there's more to the project than meets the eye, that what you see is just the tip of the iceberg, certainly resonates with Graham's Heideggerian notion of withdrawn objects. But again, I would insist that that resonance is only metaphorical. It would be a mistake to see Tom's or Payne's recent work as an architectural rehearsal or recapitulation of object-oriented philosophy.

TW: David, I'd like to go back to your work. Your Klex project [**Fig. 16.3**], shown in *Matters of Sensation* in 2008, swerved away from the curatorial theme of the show. Klex seemed to anticipate the incompleteness of sensation and its direct relational appeal in favor of the thing's mysterious depths beyond its qualities. That set of pieces was introverted, dark—even though the objects were white or mirrored—and difficult to capture. It seemed to contain a million entries, but ultimately it didn't let you inside.

I see Klex as a crossover project between the recent discourse of neo-baroque surface intricacy and a desire to establish what Graham referred to earlier as the gap between the object and its manifestations. Polar landscape, Rorschach inkblot, reptile skin: none of those/all of those. Now your work

Fig. 16.3 Ruy Klein, Klex 1 (2008).

and the work done with your students has moved toward the integration of recognizable technological and natural artifacts and away from the abstraction of Klex. You are partially retaining the legibility of the found objects—from supercolliders to body parts—and capitalizing on their specificity, even while combining them into new, alien objects, potentially pointing to a new kind of abstraction.

TG: It's clear something new is going on here. And regardless of the relation of this new work to object-oriented philosophy, it seems to represent a distinct shift in sensibility in architecture. Similar shifts in the recent past that have been marked by major exhibitions. Philip Johnson and Mark Wigley, for example, characterized their 1988 *Deconstructivist Architecture* show at MoMA in exactly such terms, as did Terry Riley with *Light Construction* seven years later, also at MoMA. The *Decon* show, according to Johnson, represented a shift from modernism's commitment to Platonic formal clarity to an interest in formal complexity and discord. *Light Construction,* for Riley, marked a shift in sensibility from an interest in formal complexity to a preoccupation with surface and material effects. The implications of that interest in surface were taken up and intensified in Spina and Huljich's *Matters of Sensation* show, in which both David and Tom participated.[17] That show is also important for marking the marriage of this surface sensibility with a trajectory of digital experimentation that grew out of *Deconstructivist Architecture* but largely bypassed *Light Construction.* Each of those exhibitions also constructed a dialogue with specific discourses in philosophy—Derrida's deconstruction, phenomenology (largely through the writing of Jean Starobinski), and Deleuze's writings on Francis Bacon, respectively—though each of the curators was careful to avoid asserting a causal relation and to maintain a distinction between disciplines.

Today we have a group of architects interested in objects as such. They're weary, maybe a little hungover, after so many years of serious sensual immersion, and they're wary of the easy integrations made possible by parametrics, BIM, and other instrumentalizations of ideas and techniques that were pursued in the '90s and '00s primarily for pleasure. I suspect, by the way, that part of what motivates the new ancients is a similar skepticism of the perceived, if not always actual, efficiencies of mainstream, professional-grade digital production. In response, we've developed an attraction to the sorts of things that resist integration into increasingly efficient conceptual and technical ordering systems. We've also found, as in earlier moments, curious parallels with a specific philosophical discourse. Maybe it's time for someone to stage an exhibition.

DR: Something that always struck me about Tom's work is how difficult it is to pinpoint what it's about. What he says about it—biomechanical articulation, novel approaches to part and whole, integrated graphic effects, etc.—never does justice to the spatial and figural sensibilities at work behind it. The projects are sublimated to the degree that they can't be explicitly articulated. In his proposal for the Kinmen project, a restraint in the design decisions forces even greater ambiguity on the architectural object. It looks familiar, but strangely so—it's familiar and not at the same time. I find this effect to be remarkably similar to the effects that natural objects can have on the viewer—a mountain, for example—but I don't think it has anything to do with biomorphism or a metaphorical reference to natural objects. Tom's projects share a problem with "natural" objects in the sense that their origins are indeterminate. If the architect refuses linguistic meaning or critical intelligence or data gathered from the context as the generator/originator of the object, what legitimizes the work?

It's interesting that there's a recent surge of interest in the historical discipline of architecture. A number of younger practitioners, including many of the new ancients, seem to believe that the only valid origin for the architectural object is another architectural object recovered from the discipline's history. Though this sidesteps the outside influences of dumb contextual, financial, or political pressures to recover some modicum of autonomy for architecture, it still kicks the can of origination down the road. Though I'm greatly sympathetic to this group for other reasons, for me it's deeply problematic that the discipline's history is understood to be legitimate by default.

Tom's work maintains the tension in the architectural object's origination. Legitimization through deferred origination is like saying, "This is good because it came from that." When it comes to "natural" objects, the history of this way of thinking becomes much clearer. This mountain I see is good because it came from that. Up until the rise of secular society in recent Western history, "that" always referred to the divine. As that article of faith breaks down, "that" only refers to some unknown. It's obvious but needs to be stated anyway that the humanities and the sciences in this regard have radically different attitudes about the problem of unknown origination.

It is a strange feature of the romantic movement that this kind of thinking merges with artistic production. The artist, like some deity, becomes a mysterious point of origin for new objects. Though the romantic movement is generally thought as something that happened way back in the past, I agree with Morton that we're still very much stuck there. As the story goes, Hans Hoffman asked Jackson Pollock, "Do you work from nature?" Pollock's now-famous reply was, "I am nature." That was a very romantic statement, but it illustrates a sentiment that burdens late modernity.

GH: Tom, I agree completely that architecture should not try to be a science, as though that were the only thing worth being. Philosophy has been trying since the 1600s to be either more like science or more like deductive geometry, and I don't think either has worked out very well. Indeed, the dominant form of philosophy in the world today—analytic philosophy—is modeled both intellectually and culturally along the lines of the natural sciences. And though it dominates departments of philosophy worldwide, very little of it is read by anyone other than themselves, and we should take a dim view of their evident pride in that fact.

Too little attention is paid to an important remark in the 1890s by Franz Brentano, a great philosopher in his own right, but most famous as the teacher of both Husserl and Freud. Brentano said something like this: In one sense philosophy is like the natural sciences, but in another, like the fine arts. He glossed this statement by explaining that in one sense philosophy amounts to an accumulation of knowledge, so that we become gradually more knowledgeable about whatever issue we study. But in another sense philosophy is not cumulative at all, but consists of alternating periods of ripeness and decadence. These are the scientific and artistic faces of philosophy, and thus the analytic and continental sides of the discipline, a chasm that is still very much with us despite all the recent misguided efforts to say that the distinction is a mere cliché. We can legitimately say that we know more about gravity in the post-Einstein world than we did during the long Newtonian era. But it makes little sense to say that we "know more" about art or "do better" art today than we did during the times of Picasso, Velásquez, or Giotto. I'm inclined to say the same about architecture. Do Peter Eisenman and Rem Koolhaas represent a "cumulative increase" in architectural knowledge over Alberti? I'm inclined to say that they are contemporary for reasons quite other than accumulation, just as Pollock was obviously not a "cumulative improvement" over Delacroix or Courbet but can still be called more advanced in some sense. In philosophy too: contemporary philosophers do not really "know more" about philosophy than Plato and Aristotle in the same way that contemporary scientists know more than Archimedes. So, I would urge architects not to try to become more scientific under any circumstances. Science has as many vices as virtues and must not be over-emulated.

David, here is my thought about the romantic concept of individual genius. Too often it seems that there are political motives for discounting this concept. Some of this has to do with the fact that the canonical figures of the European tradition in most fields are dead white males, and thus any appeal to the great tradition easily looks like the oppressive hegemony of one group. As graduates of St. John's College we are both familiar with this critique of the tradition that we both studied deeply. But I think an even more prominent political reason is that we live in an era that is just as pious about democracy and equality as an earlier era was about God. It can seem like an aristocratic affront to the equality of all if we don't realize that there are no individual achievements because everything is the product of teamwork, and so forth. I've come to think that both sides in this dispute miss the point. What is really important in history is neither human individuals nor human collectives, but nonhuman objects. You can see this from the fact that it's sometimes difficult to settle claims of priority: Who really discovered oxygen? Who really formulated the second law of thermodynamics? But you can also see it in the historical fact that rival contemporary theories often orbit the same underlying questions even when they look radically different on the surface.

Consider the pre-Socratic thinkers, generally regarded as both the first physicists and first philosophers of the West. Personally, I don't think philosophy starts until Socrates, but that's an unorthodox view that I haven't defended yet in print. Now, what you have in pre-Socratic thinking are many different views of the ultimate reality, but they really boil down to just two kinds, as Aristotle noticed. One group tries to identify the basic physical elements of which everything else is made: water, air, four elements mixed by love and hate, and atoms. But the second group thinks these are all too specific, and that they must emerge from something more formless and indeterminate, usually called the *apeiron*, though Parmenides called it *being*. But notice that both groups are united in an even deeper shared presupposition that thinking is about reducing all midsized and complicated things to some simpler underlying basis. This is what I call *undermining*. The pre-Socratics are all underminers. So in a sense, the intellectual hero of the pre-Socratic period is not any individual human—dead white male or otherwise. Nor is that period the result of egalitarian "teamwork" among various individuals. Instead, the hero is undermining itself, as an object or idea that fascinated two centuries' worth of thinkers before it gave way to a deeper, more intricate idea that was the preoccupation of the much greater period of Socrates, Plato, and Aristotle: the problem of form. To summarize, I think the proper remedy to the "romantic concept of genius" is not the polite humility of egalitarian collectives, but new nonhuman objects that silently fascinate a minority of people who are the most pained by the creeping banalities found in every present.

TW: While science, as a discipline, is often problematic for the humanities—in the sense that society often allows it to overrule those disciplines in its desire for truth and progress—the objects of science are often some of the most mysterious and productive for cultural practice. It is deep in the cosmos that we find the darkest, most unreachable entities, things that seem impossible, scales that seem ludicrous. Think of the first black hole ever discovered, Cygnus X-1, which is only known by way of its effects on objects around it rather than as something you can see with your eyes.

Discoveries in architecture are clearly different from discoveries in science, because they can only be assessed based on their cultural relevance at any given time. In science, the history of discoveries is often recounted in a different way, as if scientists were chipping away at the universe with so many axes, each coming a little closer to revealing its secrets. I prefer to think about discoveries in science in terms of how they have actually increased the strangeness of the universe by shedding dim points of light on its dark underbelly. We heard some years ago about superstrings, the newest way to simultaneously reduce the universe into the littlest of pieces and provide a "unified" theory at the same time—à la Graham's *duomining*—which reveals a desire to solve the universe as if it were a giant Rubik's Cube. Maybe superstring theory will prove to be the end-all of scientific theories, I don't know, but wouldn't that be a sad moment for imagination.

GH: Your point is well taken. The great moments in science are every bit as strange as those in aesthetics. I was speaking only of "normal science" in Thomas Kuhn's sense: as the daily incremental puzzle-solving in which most working scientists are engaged. That has its uses as well, but cannot possibly be made the model for all intellectual endeavor. Analytic philosophy has a tendency to treat the entire discipline of philosophy as a puzzle-solving normal science, and from your remarks it seems like this may be creeping into architecture as well.

DR: The architectural possibilities we have articulated here may or may not cohere into something substantial, but one thing is certain: We are each grappling with the here and now, and we're interested in taking a hard and close look at the shortcomings of our intellectual patrimony. If Deleuze addressed the inadequacies of the "linguistic turn" with his "virtual turn," Graham's work addresses the inadequacies of the "virtual turn" with his "object turn." What was inadequate about Deleuzian ontology for architecture—perhaps for the arts, in general—is precisely what Todd mentioned at the start. As the architectural object is counterintuitively deferred as a focus of attention, we're left with a hodgepodge of theories about architecture's legitimate place in the world.

It's almost comical how the virtual turn in architecture dropped architects off in a territory where we were perpetually confronted with a problem of "diagramming" virtual flows with the hope that new, more relevant objects would somehow spontaneously emerge like Athena from Zeus's forehead. I've never seen this methodology work. What I have seen is an endless parade of convoluted explanations for where the architectural object comes from. The good designers always seemed to know how to cheat and to understand that such diagrams were only compelling when they were used as a retroactive discourse of legitimization; especially in these cases, where the object actually comes from is even more mysterious.

TG: It's not that the Deleuzian project, or Deleuze, for that matter, was wrong or deficient, but rather that most of the work done under that banner, both in philosophy and in architecture, has largely run its course, at least for now. While I can return to some of the folding projects of the '90s or some of the slick rendering projects that came out of SCI-Arc in the '00s and still feel something of the excitement I felt when I first encountered them ten or twenty years ago, I don't get the same kick out of something I saw yesterday on *suckerPunch* that merely rehearses earlier achievements. I like the idea of "rallying to fresh ideas" that Graham put out there. In the end, that's what I think the current dalliance with OOO can inspire in architecture and also, I hope, what architecture can inspire in philosophy.

NOTES

1. David Ruy, "Returning to (Strange) Objects," *TARP Architecture Manual: Not Nature* (Spring 2012): 38–42.
2. In addition to Ruy's essay cited above, see Tom Wiscombe, "Discreteness, or Towards a Flat Ontology of Architecture," *Project* 3 (Spring 2014): 34–43. For a good introduction to Harman's thinking, see *The Quadruple Object* (Winchester, UK: Zero Books, 2012).
3. Manuel De Landa coined the term *flat ontology* in *Intensive Science and Virtual Philosophy* (New York: Continuum, 2002). For an important recent treatment, see Levi Bryant, *The Democracy of Objects* (Ann Arbor: Open Humanities Press, 2011).
4. Sylvia Lavin "Practice Makes Perfect," *Hunch* 11: *Rethinking Representation* (Winter 2006/07): 106–13.
5. Ian Bogost, *Alien Phenomenology, or, What It's Like to Be a Thing* (Minneapolis: University of Minnesota Press, 2012): 11.
6. See Graham Harman, "Allure," in *Guerrilla Metaphysics: Phenomenology and the Carpentry of Things* (Chicago: Open Court, 2005): 141–44.
7. See Viktor Shklovsky, "Art as Technique" (1917), in *Russian Formalist Criticism: Four Essays,* eds. Lee T. Lemon and Marion J. Reis (Lincoln: University of Nebraska Press, 1965): 3–24.
8. Dave Hickey, "Unbreak My Heart, An Overture," in *Air Guitar: Essays on Art and Democracy* (Los Angeles: Art Issues Press, 1997): 10.
9. See Graham Harman, *Weird Realism: Lovecraft and Philosophy* (Winchester, UK: Zero Books, 2012): 57–59.
10. See Wiscombe, "Discreteness," 41–43.
11. See Timothy Morton, *Hyperobjects: Philosophy and Ecology after the End of the World* (Minneapolis: University of Minnesota Press, 2013).
12. See Sylvia Lavin, *Kissing Architecture* (Princeton: Princeton University Press, 2011).
13. On planetesimals, see Jason Payne, "Variations on the Disco Ball, or, The Ambivalent Object," *Project* 2 (Summer 2013): 20–27. On Albanian bunkers, see his "Projekti Bunkerizimit: The Strange Case of the Albanian Bunker," *Log* 31: *New Ancients* (Spring/Summer 2014): 161–68.
14. Harold Bloom, *The Western Canon: The Books and School of the Ages* (New York: Riverhead Books, 1994): 25-26.
15. See Alejandro Zaera-Polo, "The Hokusai Wave," *Quaderns* 245 (2005): 77–87; also Charles Jencks and FAT, eds., *Architectural Design* 81:5: *Radical Post-modernism* (September/October 2011).
16. Sylvia Lavin, "Conversations over Cocktails," *Quaderns* 245 (2005): 88–93; and Jeffrey Kipnis, "What We ~~Got~~ Need Is – Failure to Communicate!!," *Quaderns* 245 (2005): 94–101.
17. See Todd Gannon, "Ouch or Ooooh? On 'Matters of Sensation,'" *Log* 17 (Fall 2009): 93–104.

Tabloid Transparency

with Andrew Zago, 2015

Fig. 17.1 Herzog and de Meuron, Rudin House (Leymen, 1997).

Architecture can only be political, that is, contribute to the production of another world, by being relentlessly attentive to its own discipline.
– R. E. Somol

Contemporary architecture is in the throes of an unprecedented expansion of practice types, areas of expertise, and topics of interest. Though similar proliferations of specialized niches have occurred in fields ranging from engineering to music, architecture's unique responsibilities to society as both a service profession and a cultural discipline have produced more, and more problematic, internal divergences than in other fields. Today, one is more likely to speak of the concerns of "sustainability architects," "interior architects," or "healthcare architects," than to speak of the concerns of the field as a whole. Indeed, articulating such overarching concerns has become increasingly challenging, just as constructing productive conversations between architecture's internal specializations has become more difficult.

At issue in any discussion of nascent tendencies within architecture is the status of the field's conventions of communication, its habits of speech, its discourse. The difficulty of communicating disciplinary concerns to popular audiences is well known. Less often considered is the difficulty of communication within the field, which often suffers from a similar lack of linguistic common ground. Failing to recognize important shades of meaning in familiar terms, members of specialized sub-groups in architecture—both established and emerging ones—often fail to recognize, and thus to understand and respect, the contrasting ambitions, roles, and responsibilities of architecture's varied specializations. In short, many architects today simply do not speak the same language. What follows is an attempt to clarify some basic terminological distinctions in architecture, to outline some of the field's generally accepted and less often acknowledged responsibilities to society, and to sketch the contours of a few promising developments in architecture's recent contributions to culture.

DISCOURSE COMMUNITIES

Fields of cultural production, like all social groups, develop unique vocabularies to articulate shared ambitions, to identify novel forms that emerge as the field progresses, and, perhaps most importantly, to signal an individual's membership in that group. When associated with geographical regions and socio-economic classes, these clusters of linguistic habits are commonly known as dialects. Think of Swiss-German, Québécois French, or the distinctive speech patterns of the American South. Social groups defined by shared professional responsibilities or cultural interests also develop specific dialects, which in many cases are known (often derisively) by their jargon, as in "legalese" or "art-speak."

Though sometimes bewildering to outsiders (and occasionally to the initiated), the curious inflections of meaning, structure, and syntax found in all dialects are both common and necessary. This proliferation of linguistic complexity enables not only nuanced description of topics important to the group but also the construction of the group's self-identity. The sophisticated dialects of numismatists, oenophiles, and skateboarders, for example, not only capture the intricacies of the currency, wines, and aerial maneuvers those groups esteem but also structure the very substance of the groups themselves. Submission to a dialect's vocabulary of expertise, authority, and authenticity constitutes one's membership in a group, while an ability to manipulate and direct that vocabulary establishes one's expertise. In sociology and linguistics, such groups often are referred to as "discourse communities."[1]

Like many large discourse communities, architecture has developed sophisticated dialects (and many sub-dialects) to govern its internal communications and to represent itself to society. Replete with jargon, neologisms, and obscure syntax, architecture's dialects are as necessary to the field's development as they are befuddling to the uninitiated. Consider, for example, architecture's use of the word *transparency*. As Colin Rowe and Robert Slutzky famously pointed out, the word has two main meanings in everyday English, one pertaining to material pellucidity, the other having to do with intellectual clarity.[2] To structure a particular formal debate within architecture, Rowe and Slutzky developed further inflections of the term. In architecture (at least in one if its more common sub-dialects), literal and phenomenal transparency now signify contrasting surface effects, the former having to do with the transmission of light through building materials, the latter having to do with the registration of multiple abstract patterns and illusory depth on building facades. Of course, Rowe and Slutzky used these terms not just to make categorical distinctions. More importantly, they used them to make value judgments. Literal transparency, they argued, was associated with the oblique compositional tendencies they denigrated in the work of Walter Gropius and others, and phenomenal transparency with frontal compositions, primarily those of Le Corbusier, which they supported.

Such proliferations of meaning are rampant in contemporary architecture and contribute to the difficulty of speaking of the field as a whole. Nonetheless, certain general observations can be made. One relates to architecture's ability to productively engage other disciplines and the wider world. Another has to do with the unlikely reemergence of legibility in a field long thought to have traded representational concerns for abstraction. But before turning our attention to these inflections, we must first establish an important distinction within the field, that between the profession and the discipline of architecture.

PROFESSION AND DISCIPLINE

The *profession* of architecture concerns itself with the advancement of the field as a reliable, affordable, and sustainable commodity, the *discipline* with its advancement as an art form. While those architects active in the discipline may well provide reliability, affordability, and sustainability, it is the discipline alone that takes responsibility for advancing the public imagination. This is not to say that those engaged primarily with professional concerns do not on occasion participate in architecture's cultural project, simply that when they do, they have supplanted a professional posture with a disciplinary one.

Compounding architecture's disciplinary responsibilities with the sheer size, permanence, and ubiquity of its professional output produces a unique form of politics unavailable to other art forms which also advance the public imagination. Though a person might easily avoid painting, literature, and other cultural artifacts (indeed, many do), no such option is available with regard to built form. Architecture's ubiquitous presence in the quotidian affairs of contemporary life affords it a unique political capacity irreducible to other forms of engagement, such as policy, advocacy, and social responsibility, which obtain in architecture as well as in related fields such as the political and social sciences.

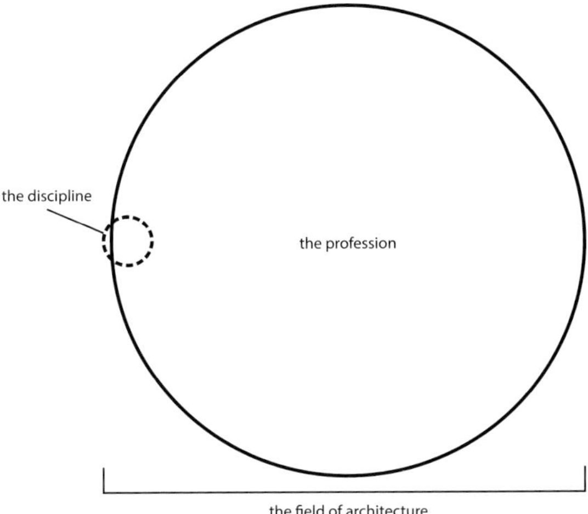

Fig. 17.2 Andrew Zago, Discipline, Profession, Field. 2011.

The diagram above [**Fig. 17.2**] illustrates the relationship of the discipline to the profession. Notice that the discipline is much smaller than the profession, lies partially outside it, and has a porous boundary. Its porosity owes to the fact that some practices work at times within and at others outside the discipline and the overlap to the fact that some extra-professional work (writing, drawing, etc.) affects architecture without being building per se. As the discipline is capable of things that the profession is not, the relationship is hierarchical. The discipline provides the evolving set of artistic concerns that, inevitably, even the most prosaic practice must draw from. This dependency is rarely acknowledged by the wider profession.

As with the broader profession, the discipline has splintered into numerous sub-interests. In the past, internal specializations within architecture such as engineering, landscape architecture, and urban planning spawned new, autonomous fields of expertise. The current proliferation of specializations may well continue to produce such distinct fields.[3] The discipline, on the other hand, is first concerned with the interrogation and reinvention of architecture's own potentials and self-definition and only later with instrumentality in the wider world. Proliferating specializations within the discipline remain embedded in the structure of the field.

Though both the discipline and the profession organize social relations through the construction of buildings, and both deploy drawings, models, diagrams, and other media to do so, their contrasting responsibilities to society point their activities in markedly different directions. The profession responds to society's immediate needs, where the discipline projects alternative possibilities for the future.

Most projects are presented to architects as problems to be solved at the level of the profession, that is, in response to society's immediate needs. Goals of course vary, but typically include functional and economic ambitions as well as site, budgetary, and programmatic constraints, among other concerns. To effectively address these challenges, architects apply the collective knowledge of the field as well as that of neighboring professions such as engineering and economics. Such relationships constructed between architecture and neighboring professions are commonly understood to be interdisciplinary. Within the discipline, on the other hand, interdisciplinarity is more complex. To project alternative possibilities to the public imagination, architecture often pursues interests parallel to those of other art forms, and at times finds itself allied with neighboring fields such as painting, literature, and philosophy to project a shared cultural agenda. Interdisciplinarity in this sense operates not in the cause of pragmatic efficiency, but rather to open new avenues of interest for the field.

Despite these differences, it is important to insist that both the profession and the discipline be understood as advancing architecture as a *material practice*, even if the former's materiality is usually manifest in the durable physicality of buildings and the latter's often is found in more ephemeral media, including the seemingly (but not actually) immaterial flux of digital design software.[4] Where the profession and the discipline deploy similar media, the former does so primarily in the cause of immediate societal needs (usually via constructed buildings), whereas the latter deploys architectural media (buildings included) as ends in themselves and to project alternative social relations. In other words, the profession instrumentalizes architectural media in order to serve society, while the discipline maintains the autonomy of those media in order to advance architecture's cultural ambitions.

CLIENTS, USERS, AND CONSTITUENCIES

There was a time when architecture was thought to address a single, general audience. Architects from Vitruvius to Le Corbusier imagined idealized subjects such as the Vitruvian Man and the Modulor Man as personifications of the collective audiences they wished to address. One of the more significant achievements of the past century of cultural production has been the critical demolition of such idealized subjectivities and with them, the hegemony of the generalized audiences they stood for. Recently, more vital groups have emerged around specific interests and proclivities within both the profession and the discipline. In the profession, increasingly complex demands have given rise to specialized service niches which address issues of programming, sustainability, accessibility, and branding as well as specific program types such as housing, prisons, hospitals, and schools. The clients who commission and finance such work, as well as the immediate users for whom the project is designed, may be understood as the direct recipient of a professional service.

The discipline, while it usually works at the behest of commercial clients and users, also addresses a broader constituency which may or may not directly inhabit or use a building. The primary concern of such constituencies is not a *building's* accommodation of utilitarian functions but rather the *architecture's* contributions to ongoing cultural projects. Where a building's users and clients are usually proximate, architecture's cultural constituencies are increasingly dispersed. Effectively addressing them requires the discipline to be particularly attentive to the full range of architectural media. Not only is architecture's proliferation as and through media crucial to its ability to impact globalized cultural constituencies, but also, the integral role of such media in architecture's ontology must be taken into account if one wishes to take seriously questions of architecture's place in cultural production.

Where a building is a concrete physical object (as are drawings, models, photographs, texts, etc.), architecture as such, the dynamic complex of habits, techniques, biases, proclivities, and, importantly, values deployed by architects, is abstract, virtual, and ineffable. As literature is irreducible to books, architecture is irreducible to buildings. And, as a mode of cultural production as opposed to a class of buildings, architecture inhabits and activates an array of media, even if buildings remain a privileged focus of our efforts. Thus, to characterize the paper architecture of the 1970s or more recent forays by the discipline into the manipulation of digital environments, the construction of pavilions, or the programming of robots as somehow less than fully architectural, as some in the field do, is to fundamentally misunderstand architecture's ontology and woefully underestimate its potential as an agent of cultural production.

Such dismissive characterizations also fail to recognize the spectrum of constituencies that has arisen within and through architecture's recent disciplinary achievements. As in music, the diversity of audiences addressed by contemporary architecture has increased dramatically. In response, the discipline has evolved a host of specialized genres through which to address them. Given the breadth of interests, limitations of space, and the fact that many of these nascent tendencies are not yet fully formed, we will not attempt a comprehensive overview of such practices here. Instead, we will devote our remaining space to a discussion of themes with which the more promising of these new practices are all in some way grappling.

LEGIBILITY AND ABSTRACTION

The return to questions of legibility today can be seen in a wide sampling of contemporary work, including the neo-post-modernism of FAT (the now defunct practice led by Sam Jacob, Sean Griffiths, and Charles Holland), the frank clarity of typological forms in projects by Herzog and de Meuron or Atelier Bow Wow, and the regional symbolism deployed in recent projects by BIG, FOA, and others. At the same time, one sees a resurgent and diametrically opposed interest in overt, neo-modernist, abstraction, as in the fluid expressionism of Zaha Hadid Architects, the stark minimalism of John Pawson, or the seeming return to the themes of 1970s "paper architecture" in the work of young practices in Los Angeles, Chicago, and elsewhere.[5]

In 2011, the principals of FAT made their case for a resurgent "Radical Post-Modernism" by calling into question modernism's associations with abstraction. Citing observations by the novelist Gabriel Josipovici, they write,

> The essential characteristics of Modernism can be limited to neither abstraction nor technological innovation and, indeed...the kind of abstraction promoted by the likes of Abstract Expressionist high priest Clement Greenberg did not represent the essence of Modernism at all, but acted merely as a sign of it.

Modernism's key characteristic, they continue, was instead "the recognition of a loss of authority after the Reformation," which caused modernist artists to adopt exactly the values pursued by the postmodernists of the 1970s, that is, "those of multiple authorship, multivalence, collage, quotation, and decentered authority."[6] Modernists, they claim, preached abstraction but in fact practiced postmodern legibility.

In this, the authors are half right. Though Greenberg certainly promoted Abstract Expressionists in the 1950s, he was by no means convinced of abstraction's necessity to modernism. In a seminal 1960 essay, he wrote, "Abstractness, or the non-figurative, has in itself still not proved to be an altogether necessary moment in the self-criticism of pictorial art, even though artists as eminent as Kandinsky and Mondrian have thought so."[7] Indeed, it was self-criticism, not abstraction, that Greenberg saw as modernism's essence.[8] Self-criticism had to do primarily with self-definition, with establishing the "unique and irreducible" qualities of each art, which in painting issued from the flatness of the picture plane. For Greenberg, the key feature of modern painting was not abstraction, but rather the legibility of a painting's irreducible flatness.

Twenty years after Greenberg, Peter Eisenman addressed the question of modernism in architecture and attempted a similar self-definition of the field. Once again, the central concern was legibility, not abstraction. Modernism, he argued, was distinguished by an "object's tendency to be self-referential."[9] Indeed, for Eisenman, it was not just modern architecture but architecture as such for which legibility was a necessary precondition. To distinguish itself from geometry, he argued, architecture required legible intentionality. To distinguish itself from sculpture, it required a legible relationship to function or use. Finally, to distinguish itself from building, architecture had to "overcome" its function through self-referential signification, as when a classical column both carries a load and simultaneously represents the act of structural support. Like Greenberg, Eisenman saw no need to include abstraction in his formulations. In his view, architecture does not, indeed cannot, deal in abstract forms such as planes and volumes. Rather, architecture's elements—walls, roofs, floors, et cetera—are always already legible signs associated with shelter, structure, or use.

More than thirty years on, Eisenman's self-referential conception of modern architecture remains more convincing than other views that understand modern architecture as a visual style based on Platonic forms and blank surfaces.[10] In Eisenman's (and, it turns out, Josipovici's) view, modernism is not a style particular to a specific medium, but rather a pervasive cultural condition manifested across creative fields. As Eisenman put it, "modernism is a state of mind."[11]

On this, the principals of FAT seem to agree, and indeed they see postmodernism not as a "disavowal of Modernism," but rather as "the continuation of it under different conditions and armed with new weapons."[12] They are also correct in their assessment that modernist abstraction is not abstraction as such but rather a sign of abstraction. Their dismissal of abstract formal vocabularies on such grounds, however, is specious. The question is not whether abstraction has been achieved, but rather how to overcome architecture's pre-existing associations with shelter, structure, and use. FAT's neo-postmodernism works to overcome these associations by pointing beyond architecture toward other resonances with culture. Their outwardly referential project is served well by a formal vocabulary freighted with easily legible content. Eisenman's modernism, on the other hand, works to overcome architecture's pre-existing associations by directing attention inward toward architecture's "unique and irreducible" qualities. At least through the 1970s, this self-referential project was best served by a vocabulary of elements with minimal symbolic associations.[13]

The suitability of non-figurative vocabularies to disciplinary self-reflection by twentieth-century artists and architects is well known.[14] Equally well known is that by the 1960s, abstraction in both painting and architecture was on the verge of exhaustion. The reductive vocabularies of Mondrian and Corbusier, adopted by each as means to direct attention away from representational clichés toward core disciplinary questions in their respective fields, began, after decades of imitation, to appear as legible and clichéd as the symbolic vocabularies they had been developed to replace.[15] By the 1970s, many architects had turned away from the Platonic forms of orthodox modernism toward a vocabulary of legible historical types. For some, the use of identifiable typological forms was a means to counter modernism's abstract self-reflections with overtly symbolic and often nostalgic outward associations.[16] Others wagered that an engagement with historical types offered the best chance to recover the exhausted disciplinary ambitions of modernism. As Anthony Vidler explained in 1977, "the issue of typology is raised in architecture, not this time with a need to search outside the practice for legitimation in science and technology, but with a sense that within architecture itself resides a unique and particular mode of production and explanation."[17] While Vidler claimed this new, "third typology" "refuses any "nostalgia" in its evocations of history,"[18] subsequent production demonstrated just how difficult it was to avoid nostalgia and sustain serious disciplinary reflection when using historical types. Indeed, even the formal abstraction of Eisenman and the New York Five was susceptible to charges of nostalgia, in their case for the historically identifiable vocabulary of Le Corbusier's *lait de chaux* villas of the 1920s and '30s.[19]

The dispute between "abstract" neo-modernist autonomy and "legible" postmodernist engagement raged through the closing decades of the twentieth century. On one side, the unavoidable fact of legibility was embraced and used to sanction a broadly engaged populism. On the other, architects (particularly in the 1980s) allied themselves with philosophers such as Jacques Derrida not to evade legibility but rather to destabilize it an attempt to maintain architecture's inwardly focused autonomy. By the 1990s, new architectural interests rooted neither in populist legibility nor in autonomous abstraction began to come into focus. Terence Riley's 1995 exhibition, *Light Construction,* at the Museum of Modern Art in New York, showcased an array of projects that focused instead on specific material effects, particularly those of glass.[20] In 2008, the exhibition *Matters of Sensation,* curated by Marcelo Spina and Georgina Huljich at Artists Space in New York, built on this renewed interest in material effects and directed attention toward architecture's affective, as opposed to representational, potential.[21] The latter exhibition drew significant inspiration from the writings of Gilles Deleuze on Francis Bacon. In Bacon, Deleuze saw a painter who rejected both representation (what Deleuze referred to as "figuration") and abstraction as viable options for contemporary painting. Instead, Bacon deployed what Deleuze called "the Figure," which he described as "the sensible form related to a sensation; it acts immediately upon the nervous system, which is of the flesh, whereas abstract form is addressed to the head and acts through the intermediary of the brain."[22]

Through the first decade of this millenium, appeals to affective figures and visceral sensation (as opposed to indexical forms and conceptual intellection) were common in architecture, particularly among younger practitioners engaged in speculative projects executed in unbuilt work and gallery installations. At the same time, firms such as BIG and FOA began to make overt appeals to legible symbolic content, claiming to do so in order to seduce clients and competition juries. In an important 2005 text, Alejandro Zaera-Polo of FOA made a case for a "double agenda" that wedded the firm's long-standing interest in formal abstraction and indexical process with their clients' desire for legible symbolic identity.[23] Though Zaera-Polo attempted to distance his approach from the earlier postmodernist positions, his argument distinctly resonated with Charles Jencks's idea of "double-coding,"[24] and drew pointed responses from Sylvia Lavin and Jeffrey Kipnis. Lavin criticized Zaera-Polo's appeal to metaphors, which, she argued, were inevitably bound up with meaning and thus vulnerable to falsification. As an alternative, she proposed the use of seductive but ultimately meaningless forms "that have no logic of verifiability, truth, or even use," offering fishnet stockings and Pereira and Luckman's 1961 Theme Building at Los Angeles International Airport as examples.[25] Like Lavin, Kipnis also suggested non-signifying forms as an alternative to Zaera-Polo's mimetic paraphrase, arguing that these should aim to elicit irreducibly architectural effects. Though he offered Deleuze's reading of Bacon as a model for how such effects might be pursued (with the caveat that architecture could not achieve its ends by imitating painting), he noticed that Bacon's paintings did not fully overcome the legacy of abstraction due to the traces of the process of painting evident on the surface of his canvases. Better, in Kipnis's view, were recent works by Damien Hirst, Jeff Koons, and others that, by effacing all evidence of process, proved startlingly resistant to the clichés of both representation and abstraction. Works such as Koons's *Balloon Dog* [**Fig. 17.3**], he argued,

> do not mean anything, they do not say anything, but neither are they silent. ...It is not that they have nothing to say, it is that they do not say; they belong to a world, to an ontology that has no place for saying, even as a possibility. This effect, made possible only by the figural, suggests an un-theorized power of the figure.[26]

Writing in 2005, Kipnis found little work on the figure in architecture beyond the writings of R. E. Somol.[27] In the ensuing decade, a number of architects have taken up the problem. And if contemporary rehearsals of neo-modernist abstraction and neo-postmodernist legibility appear ill-equipped to open new avenues of disciplinary exploration, these novel figural speculations signal just such a possibility.

TABLOID TRANSPARENCY

To distinguish recent experiments with the figure in architecture from those pursued in painting and sculpture, we propose the term *tabloid transparency.*[28] In this, we take a cue from tabloid newspapers, in which the content is so vapid that it cannot possibly bear scrutiny as meaning. The presence of content provides raw materials to perception, while the vapidity of that content allows

Fig. 17.3 Jeff Koons, *Balloon Dog (Blue)*. 1994-2000.

one's attention to shift toward the material fact of the tabloid as an object—to the letter forms, the patterning of dot-screen printing, the materiality of the paper, et cetera. Meaning in such works is so inconsequential that it collapses and, in effect, becomes transparent. In the object's absolute lack of ambiguity, questions such as, "what is this?" or "what does it mean?" are suspended. Thus, tabloid transparency does not proliferate ambiguities or otherwise destabilize meaning, but rather disarms it by rendering it insignificant. Where Deleuze aimed to bypass both abstraction and figuration via the Figure, tabloid transparency dissolves the obvious in order to access what might be referred to as the Abstract.

The Abstract, we submit, stands for an ineffable but nonetheless specific disciplinary condition, akin to Greenberg's "unique and irreducible" qualities, or Kipnis's "ontology that has no place for saying." Though closely linked to questions of form, the Abstract exceeds mere description of physical shapes. As an analogy, imagine an accomplished athlete, say, a competitive diver or gymnast. While such athletes are likely to be "in shape," their performance is ultimately judged in terms of good or bad "form." In this sense, form, as a function of the Abstract, disciplines physical shapes.

Though a function of physical materials (e.g., paint and canvas, steel and glass) the Abstract cannot be reduced to its physical manifestation—the material object only alludes to its ineffable qualities.[29] Where the distilled palettes of early twentieth-century painting and ideal geometries of early twentieth-century architecture were able, temporarily, to sustain the illusion of being "content-free," that is, of appearing to operate somewhere beyond language or indexicality, they ultimately collapsed into legibility. Ironically, abstraction precluded access to the Abstract. Equally ironically, tabloid transparency's awkward embrace of the banal legibility of cartoons, contortionists, funny faces, and other trivial figures points toward novel abstract achievements.[30] Such projects do not attempt to evade meaning, but rather wager that overt triviality might render the question of meaning moot.

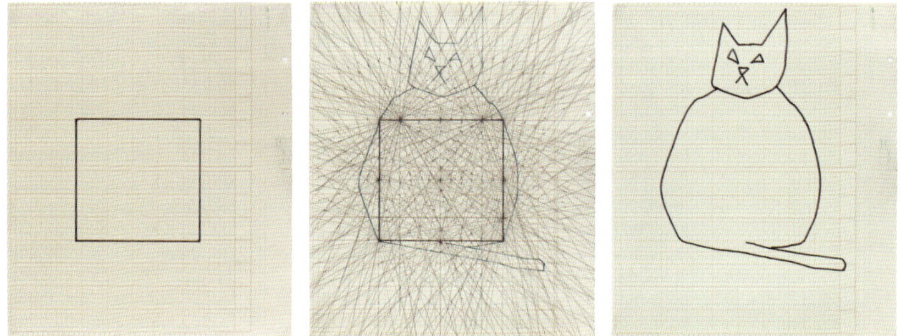

Fig. 17.4 Mike Kelley, *Square, Tangents and Cats (from The Little Girl's Room)*. 1980.

In the art world, the conundrum that links abstraction to figure is hilariously diagrammed in Mike Kelley's 1980 triptych, *Square, Tangents and Cats.* [**Fig. 17.4**] The effect can also be seen in much of Kelley's later work as well as in Koons's *Balloon Dog* and other of his pieces. Koons and Kelley are typically understood as pursuing widely different, even antagonistic, ambitions, and both are well known for including overt narratives of their respective subjectivities in their work (cf. themes of autobiography and suppressed memory in Kelley and of seeming narcissism and ironic self-promotion in Koons). In the present context, however, both are notable for their keen understanding of their position within current and broader historical trends in the art world and for their cunning ability to leverage that knowledge toward the development of novel abstract effects. If the postmodernist argument (in both architecture and art) holds that legibility is unavoidable and therefore should be embraced, works such as *Balloon Dog* and *Square, Tangents and Cats* demonstrate that abstraction is equally ever-present and, in fact, more powerfully unavoidable. These works demonstrate that no amount of literalness can remove the fundamentally abstract nature of everything, and that the more obvious the content, the more efficiently it can offer access to the Abstract.

Since at least the late 1970s, a number of architects have deployed familiar forms to open similar avenues of exploration in architecture. Early experiments can be seen in James Stirling's use of typological forms at the Berlin Wissenschaftszentrum (1979–87). While one can easily identify the fortress, theater, and church forms in the building's plan and massing, the interior arrangement and facades both work to undermine the clarity of those type-forms. It is not that their historical significance is effaced, but rather that it is rendered inconsequential to Stirling's other organizational and material ambitions. This is particularly apparent in plan, where the interior organization often diverges sharply from the massing of the typologically legible volumes. With questions of quotation or meaning thus largely suspended, novel organizational and material possibilities, such as the axial connections constructed between the type-forms or the undulating shapes of the building's perimeter (rendered continuous with banded and cartoonishly flat stone surfaces) come to the fore.

Certain of Frank Gehry's projects from the same period operate similarly. At the Loyola Law School in Los Angeles (1979–84), Gehry deployed a collection of typologically legible forms—church, temple, basilica, et cetera—to accommodate a large expansion of the campus. Filtered through the lens of modernist abstraction, Gehry's legible forms resonate with Vidler's idea of the "third typology." And, like contemporaneous works by Aldo Rossi, Georgio Grassi, and others, the strong associations between these forms and the programs they house (e.g., the relation of ancient basilica and temple forms to law courts) remain intact. In this, the project produces something akin to Jencks's idea of "double-coding," in which one's attention oscillates between the legibility of the shapes and the abstraction of their material and organizational effects. Gehry's Chiat/Day Building in Venice (1991), with its distinctive overscaled binoculars by Claes Oldenburg and Coosje van Bruggen, comes closer to achieving tabloid transparency. The triviality of the binoculars undermines (but does not completely eradicate) one's ability to tie them to metaphorical narratives related to the program or context and hastens a shift in attention to the object's unexpected voluptuousness. In more recent projects such as the Lewis House project near Cleveland, the Guggenheim Museum in Bilbao, or the Disney Concert Hall in Los Angeles, Gehry's formal sources, whether borrowed from painting, folded fabrics, billowing ship's sails, or allusions to the building's immediate context, are relaxed to the point of non-recognition. Though exhilarating, Gehry's recent work has become an identifiable signature, making it increasingly difficult to separate the abstract achievements of individual buildings from their legible associations with the architect.

Something closer to the effect currently under discussion can be found in Gehry's serial use of various animal forms, such as fish and serpents, and more emphatically in his experiments with the form of the Horse's Head in the Lewis House, the DZ Bank in Berlin, and elsewhere.[31] Herzog and de Meuron have conducted a similar series of experiments with the archetypal house form dating at least to their 1985 House for an Art Collector in Therwil, Switzerland. Here, as in their 1997 Rudin House in Leymen, France [**Fig. 17.1**], the architects adopt the banal massing of a gable-roof house only to dissolve its prototypical associations through unconventional materials, detailing, and a curious disengagement from the ground. A number of other architects also have taken up the archetypal gable form in recent years, but in most cases, their projects fail to achieve the tabloid transparency found at the Rudin House. In MVRDV's Ypenburg Master Plan in The Hague (1998–2005) and Sou Fujimoto's House 7/2 in Hokkaido (2006), for example, clear associations to traditional ideas of "house" remain firmly intact and the projects ultimately fail to overcome the banality of their elements. These latter projects, and others like them, rely too strongly on reductive tactics, similar to the Platonic abstractions of the 1920s and '30s, which have lost their efficacy and no longer offer a viable means of approaching the Abstract.

Herzog and de Meuron's achievements notwithstanding, most recent "typological" projects, as well as the commercial popularity and lack of significant disciplinary purchase of neo-minimalism (whether manifest in John Pawson's luxury asceticism or *Dwell* magazine's fashionable populism), suggest that the discipline's reductive project of the early twentieth century, as well as its typological one of the late twentieth century, have been completed. Rather than rehearse well-known successes, today's more inventive practices have concerned themselves with other possibilities, particularly those that arise from complex geometries that superficially "look like something," left unexplored by earlier innovators. Johnston Marklee's House House project for Ordos (2008) [**Fig. 17.5**], Jason Payne's Raspberry

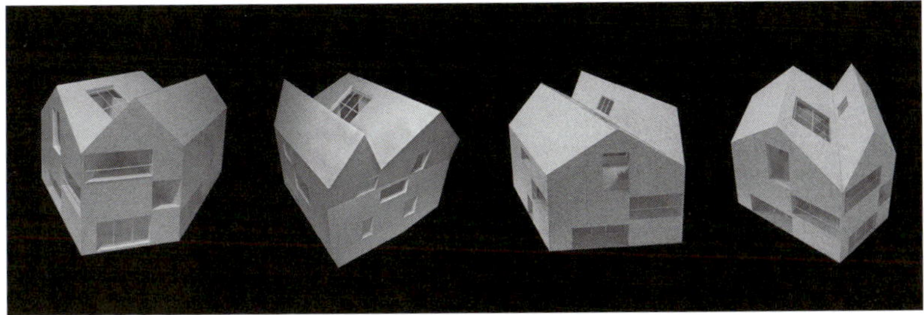

Fig. 17.5 Johnston Marklee, House House (2013).

Fig. 17.6 Zago Architecture, Arup Downtown Los Angeles (2014).

Fields in rural Utah (2008) [**Fig. 5.1**], and Herzog and de Meuron's Vitrahaus in Weil am Rhein (2009) are promising examples. Though each begins with an archetypal gable form, each then aggressively manipulates that massing and deploys curious surface treatments to loosen familiar associations.

Whether deployed at the level of the element or the massing, the "content" of each of these projects is immediately apprehensible but, owing to its utter lack of ambiguity, quickly fades from attention to allow more sophisticated organizational and material effects to take over. In them, typological forms serve simply as a means of entry into a discussion of the Abstract. Of course, typology is but one way to enter into such discussions. Other methods, such as cartoons or contortions, offer other ways, which Zago Architecture has explored in recent projects [**Fig. 17.6**].

Though these latter tactics are sometimes nurtured as inevitable endgames by neo-postmoderists and are easily coopted by those interested in producing a kind of meta-critical irony, the projects to which we refer here deploy tabloid transparency and an interest in the Abstract to introduce a reinvigorated sense of *authenticity* into progressive architectural discourse. Tabloid transparency points toward the possibility of a post-ironic "stealth authenticity," which, by pressing the banal, the ordinary, and the dull into the service of the Abstract, avoids both the skepticism of neo-postmodernism as well as the well-known pitfalls of traditional authenticity.[32]

PROJECTING INTERDISCIPLINARITY OUTWARD

Armed with such a concept, architecture might finally begin to move beyond the longstanding insecurity felt by many architects over the field's relation to neighboring areas of cultural production. As we noted above, interdisciplinary collaboration has become a central feature of contemporary practice. Though it greatly increases the effectiveness of building design and construction, this very effectiveness has led to unfortunate consequences. Routine injections of efficacy from outside architecture have led many architects to view their own field as fundamentally inadequate. In the hands of some within the discipline, architecture has become little more than a thinly veiled paraphrase of philosophy, computer science, or studio art. In the profession, one finds engineering, sustainability, and humanitarianism overshadowing specifically architectural concerns. The effect is tantamount to draining the architecture from architectural projects.[33] Feelings of disciplinary inadequacy have also inspired some architects to retreat from engagement with the broader world to aim exclusively at disciplinary concerns. Taken to extremes, this approach can result in isolation, acrimony, and, ultimately, irrelevance.

Today, though architecture enjoys a general admiration by society, it is difficult to find instances where a specifically architectural issue is recognized as making a valuable contribution to the world. This is not the case for law, engineering, medicine, or, for that matter, painting, music, literature, or any number of other fields. Though this state of affairs might be attributed to the fact that some of architecture's most potent effects operate beneath the threshold of conscious attention,[34] a more convincing reason is that architecture tends to engage the world on the world's terms, not its own. As they generally are not seen to offer an immediate public health, safety, and/or welfare "service" to society, painting, music, literature, and other art forms are valued primarily for their specific disciplinary contributions, that is, for their form as opposed to their function. Architecture, on the other hand, though it offers society both functional "service" and formal enrichment, generally is understood solely in terms of the former, even though its greatest strengths issue from the latter. In short, most people (many architects included) miss architecture's point, and as a result, many architects have tacitly or explicitly accepted a position of apparent impotency and have constructed alternative constellations of values in compensation. R. E. Somol forcefully counters such tactics in a recent essay. "If architecture has lost its ability to operate in the world," he opines, "it's not because architecture has become too self-involved, but because it has not been attentive enough to its own protocols, techniques, and forms of knowledge." His argument hinges on the unrecognized potential of architecture's disciplinary abstractions. Too many architects, he continues,

> seem afflicted by the assumption that the abstractions of other fields are real (for example, the bookkeeping tricks that allowed Enron to count potential future profits as if they were actual—conceptual accounting?), while the abstractions of architecture are not. Architecture, if it is to operate in the world, first needs to overcome this reality envy of other fields, and take its own abstractions as literally as it accepts those of others.[35]

The form of disciplinarity we have outlined here, one not insulated by neo-postmodernism's ironic detachment but rather galvanized by stealth authenticity, offers a potent means to answer Somol's call to action. Though we respect architecture's very real and important professional responsibilities, we insist that the field's most valuable contributions to culture have been and will continue to be made in terms of architecture's disciplinary ambitions. Today, the discipline of architecture can best "serve" society by continuing to explore counterintuitive, risky, and abstract possibilities which for various reasons the profession is unable to explore. Only by taking seriously architecture's disciplinary responsibilities, and by relentlessly proliferating formal and rhetorical dialects through which to articulate them, can we meet architecture's obligation to "provoke other fields (ecology, law, economics, politics and policy, and so on) to challenge their own limitations that have been unconsciously and pervasively founded on ours."[36] Projecting architecture's abstractions on other fields, as opposed to absorbing those of other fields into our own, is a model for a new, more productive mode of interdisciplinarity, one founded not on pragmatic efficiency, aversion to risk, and the solution of known problems, but rather on counterintuitive experimentation, calculated risk-taking, and the invention of new problems from which new possibilities—of built form as well as political life—might emerge.

NOTES

1. For an excellent treatment of the politics of discourse communities, see David Foster Wallace, "Authority and American Usage," in *Consider the Lobster and Other Essays* (New York: Little Brown and Co., 2006): 66–127. For more general treatments of the concept, see *Communities of Discourse: The Rhetoric of Disciplines*, eds. Gary D. Schmidt and William J. Vande Kopple (New York: Prentice Hall, 1992).
2. Colin Rowe and Robert Slutzky, "Transparency: Literal and Phenomenal" [1963], in Rowe, *The Mathematics of the Ideal Villa and Other Essays* (Cambridge: MIT Press, 1976): 159–83.
3. Given the complex technical, legal, and bureaucratic contexts within which architects now operate, many tasks that traditionally have fallen under the purview of standard architectural services (e.g., programming, accessibility, cost estimating, permitting, specifications, sustainability design, and construction administration as well as rendering, model-making, digital animation, and other "pre-visualization" techniques) are now increasingly handled by outside consultants who, like engineers and landscape architects, bring significant extra-architectural expertise to the table and are rapidly developing specific disciplinary habits and conventions within their respective areas of expertise.
4. Cf. N. Katherine Hayles and Todd Gannon, "Virtual Architecture, Actual Media," 174–99 in this volume.
5. Cf. *Log* 31: *New Ancients* (Spring/Summer 2014), edited by Dora Epstein Jones and Bryony Roberts.
6. FAT, "Post-Modernism: An Incomplete Project," in *Architectural Design* (Sept/Oct 2011): 18. The issue, *Radical Post-Modernism*, was edited by Charles Jencks and FAT. Josipovici's arguments are from *What Ever Happened to Modernism?* (New Haven: Yale University Press, 2011).
7. Clement Greenberg, "Modernist Painting" [1960] in *Clement Greenberg: The Collected Essays and Criticism, Volume Four, Modernism with a Vengeance, 1957–1969*, ed. John O'Brian (Chicago: Univ. of Chicago Press, 1993): 87.
8. "The essence of Modernism lies, as I see it, in the use of characteristic methods of a discipline to criticize the discipline itself, not in order to subvert it but in order to entrench it more firmly in its area of competence." Ibid., 85.
9. Peter Eisenman, "Aspects of Modernism: Maison Dom-ino and the Self-referential Sign" [1980], in *Eisenman Inside Out: Selected Writings 1963–1988* (New Haven: Yale University Press, 2004): 112–13.
10. Cf. Henry-Russell Hitchcock and Philip Johnson, *The International Style* [1932] (New York: W.W. Norton, 1995).
11. Eisenman, "Aspects of Modernism," 112.
12. FAT, "Post-Modernism," 21.
13. Of course, by the 1980s, Eisenman would routinely deploy more legible elements as part of his formal vocabulary, as in the "as-found" elements at the Wexner Center for the Arts and Cincinnati DAAP.
14. In painting, recall Mondrian: "All art employing naturalistic appearance becomes weakened in its true function. All representation, even using abstract forms, is fatal to pure art; that is why purely abstract art is expressed exclusively through relationships." (Piet Mondrain, "Purely Abstract Art" [1926] in *The New Art—the New Life: The Collected Writings of Piet Mondrian*, eds. Harry Holtzman and Martin S. James [Boston: Da Capo Press, 1993]: 200). And in architecture, Le Corbusier: "cubes, cones, spheres, cylinders, and pyramids are the great primary forms that light reveals well...*these are beautiful forms, the most beautiful forms.* Everyone is in agreement about this: children, savages, and metaphysicians." (Le Corbusier, *Toward an Architecture* [1923] [Los Angles: Getty Research Institute, 2007]: 102, emphasis in the original.)
15. On the problem of cliché in architecture, see Todd Gannon, "Five Points for Thesis," 259–77 in this volume.
16. Cf. Charles Jencks, *The Language of Post-modern Architecture* (New York: Rizzoli, 1977).

17. Anthony Vidler, "The Third Typology" [1977] reprinted in *Architecture/Theory since 1968*, ed. K. Micahel Hayes (Cambridge: MIT Press, 1998): 288.
18. Ibid., 293.
19. See Colin Rowe, "Introduction," in *Five Architects* (New York: Wittenborn, 1972): 3–7.
20. See Terence Riley, *Light Construction* (New York: Museum of Modern Art, 1995).
21. See Marcelo Spina and Georgina Huljich, "Matter, Sensation, and the Sublime," in *PATTERNS: Embedded* (Beijing: AADCU, 2010): 208–17.
22. Gilles Deleuze, *Francis Bacon: The Logic of Sensation* [1981] (Minneapolis: Univ. of Minnesota Press, 2003): 31.
23. Alejandro Zaera-Polo, "The Hokusai Wave," *Quaderns* 245 (2005): 77–87.
24. Cf. Jencks, *The Language of Post-modern Architecture*, 6.
25. Sylvia Lavin, "Conversations over Cocktails," *Quaderns* 245 (2005): 90.
26. Jeffry Kipnis, "What We ~~Got~~ Need Is—Failure to Communicate" *Quaderns* 245 (2005): 96–97.
27. See R. E. Somol, "12 Reasons to Get Back into Shape," in *Content*, eds. Rem Koolhaas and OMA/AMO (Cologne: Taschen, 2004): 86–87.
28. Though he never used it in publication, we suspect credit for coining this term goes to Kipnis, with whom we recall discussing the idea several years ago.
29. A useful parallel might be drawn here with the writings of Graham Harman, who posits allusion as a means to intuit the qualities of "withdrawn objects" otherwise inaccessible to perception. See Harman, *The Quadruple Object* (Winchester, UK: Zero Books, 2011).
30. For a discussion of these tactics, see Andrew Zago, "Awkward Position," *Perspecta* 42 (2010): 209–22.
31. For an informative treatment of Gehry's development of the Horse's Head, see Sylvia Lavin, "Twelve Heads are Better than One," in *Fragments: Architecture and the Unfinished, Essays Presented to Robin Middleton*, eds. Barry Bergdoll and Werner Oechslin (London: Thames and Hudson, 2006): 343–52.
32. For a more developed discussion of stealth authenticity, see Andrew Zago, "Real What?" *Log* 5 (Spring/Summer 2005): 100–5.
33. In a recent lecture, Sarah Whiting outlined a compelling indictment of this situation. See "Engaging Autonomy," lecture at the Southern California Institute of Architecture, 6 Nov 2013. David Ruy persuasively articulated similar concerns in "Returning to (Strange) Objects," *TARP Architecture Manual: Not Nature* (Spring 2012): 38–42.
34. For discussions of such subliminal effects, see Todd Gannon, "Grand Gestures and Intelligent Plans," 120–24 in this volume.
35. R. E. Somol, "Shape and the City," *Architectural Design* 82, special issue, *City Catalyst: Architecture in the Age of Extreme Urbanisation* (Sept/Oct 2012): 113.
36. Ibid.

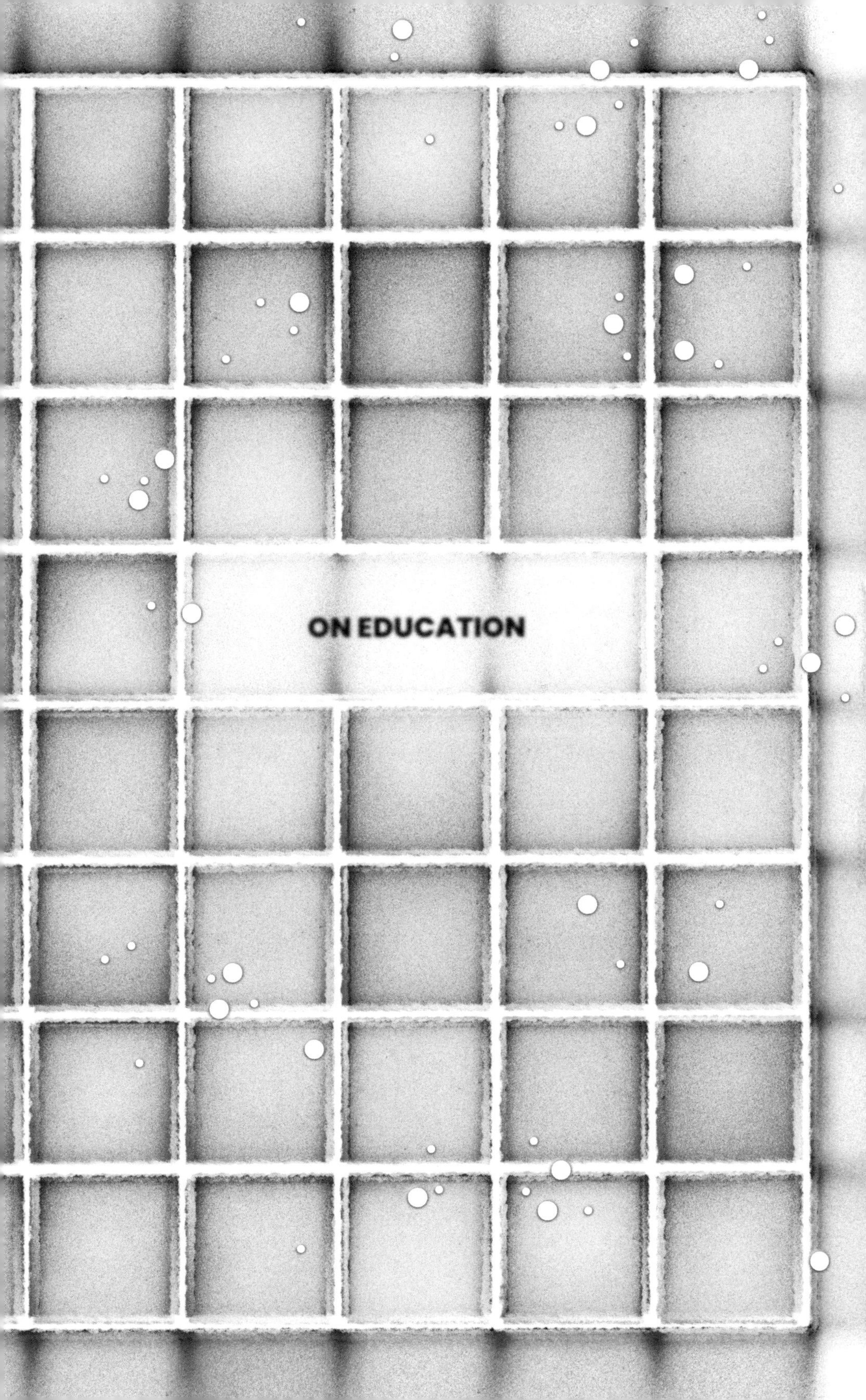
ON EDUCATION

Of Prophets and Professionals

2016

Fig. 18.1 SCI-Arc student presentations, c. 1974.

Though I share some of his concerns about the state of contemporary architectural education, I was taken aback by comments from my friend and colleague Peter Zellner in a recent editorial.

In "Architectural Education Is Broken—Here's How to Fix It," Peter offers a five-point critique of contemporary education and a matching five-point prescription for a "post-studio and post-digital architectural education."[1]

The criticism, gleaned from twenty-five-year-old comments by John Baldessari about the artist's development of a "post-studio" course at CalArts nearly fifty years ago, takes aim at hierarchical master-disciple relationships between teachers and students, at the proliferation of academic styles that often result from them, and at the suppression of dissenting opinions such situations often entail. His prescription for change unfolds along a familiar, if vague, trajectory that valorizes shared knowledge, free experimentation, and egalitarian exchange among students and teachers.

Some of Peter's criticisms are justified, if a bit overblown. "Various forms of academic cult worship" indeed exist in architecture schools today, and this "pied-piperism," to borrow a term from Eric Moss, has led many a promising student into unproductive territory. In my experience, though, most of those lost sheep eventually find their way home, and more often than not they return primed to parlay experience gained in foreign fields into significant contributions within the disciplinary fold.

Peter's complaints about the nefarious forces of digital technology, on the other hand, lack both specificity and substance. He merely states, rather than argues, his contention that digital tools foreclose creativity, and dismisses without comment not only the obvious achievements of several decades of innovative work at schools around the globe but also of his own students. Worse, the statement is not his own, but rather a quote from Peter Eisenman, which adds to an air of older generations kvetching about newfangled habits and, like his invocation of Baldessari, undermines his admonition against undue authority invested in the pronouncements of elder statesmen.

However problematic, Peter's criticisms are for the most part innocuous. I have more serious concerns about his proposals for change. His recipe for post-studio education rests on a specious, if common, elision of art and architecture and a ludicrous, if equally common, contention that architecture "can't be taught." Such arguments brush aside significant differences between art and architecture and perpetuate damaging mystifications about the nature of architectural practice and education.

I agree with Peter's assertion that architecture is an art form. But unlike painting, literature, music, and other modes of artistic production, it is also a *profession* with significant ethical and legal responsibilities, and a *discipline* with cultural ambitions to advance the public imagination. The latter aspect distinguishes the practice of architecture from the craft of building. The former distinguishes it from the production of fine art.

Peter and I share a deep commitment to architecture understood as a cultural practice with professional responsibilities, as opposed to a design profession with cultural ambitions. Nonetheless, I take issue with his proposals, which, despite his criticism of a supposedly style-obsessed status quo, continue to portray architecture almost exclusively in aesthetic terms, pay only passing lip service to "technical knowledge," overemphasize issues of style and individual expression, and disregard questions of professional competence. Any serious proposal about architectural education must take the full gamut of architecture's professional and disciplinary responsibilities into account.

More damaging is Peter's proposition, also borrowed from Baldessari, that architecture cannot be taught. Apparently, the best we can do is to "set up a situation where [architecture] might happen." This is a bizarre idea to be put forward by such an intelligent and effective teacher as Peter Zellner.

Peter proposes that we can't teach architecture because he conceives of architecture, as Baldassari apparently conceives of art, as a mystical quality, a transubstantiation of physical matter into some higher form of existence. This is the sort of stuff that routinely pours from the mouths of those academic shamans Peter rails against in his essay. It can be seductive, to be sure, but it is nonsense.

Architecture doesn't just *happen*. Architecture is *made*. Architecture can be made, and its methods taught, because "architecture" refers not to a specific object but rather to evidence that an object—usually but not always a building—has been produced in terms of a specific way of working. Just as literature cannot be reduced to books, architecture cannot be reduced to buildings. Neither can it be reduced to drawings, models, or digital animations. Architecture is method all the way down. The *Oxford English Dictionary* defines architecture not as a kind of building but rather as "the art or science of building." Another Peter, the historian better known as Reyner Banham, put it better: "What distinguishes architecture is not *what* is done...but *how* it is done."

Understanding architecture as having to do with *how* rather than *what* makes it easier to see that architecture is, like all academic disciplines, a cultural construct. Its techniques and methods, its history and theory, the habits and conventions of those who practice it, can and routinely are taught and learned, as evidenced by the surfeit of students who quickly master the tactics of their teachers that Peter laments in his essay. Of course, those techniques, histories, habits, and conventions also can be developed, transformed, thrown out, and replaced as needed. Such activities rank among the most important work that takes place in architecture schools.

Understanding architecture this way also makes it easier to see that the field's value system, its internal methods for identifying what constitutes good and bad work, is always a work in progress. Architectural quality, like architecture itself, is determined not by the presence or absence of some quasi-spiritual attribute in an object but rather by consensus. Constituencies in support of any architectural work must be constructed long before the project can be built, and even if constructed buildings are not one's aim, it is an ability to assemble such constituencies, and little else, that transforms individual interests into relevant contributions and, in some cases, canonical achievements.

In other words, architecture's aesthetic ambitions are deeply political. And the disciplinary politics of architectural education, as Peter intimates in his essay, can make for some pretty ugly situations. Luckily, contemporary architecture can and does support a wide range of coexisting genres and associated value systems. In the best schools, a handful of them vie for dominance, motivating proponents of each to hone their political as well as their aesthetic and technical chops as they make their respective cases and build their respective constituencies. In the worst ones, well-meaning but misguided faculty utter empty pronouncements like "you can't teach architecture."

There are plenty of issues with contemporary architectural education today, and I commend Peter for having put some of them on the table. But at the top of any list of things to fix in architecture schools must surely be the abdication of so many faculty of their responsibility to teach it.

NOTE

1. Peter Zellner, "Architectural Education Is Broken—Here's How to Fix It," *The Architect's Newspaper* (16 Sept 2016).

Mind the Gaps!

2020

Fig. 19.1 Instructors S. Kochar and E. Herrmann, A Thing Inside a Thing Inside a Thing models, 2019.

They appear just after Thanksgiving, around the time when everything in Columbus begins to fade to wintry gray. There are usually about twenty-five of them—squat, vaguely cubic, roughly milk crate sized—arranged in an alien phalanx on the Big Steps in Knowlton Hall, the Mack Scogin Merrill Elam Architects-designed home of the Knowlton School at The Ohio State University, where I lead the architecture program. Easter-egg colors predominate and starkly contrast with the coolness of Mack and Merrill's interior concrete and the clouds gathering outside. The objects exhibit a curious density; their masses are less solid than stuffed with squishy sleeves of space. Moving in for a closer look, notice that they appear to have been sliced from larger wholes to reveal hints of building-like orthogonality—a stair here, a balcony there, the occasional stack of boxy rooms—nestled into otherwise plump, invaginated volumes.

They are the final models of Knowlton's first semester, second-year graduate architecture studio (G2 for short). As it turns out, they represent hotel designs for an urban site in Cincinnati, but you would be hard pressed to figure that out on your own. The drawings pinned up nearby uniformly eschew labels, and the syllabus, assembled by instructors Erik Herrmann and Sandhya Kochar and clotted with allusions to the work of philosophers

(Graham Harman, Martin Heidegger, Bruno Latour), art critics (Michael Fried, Dave Hickey), and mostly young architects (Andrew Atwood, Jennifer Bonner, Jimenez Lai, Michael Meredith, Anna Neimark, Hilary Sample), speaks not of hotels but rather, and rather cryptically, of "a thing inside a thing inside a thing."

Each year, the models trigger a wave of excitement that ripples through the school. On final review day, undergraduates who normally hang out on the Steps gawk at the curious invaders that have commandeered their lunch spot. G2 students lean gregariously on one another with the air of postcompetition athletes. G1s chatter nervously, wondering if they will be able to pull it off next year. Flinty-eyed G3s look on in silence, like war veterans.

Studio reviews are uniformly lively and generate their share of criticism, some of which—the kind that whines like tinnitus at Ohio State, SCI-Arc, Penn, Pratt, UCLA, and other institutions where advanced formal speculation remains the norm—I'll use as a jumping-off point here. The criticism takes aim at the purportedly problematic relationship of speculative work to the realities of conventional building tectonics and functional performance. Critics (often the same students who produced the models!) are quick to point out that, while interesting, these models tend to be long on form and short on function, underdeveloped in terms of structure and program, and, in some cases, improbable as buildings, raising thorny questions as to their ultimate value to the education of an architect.

True enough. In this studio, faculty suspend some technical questions and encourage students to pursue compositional and spatial effects unperturbed by the often-stifling realities of structure, program, and budget.[1] If architecture is understood merely in the traditional (and dictionary) sense as the art and science of building, a case can be made that these models fall short. But if architecture is understood more broadly as "an unfolding investigation into the possibilities of occupying material form," as Jeffrey Kipnis memorably puts it, these models are right on the money.[2]

To achieve this broader understanding of the discipline, Knowlton faculty often encourage students to proceed via counterintuitive experimentation and calculated risk-taking. In other words, we sometimes ask them to do things the wrong way on purpose. We do so not out of recklessness but out of a desire to produce new forms of rightness. If all we asked was for our students to conform to best practices, all they would ever do is repeat known successes. If we want new successes, we need new practices. That, in a milk crate, is what these models are about. If it ain't broke, break it!

A key difference between our position and that of our critics is that the latter generally want to close gaps they identify in the work—gaps between the models and the buildings they represent, between education and the professional practice it predicts, and even those pesky gaps between materials that signal poor craft in models and allow the rain into and the heat out of poorly made buildings. Though we agree that craft-related gaps should be eliminated, at Knowlton we usually aim to open gaps—between models and buildings, schools and offices, theory and practice, discipline and profession—in order to demonstrate that the most interesting work in any field tends to emerge from the dissonance between the polarities by which that field is defined. As I have argued elsewhere, a defining polarity in architecture is that between a profession understood as a technical pursuit and a discipline understood as an art form.[3] By denying the assumption that an architect's job is to resolve the inherent misalignment of these aspects of architecture, we aim to teach our students how to exploit the inevitable gaps between them to generate new possibilities for the field.

All architecture is a function of a gap between concepts and actuality, as even the dullest project architect will confirm. You know who I am talking about, that grouchy guy (it's always a guy) in every office who can't stop telling the interns to forget about that theory stuff they learned in school and face up to the real world. Next time you visit a building with that guy, point out a flaw. A misaligned light fixture, a badly finished wall surface, any punch list item will do. As if on cue, he will protest: "Well, it's not supposed to be like that." In this, our rock-ribbed realist draws attention away from the supposedly real world of the building to an apparently realer one of its architecture. The conceptual doppelgänger that haunts all material form, what Rosalind Krauss once labeled the "hermeneutic phantom," is not an irrelevant example of obscure theorizing, as our hapless P.A. might have it, but a precise description of his favorite excuse for slipshod construction.[4] And though he might not believe it, his protestations make it clear that he at least intuitively understands that architecture cannot be reduced to buildings. Rather, architecture must be understood in terms of the persistent gap between material form and immaterial concepts.[5]

In my drawing attention to gaps, readers may notice an echo of Harman, whose book on H. P. Lovecraft centers on the philosophical implications of the production and destruction of gaps.[6] Less obvious, but perhaps more important to my argument, is the debt I owe to the late sociologist Murray S. Davis. In an influential 1971 essay, Davis points to the importance of denying the expectations of one's audience in order to produce interesting social theories.[7] Here, theories have to do primarily with the relationship between what seems to be and what is. That is, in its most basic form, a theory states whether phenomenology aligns with or diverges from ontology. Whether a theory is found to be interesting, by contrast, has more to do with its audience, and occurs when a prevailing assumption about the relationship between seeming and being is denied.[8]

Most theories, like the common sense into which successful ones degrade, work to eliminate gaps to make the world more manageable, understandable, and predictable: if it seems too good to be true, it probably is; humans evolved from apes; $E = mc^2$. Interesting theories, on the other hand, "constitute an attack on the taken-for-granted world," and always upset prevailing assumptions.[9] *Humans evolved from apes?!? Mass is equivalent to energy?!?* Of course, interest is always context dependent. However shocking they once were, Darwin's theory of evolution and Einstein's theory of special relativity have, for most of us, long since slouched into the comforting familiarity of common sense.

Davis's formula for interesting social theory is simple and is easily transported to other fields: "What is accepted as *X* is actually non-*X*."[10] Importantly, Davis is careful to point out that theories need not be true to be interesting. (His opening lines ought to be tattooed on the inner forearm of every aspiring theorist and PhD student: "It has long been thought that a theorist is considered great because his theories are true, but this is false. A theorist is considered great, not because his theories are true, but because they are *interesting*."[11]) In fact, theories that merely verify prevailing assumptions are generally dismissed as their truth is affirmed. "That's obvious," we huff and move on.[12]

As responsible professionals, architects often, and rightly, work to eliminate gaps by aligning phenomenology with ontology. This column *seems* sufficiently strong to carry the load placed on it and, in fact, *is* sufficiently strong. This window *seems* to be the right size to provide light and air to this room and, in fact, *is* the right size. Useful buildings often result from the application of such commonsense thinking. Interesting architecture requires more.

Interesting architecture (which is to say, architecture) most often results when architects deny prevailing assumptions. Henri Labrouste understood as much when he specified columns that appear insufficiently strong to carry the vaults they support in the reading room at the Bibliothèque Nationale in Paris. Colin Rowe knew it too when he quipped, "If you see a building with windows of a size to admit an appropriate amount of light, it may or may not be a work of architecture; but, if the windows are definitely too big or definitely too small, then you can be almost certain that you are in the presence of an architectural endeavor."[13] The implication is startling. Adherence to convention only sometimes leads to architecture; affronts to convention nearly always do.[14]

The G2 models should be understood in the same spirit. If you see a model with interior spaces appropriate to their intended uses, it may or may not be a work of architecture; but, if you see a model with interior spaces that wildly exceed what is appropriate for their intended use, you can be almost certain that you are in the presence of an architectural endeavor. I allow that some (but not all) of these models are implausible as buildings. I also submit that most (if not all) of them point to exciting new possibilities for architecture.

Fig. 19.2 Mack Scogin Merrill Elam Architects, Knowlton Hall (Columbus, 2004).

In this, our students take up the challenge Mack and Merrill posed to them with Knowlton Hall, which my colleagues and I often hold up as a model for speculative practice [**Fig. 19.2**]. The building, with its undulating curves, odd shingles, and crystalline voids chiseled into its marble mass, flies in the face of its staid, brick-clad context to open a yawning chasm between what it is and what campus buildings are expected to be. Where most buildings at Ohio State offer bland stacks of single-height classrooms clipped to double-loaded corridors, Mack and Merrill conjure an architecture of dizzying volumetric complexity. Triple- and even quadruple-height spaces soar up past faculty offices, through design studios, and around glass-clad laboratories that cling to the ceilings like wayward balloons. Outlandishly long ramps guide visitors up through a section torn open by split-level floor slabs pinned in place by concrete columns. Resisting the regimentation of an orthogonal grid, these columns are distributed loosely across the plan and scaled like oaks. On entry, first-time visitors typically raise their eyes skyward and fall reverently silent. Only after they have collected themselves do they begin to scratch their heads and wonder how the hell they are supposed to find the lecture hall. (Don't worry, just head up the ramp!) Once occupants have spent a little time figuring the place out, new possibilities begin to emerge. Curious nooks offer cozy spots to cram for a quiz or sneak in a nap. Gaps between floor levels provide more than just spatial excitement, they foster casual communication between normally isolated floors, with students exchanging tips or gossip and occasionally lobbing snacks across the void.

Where most buildings segregate occupants into clearly defined rooms, this one joins them in loosely layered, overlapping zones. The G2 models attempt something similar. Though they may not yet exhibit professional control to the degree that is everywhere apparent in Knowlton Hall, they signal a commitment to speculative possibility that is utterly lacking in far too many buildings today. Reliance on conventional methods and best practices alone, which manage expectations by foreclosing uncertainty, quite simply cannot produce possibilities like these. Indeed, the more we adhere to them, the less likely we are to produce architecture at all.

NOTES

1. These technical questions are pursued more pointedly elsewhere in the curriculum, including in the comprehensive studio that immediately follows this one. Beth Blostein and I taught that studio last spring. Recent student work from both studios can be seen at https://knowlton.work/G2.
2. Aphorism 14 in Jeffrey Kipnis, *In the Manor of Nietzsche: Aphorisms around and about Architecture* (New York: Calluna Farms Press, 1990): np.
3. See Todd Gannon, "Figments of the Architectural Imagination," 22–26 in this volume. For a more expansive treatment of the relationship of the profession and the discipline, see Andrew Zago and Todd Gannon, "Tabloid Transparency," 226–45 in this volume.
4. See Rosalind Krauss, "Death of the Hermeneutic Phantom: Materialization of the Sign in the Work of Peter Eisenman," in Peter Eisenman, *Houses of Cards* (New York: Oxford University Press, 1987): 166–84.
5. For an elaboration, see N. Katherine Hayles and Todd Gannon, "Virtual Architecture, Actual Media," 174–99 in this volume.

6. "One of the most important decisions made by philosophers today concerns the production or destruction of gaps in the cosmos. That is to say, the philosopher can either declare that what appears to be one is actually two, or that what seems to be two is actually one." Graham Harman, *Weird Realism: Lovecraft and Philosophy* (Winchester: Zero Books, 2012): 2.
7. Murray S. Davis, "That's Interesting! Towards a Phenomenology of Sociology and a Sociology of Phenomenology," *Philosophy of the Social Sciences* 1: 2 (June 1971): 309–44.
8. In the interest of brevity, I will refrain from swerving through the literature on "interesting" as a concept and a category. Those who wish to do so ought to begin with Sianne Ngai's *Our Aesthetic Categories: Zany, Cute, Interesting* (Cambridge: Harvard University Press, 2012), which is required reading for anyone wishing to use the term intelligently; Mark Dorrian's "What's Interesting? On the Ascendency of an Evaluative Term," *Architecture and Culture* 4:2 (Sept 2016): 173–84, which provides an incisive analysis of the term's recent use in architecture; and Andrew Atwood's *Not Interesting: On the Limits of Criticism in Architecture* (San Francisco: AR+D: 2018), which, in spite of its arguments, is interesting in exactly Davis's sense of the term.
9. Davis, 'That's Interesting!" 311.
10. Ibid., 313. Cf. Harman's take on philosophical gaps, quoted in n. 6 above.
11. Ibid., 309. Emphasis in the original.
12. Ibid., 311.
13. A Questioner, "Questions for Colin Rowe," *ANY: Architecture New York* 7/8: *Form Work: Colin Rowe* (1994): 34, reprinted as "Interview: 1989," in Rowe, *As I Was Saying: Recollections and Miscellaneous Essays*, vol. 2 (Cambridge: MIT Press, 1996): 356. Here, Rowe guesses that the anonymous questioner was Richard Ingersoll.
14. If architecture exists as an affront to building, it also sometimes finds itself at odds with theory, which too often is expected to serve as a model for practice. Normally, architectural theories become interesting when individual buildings conform to a theory's general principles. Individual buildings, on the other hand, become interesting when they confound a theory's necessary generalizations. For proof, compare the built work of any architect who has written a theory to the general principles of that theory. You will find that the work is most interesting when the gap between the architecture and the theory is most pronounced. Given this, we should return to understanding (and teaching!) building as a cause for, not an effect of theory, at least until that approach ceases to be interesting.

Five Points for Thesis

2017

Fig. 20.1 Frank Gehry, Peter B. Lewis building (Cleveland, 2002).

The following is an edited transcript of a lecture first given to SCI-Arc's graduate thesis class in the spring of 2014.

I think the philosopher Richard Rorty was onto something when he wrote:

> Interesting philosophy...usually...is a contest between an entrenched vocabulary which has become a nuisance and a half-formed new vocabulary which vaguely promises great things.

This phrase resonates with contemporary architecture in general and SCI-Arc thesis in particular, as I'll try to show. But first, following Rorty, I want to encourage all of you to vaguely promise great things with your thesis projects—and to avoid being a nuisance. For this talk, I came up with five points for thesis, which I hope will help in both regards. We'll start with this:

PART ONE: SIMILARITY AND DIFFERENCE

There is nothing new under the sun.
– Ecclesiastes 1:9

This is a phrase we hear often around architecture schools. It's an inoculation against naïveté and superficial valorization of novelty. It's also pretty easy to demonstrate. If we look at something like Frank Gehry's Peter B. Lewis Building in Cleveland [**Fig. 20.1**], for example, we could say that there's not much new here. We've seen it in Bilbao. We've seen it in Downtown Los Angeles. If we follow Peter Eisenman, we could say that Gehry got the idea from Schinkel. From there, it's pretty easy to lock Gehry's project into a trajectory that goes back through Stirling's Staatsgalerie to Le Corbusier's Capitol at Chandigarh through Schinkel's Altesmuseum to Lord Burlington's Chiswick House and Palladio's Villa Rotunda. Each of these projects conforms to a similar plan diagram: central rotunda, U-shaped wrapper, and porch [**Fig. 20.2**]. With a few more steps, we could take Gehry all the way back through the Parthenon to the Primitive Hut. Trajectories like these are fairly common and tend to have a domesticating function: works are validated in terms of what came before.

Of course, we could look at it another way. Rather than point out the similarities between projects, we could draw attention to the differences. The Primitive Hut, for instance, is a novel arrangement of trees in a forest. With the Parthenon, whether we look at it in terms of the conversion of wood detailing to stone or as the conversion of myth to reality, we find plenty that is absent in the Primitive Hut. If we look at Palladio, we'll discover an almost unprecedented use of temple architecture for a residence. We'll also see a whole collection of rooms in the plan, something absent in the earlier temples. At Chiswick, the rooms become much more specific—the Green Velvet Room, the Red Velvet Room, et cetera—contrasting Palladio's seeming disinterest in specifically programmed spaces. Chiswick is also emphatically frontal, a significant swerve from earlier schemes. Moving on to Schinkel, notice the appearance of the voids on either side of the central rotunda. We see those voids expanding in Chandigarh, with the columns in Schinkel's outer wrapper becoming a free-plan field. At the Staatsgalerie, all of the pieces are still present, though the porch has turned back into trees and the rotunda has lost its dome. With Gehry, the central rotunda either compresses into a desk, or divides into two elements, depending on how you look at it. You get the idea: we can portray the sequence as moving from novelty to novelty to novelty.

So, it's not a question of whether or not something is new, it is a question of how something is described. In school, we have a tendency to describe things in terms of domesticating similarities. For thesis, I want to encourage you to talk about projects in terms of novelties and differences. Look for those moments where the examples start to move into new territory as opposed to looking for ways to circle them back into the fold. So, Point Number One is *Privilege Difference over Similarity.*

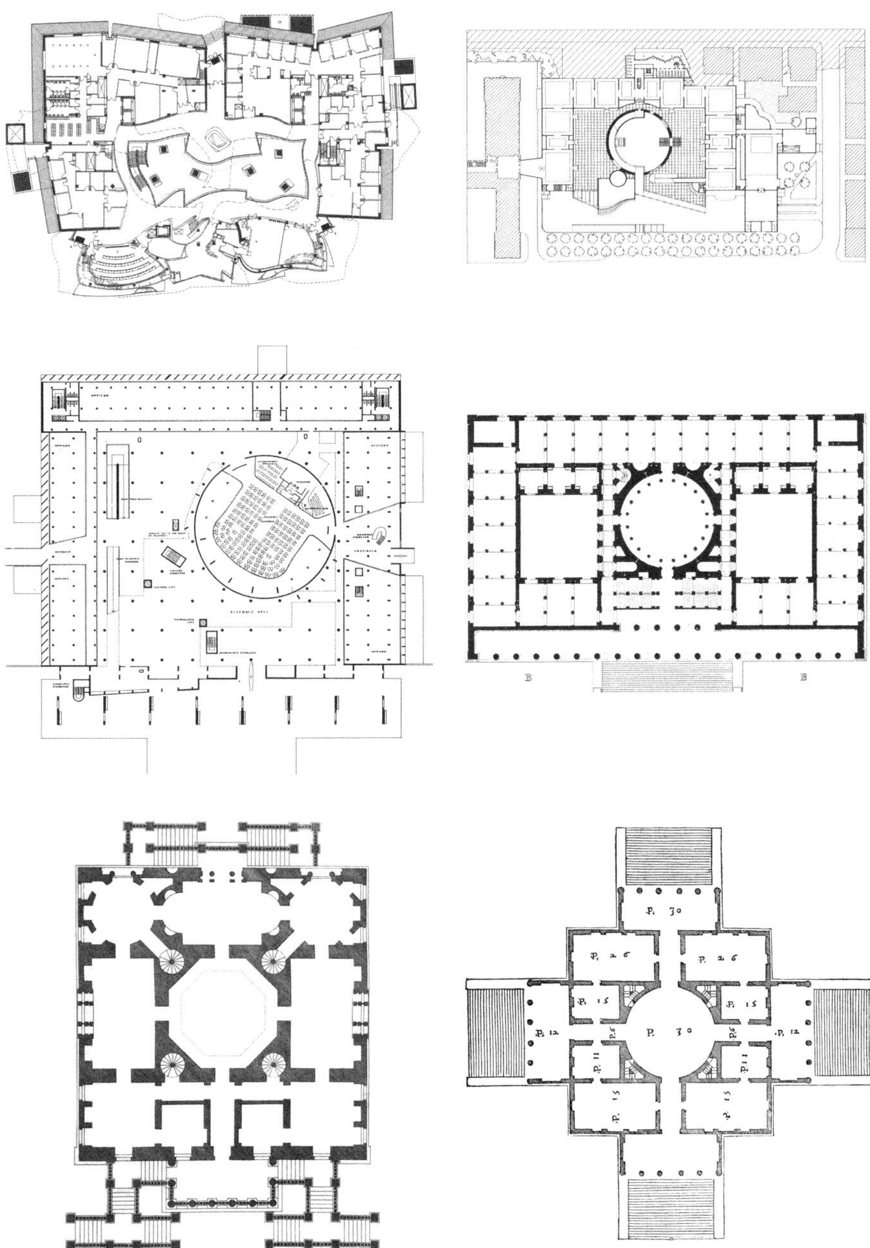

Figs. 20.2a–f *top left to lower right*: Frank Gehry, Peter B. Lewis building (Cleveland, 2002); James Stirling and Michael Wilford, Neuestaatsgalerie (Stuttgart, 1984); Le Corbusier, Palace of Assembly (Chandigarh, 1962); Karl Friedrich Schinkel, Altesmuseum (Berlin, 1830); Lord Burlington, Chiswick House (London, 1729); Andrea Palladio, Villa Rotonda (Vicenza, 1571).

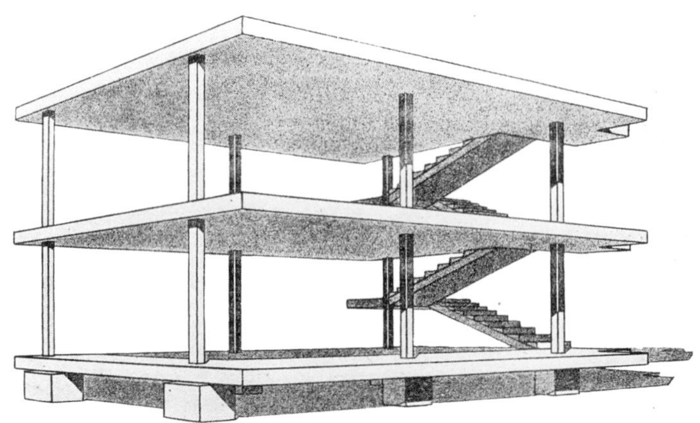

Fig. 20.3 Le Corbusier, Maison Dom-ino (1914–15).

PART TWO: CLICHÉS

"Nothing new under the sun" is both correct and incorrect, depending on your point of view. It's also a cliché. The word *cliché* originated among French typesetters. To speed up their work, they would gang together the letters for commonly used phrases into single units. Another word for this is *stereotype.* It is thought that cliché comes from the sound produced when the letters were melted together. Over time, it has come to mean the overuse of common conventions and phrases. "Once upon a time," for instance, is a cliché. So is "thinking outside the box." In design, think of the overuse of historical quotation in certain strains of postmodernism, or, closer to home, recent overindulgence in things like parasites.

If we look more carefully, we can see that clichés have three main characteristics: They operate by repetition. They eradicate authorship. And they follow a formula.

Think back to that phrase, "Once upon a time." Despite its prevalence, nobody knows who first wrote it. There has been a lot of debate over its attribution. My favorite theory is that it comes from Charles Perrault, the brother of the French architectural theorist, Claude Perrault. Charles used the phrase, *Il était une fois,* in all of his fairy tales. I'm not sure if he used it in *Parallèle des anciens et modernes.* But, in any event, you can see that clichés are by definition repetitive and that they tend to eradicate authorship. They also follow a five-point formula:

Innovation → Repetition → Codification → Parody → Cliché

Fig. 20.4 Crapi Apartments, Los Angeles, 1960.

Fig. 20.5 Richard Meier, Getty Center (Los Angeles, 1997).

Let me demonstrate how this works. Consider Le Corbusier's Maison Dom-ino [**Fig. 20.3**]. This was not a brand-new use of reinforced concrete, but it is a nice compression of several concurrent innovations into one tidy package. Let's take it as the *innovation*. We're all familiar with the *repetition* in Corbusier's white villas. We're also familiar with the *codification*: Corbusier's Five Points of 1926—the *pilotis*, the free plan, the roof garden, the free façade, and the ribbon window. Notice there are two points for facades, no points for doors, and notice how he almost cancels the point about free façade with the one about ribbon windows. From the beginning, he's stacking the deck, pointing you in a certain direction.

The part we really need to pay attention to is *parody*. Once the codification is in place, it's very easy to just keep doing it. Parody is a way to break the cycle. Here is a low-brow parody, the Crapi Apartments in West L.A. [**Fig. 20.4**]. The Getty Center, just a little bit further west, is a high-brow parody [**Fig. 20.5**]. Both are parodic repetitions of Le Corbusier's five points. We can see the trajectory hardened into *cliché* in just about every issue of *Dwell*.

Fig. 20.6 Hugo Sanchez, Gangnam Style!!! The 5 Basic Steps (2012).

Let's run through the formula again in a different context. The *innovation* in this case is Psy's Youtube hit, *Gangnam Style.* It went from ninety million to a billion views in about a month and a half, so we have *repetition.* The *codification* came very quickly: the Five Points of Gangnam Style [**Fig. 20.6**]. Just as quickly we begin to see many low- and high-brow *parodies* [**Figs. 20.7, 20.8**]. And finally, we see it become a *cliché* with the birth of a new kind of wedding dance [**Fig. 20.9**]. My point is that it's a slippery slope from the Maison Dom-ino to the Electric Slide.

Now, let's look back at these five steps. The first four, innovation, repetition, codification, and parody, are all perfectly reasonable places to locate your thesis. In general, most thesis projects are two or four. There are a couple of ambitious threes. Every once in a while, we get a one. We get a bunch of fives, which I would like to eliminate. I think it's very useful to do a good repetition project, that is, a development or refinement of a current problem. Some among you might be suited to attempt the codification project. I think parody is probably where we're most exciting. I don't mean taking something and making fun of it. Parody in this sense means to understand something and begin to twist its principles, to swerve them toward something that wasn't intended, like the Crapi Apartments or the Getty Center.

There is another story about clichés. We've all read Gilles Deleuze's book on Francis Bacon, in which Deleuze attacked the clichés he saw

Fig. 20.7 Michael Mayne, Ganon Style (2012).

Fig. 20.8 Ai Wei Wei, Gangnam Style protest video (2012).

Fig. 20.9 Gangnam Style wedding dance (2012).

forming of both representational and abstract art. His answer was the idea of the Figure—something that stepped over intellection and was able to impress itself directly on the central nervous system. That's what he saw in Bacon's paintings.

We have spent a fair amount of time at SCI-Arc talking about cliché breaking, which is something parodies can do. Lately, I've noticed another problem beginning to develop, which I'll call *inadvertent cliché making*. Something like *suckerPUNCH*, for example, which is great for getting a lot of information out into the world, has an unfortunate side effect of helping to produce clichéd versions of significant innovations very quickly by encouraging thoughtless copying. I think we have to be careful about that. So, Point Number Two is *Avoid Clichés*.

Fig. 20.10 Norman Foster, Willis Faber & Dumas building (Ipswich, 1974).

PART THREE: WHAT VERSUS HOW

One way to avoid clichés is to shift our point of view, to look at the problem differently. We can illustrate this point with Norman Foster's Willis Faber and Dumas Building in Ipswich [**Fig. 20.10**]. It's a kind of parody—Foster follows seemingly antithetical rules that were set down before him—Corbusier's Five Points, Gordon Cullen's Townscape Casebook—to produce something that no one would have predicted. It's hard to determine exactly *what* it is—is it modern? Is it traditional? But it's incredibly instructive when we study *how* it does what it does. Contrasting the critical tendency to say "no" to prevailing doctrine, Foster cunningly says "yes" to all of them.

Most of your attention through thesis will be devoted to the specifics of *how* you will do your projects, but your presentations tend to focus on *what* your project is. I think it's a good idea to break that habit. The third point, *Privilege How over What,* can help to do that.

PART FOUR: NEW VOCABULARIES

In talking to the students this semester, I have noticed a very consistent pattern, not in the work itself, but in the way that the work is described. Especially early on, project descriptions tend to be too general, too abstract, and too familiar. I'd like to change that. Some of these habits probably come from thesis prep, so we instructors have some work to do, too.

We're getting better in terms of generalizations—we don't have as many projects about light or nature or things like that—but we could be more specific. As for abstraction, here is a hint: Any time your thesis is driven by a term that ends in -ism, -ity, -ology, -tion, or any of those suffixes that turn a verb into a noun, you're probably on thin ice. That's because these generalized, abstract categories actually produce familiarity. A good way to avoid that problem is to follow the advice of Colin Rowe. In the 1950s, Rowe proposed the "particular," the "personal," and the "curious" as antidotes to systematic architectural formulas. I think these are great qualities to shoot for in a thesis: try to develop your projects so that they are *specific*, that they are *yours*, and that they are a little bit *weird*.

As I said, I think cliché has a lot to do with the vocabulary we use. The vocabulary we use most of the time remains that of critical theory. We tend to speak in the vocabularies of cultural criticism, linguistic theory, and philosophy from, say, the 1960s into the '90s. That language is what, in Rorty's terms, is becoming a nuisance to me.

Now, I want to make sure that this is not taken as just another in a long series of attacks on "the critical." Rather, I want to identify what critical theory is good at and, hopefully, what some of its blind spots are. Then I want to lay out an alternative trajectory that sheds a little light on those blind spots. We'll use this chart as a guide:

<table>
<tr><th>Paradigm</th><th>Root</th><th>Mode</th><th>Technique</th><th>Character</th><th>Aim</th></tr>
<tr><td rowspan="2">Critical Theory</td><td>Krinein:
division,
judgement</td><td>Ontological
(What it is)</td><td rowspan="2">Analysis</td><td rowspan="2">Distant,
Reactive</td><td rowspan="2">Classification
&
Judgment</td></tr>
<tr><td>Theoria:
contemplation,
speculation</td><td>Representational
(What it means)</td></tr>
<tr><td rowspan="2">Narrative Discourse</td><td>Gnarare:
knowledge,
skill</td><td>Operational
(What it does)</td><td rowspan="2">Description</td><td rowspan="2">Proximate,
Current</td><td rowspan="2">Action
&
Making</td></tr>
<tr><td>Discurrere:
to run over
a region</td><td>Organizational
(How it works)</td></tr>
</table>

Let's begin with the words themselves. The word *critical* comes from the Greek word *krinein*, which has to do with division and judgment. *Theory* also comes from a Greek word, *theoria*, for contemplation and speculation. If you keep going, you arrive at *theoros*, meaning spectator. The word is also related to the theater. If you go back further, you'll find resonances with a pre-Greek word, *thauma*, which has to do with marvel. This gives us a hint at the source theory's associations with falsehood, as in, "Well, that's only a theory," or "I want facts, not theory." A slight detachment from reality is built right into the word.

If we look at critical theory as a mode of intellection, we see that it is used primarily to ask ontological and representational questions. That is, critical theory tends to make us want to ask questions like, "What is it?" and, "What does it mean?" These are important questions, but they are not always the most pressing ones in the design studio.

The *technique* that we use to ask these questions tends to be logical analysis. Critical theory demands that ideas hold together, that principles be sensible and apparent, that we can understand how the whole thing unfolds. All these aspects give critical theory a distancing character. Critical distance takes you out of the heat of the moment in order to allow calm and considered opinion-making.

Finally, the *aim* of critical theory tends to be classification and judgment. It's very useful to be able to classify things—to put things in their places and make sense of them through a kind of divide-and-conquer technique. It's also very important to be able to judge things, to be able to say, "That's a good one and this is a bad one and here's why." Critical theory is very useful in bringing discipline and rigor to those kinds of questions, and it works because of its twofold ability to break a thing down into its parts and to contemplate a unified whole from a distance.

Of course, critical theory has shortcomings. It tends to be non-participatory or, at least, distant. The action tends to be elsewhere when we're having a theoretical conversation. You don't do theory on the battlefield. Critical theory is also reactive. The critic watches from the audience and makes judgments after the fact. An architect also needs techniques that allow her to participate in real time. Design happens before the fact.

I have been thinking about these issues a lot lately. In my graduate seminars, we're reading a lot of literary criticism written by authors as opposed to literary criticism written by critics. We're trying to shift the lens, and we're just beginning to articulate an alternative paradigm I'll call *Narrative Discourse.*

Let's look again at some etymology. *Narrative* comes from the Latin, *narrare,* meaning to relate, recount, or explain. It can be traced back to a pre-Latin root, *gnarare,* which has to do with knowledge and skill. Discourse comes from the Latin, *discurrere,* meaning to run about. The root verb, *currere,* is related to current, which gives it a relation to flowing, to currency, and to timeliness. When it first came into English in the sixteenth century, discourse meant to run over a region.

If we look at the *mode* of Narrative Discourse, its questions are more operational and organizational: "What does it do?" and, "How does it work?" as opposed to, "What is it?" and, "What does it mean?" The *technique* has to do with detailed description, another idea I borrow from Richard Rorty. Vladimir Nabokov discussed the necessity of fondling the details when you are working with literary texts; a good reader was attentive to the particularities of the text. I want to you to bring that kind of detail-oriented attentiveness to your thesis projects. The *character* I'm after is proximate and current—intimately bound up with details as opposed to generalities and with the present as opposed to the past. Finally, the *aim* has to do with action and making as opposed to classification and judgment.

A solid, well-rounded architect should be nimble in both paradigms. I think most of us tend to be pretty nimble in the upper part of the chart because that's where most of the sacred texts of the discipline come from. But I think we could learn a lot by paying attention to the bottom part.

Now, this chart doesn't get too close to the question of how to do it. For that, I want to introduce two more terms: *character* and *composition.* Colin Rowe used these terms in the 1950s to specify his interest in the particular, the personal, and the curious. I'd like to follow in his footsteps here. Let's start with composition.

Douglas Graf, who has been a very big influence on me, provides a useful starting point for speaking of architectural composition. Graf's ideas aren't exactly new, but they operate somewhere outside of conventional critical vocabularies and attend instead to the specifics of how a building is put together. He is very attentive to architecture's fundamental elements. In these diagrams [**Fig. 20.11**], Graf demonstrates how any perimeter will always also suggest a center, that any set of modules will begin to suggest an axial alternative, that if you look at things carefully and study them long enough, they will tend to turn into their opposites. With these ideas in mind, we can look at something like the Temple of Khons, as Graf did, and see it as both a procession and a barrier, as simultaneously one thing and two [**Fig. 20.12**]. We begin to see something we might have written off as old and boring as quite odd and ambiguous in terms of its composition.

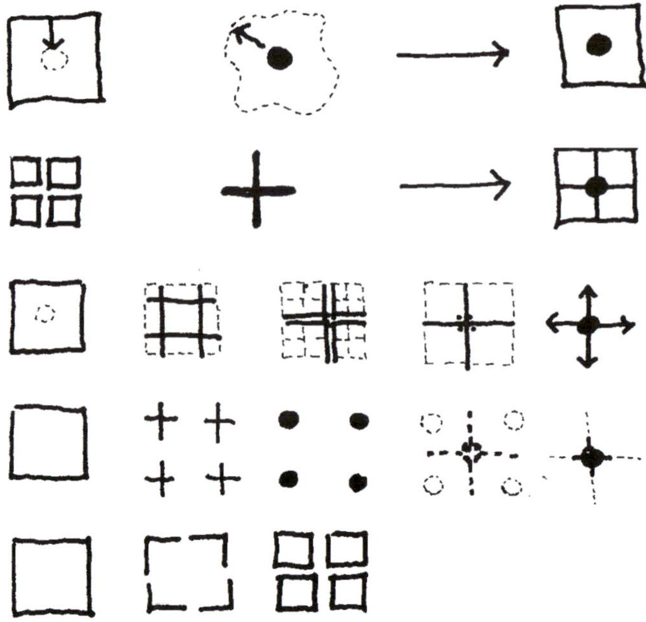

Fig. 20.11 Douglas Graf, from "Diagrams," 1986.

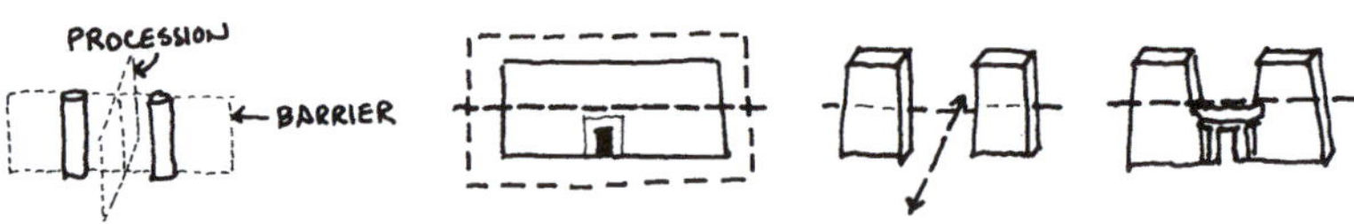

Fig. 20.12 Temple of Khons (Karnak, c. 1500 BCE).

Or look again at Peter Eisenman's diagrammatic analysis of the Maison Dom-ino [**Fig. 20.13**]. Now, we know Eisenman was making a serious argument about the nature of form and the essence of architecture. But he also was inventing another creation myth for the field. The way he developed his story was by being incredibly specific about compositional details. The difference between a square and a rectangle is significant. The distance between the edge of the slab and the columns is significant. Eisenman's story unfolds narratively. It has a beginning, it has a middle, it has an end. So, I like to look at an analysis like this not as a statement of truth, but rather as a kind of story, as a fairy tale written in form.

Fig. 20.13 Peter Eisenman, Le Corbusier's Maison Dom-ino, from "Aspects of Modernism," 1980.

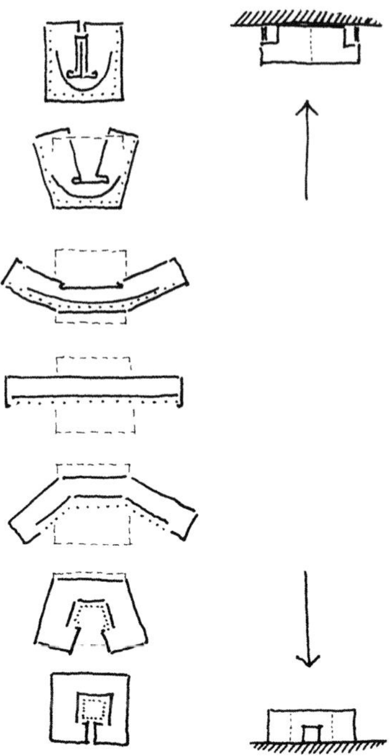

Fig. 20.14 Douglas Graf, from "Diagrams," 1986.

There are other, weirder things. Here is Graf's transformation of the Villa Savoye into the Palazzo Farnese [**Fig. 20.14**]. It passes through the Stoa of Attalos along the way. Now, it would be very easy to look at something like this and think, "Well, that's not very serious." Maybe, but this is exactly the sort of inventive play that excites the architectural imagination, and it only works by being very attentive to compositional particulars. It's also exactly the same technique that Jeff Kipnis and his team used to produce some of the figures in the Figure Ground Game exhibition. They took Andrew Zago's MOCAPE scheme and unfolded it to produces the White Walkers [**Figs. 20.15, 20.16**]. You can understand it through a narrative: "Once upon a time there was a building. It desperately wanted to be a real building, but it was never built. Then, somehow, it came to life at the Venice Biennale, and now it's walking around in Rome and at SCI-Arc." I like that the story is told with form, not with footnotes. This is the kind of attentiveness to and inventiveness with the particularities of form and organization I think all of you should work toward.

Fig. 20.15 Zago Architecture, MOCAPE (Shenzhen, 2007).

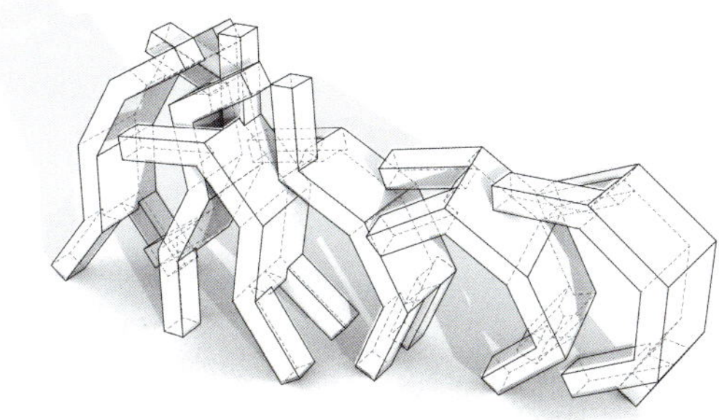

Fig. 20.16 Jeffrey Kipnis and Stephen Turk, White Walkers, 2013.

Now, let's move on to character. If composition has to do with architecture's organizational and formal structure, character has to do with its experiential qualities and effects. Here is Jason Payne's Raspberry Fields [**Fig. 20.17**]. In this project, Payne develops a story about the material properties of wood. He looks at twisting and warping and all those things we usually work very hard to keep wood from doing. He makes a project out of them by linking those material qualities to his longstanding interest in hairy things. To do that, he has to mobilize a lot of architectural intelligence. We're all very familiar with the story of the fur, so I want to turn attention toward Payne's study of the building's posture. To develop the posture of the building, Payne wasn't just studying the form of cows lying in pastures. He was also studying William Gilpin's eighteenth-century drawings of cows lying in pastures [**Fig. 20.18**]. From these, he develops a specific relationship between the posture of the cow and the posture of the house. It's important to understand that this is not a recapitulation of a cow nor is it a quotation of Gilpin's picturesqueness. Rather, it is a translation of a complex set of character traits from various sources into something new.

Fig. 20.17 Hirsuta, Raspberry Fields (Northern Utah, 2008–2012).

Fig. 20.18 William Gilpin, "How to Group Cows," 1772.

Fig. 20.19 Jeffrey Kipnis and Stephen Turk, White Walker, 2012.

There are a number of architects looking into posture today. Payne studied the posture of cows. Andrew Zago has been looking at the awkward posture of contortionists for some time, and Kipnis is developing an interest in torpid postures in his recent projects with Stephen Turk [**Fig. 20.19**]. As some of you take up the problem of posture, I want to make sure we don't devolve into generalities like "posturism" or "posturicity." Much better to elaborate a particular instance of whatever abstraction you're interested in than to construct your thesis as a kind of umbrella over the entire category. These posture projects are interesting not because of posture as such, but because of the specific forms of posture they develop. They have specific attitudes about posture and require different, highly specific vocabularies to discuss them. You will need these, too. So, Thesis Point Number Four is: *Develop New Vocabularies.*

PART FIVE: ENFRANCHISEMENT

The last point has to do with something Kipnis has been talking about recently. Here is a quote from a recent interview:

> I have a certain prejudice against rectitude. I'm tired of every building telling me I should be young and fit and have good posture. I'm not young, I'm not fit, I like sitting hunched over, I'm often drunk and I like to lean on stuff. So, just once, I would like to walk into a city and have a few buildings tell me: You're OK, you're a part of the world and you belong in it.

Writing in the early 1990s about Robert Mapplethorpe's work, which at the time was under serious attack from Jesse Helms and certain conservative groups, Dave Hickey said something very similar:

> The task of beauty is to enfranchise an audience and to acknowledge its power—to designate a territory of shared values between the image and its beholder and then, in this territory, to advance arguments by valorizing the picture's problematic content.

I want to insist that these are not critical attacks on standing up straight or being straight, but rather celebrations of possibilities that are excluded from dominant paradigms. There's no attack here, and there's no apology here. The point, as Kipnis makes it, is that something like the Empire State building celebrates a community that valorizes standing up straight, and that something like the White Walker says that there is a community in which it's OK not to stand that way.

Bernard Tschumi made a similar point in his *Advertisements for Architecture* [**Fig. 20.20**]. This comes out of the heyday of critical culture, but I want to point out how Tschumi uses re-description to make his point. The constraints he describes are not necessarily bad—in fact, in his view, they're not even constraints. Rather, they become a catalyst for a new kind of freedom.

All these examples point toward the proliferation of communities. They demonstrate that architecture does not need to aim at total world domination, which is what -isms and -itys usually do. Too often, sticking an -ism or an -ity on the end of a word becomes a license to say, "This is good for everyone at all times. Everybody do it this way." I think we should resist that. I think we should push for smaller, more devoted audiences—and more of them—as opposed to a single, one-size-fits-all audience. Thesis Point Number Five, *Enfranchise New Constituencies,* is about doing just that.

So, to conclude, let's quickly review the Five Points for thesis:

Privilege Difference over Similarity.
Avoid Clichés.
Privilege How over What.
Develop New Vocabularies.
Enfranchise New Consistencies.

I hope you find them useful. Thank you for listening.

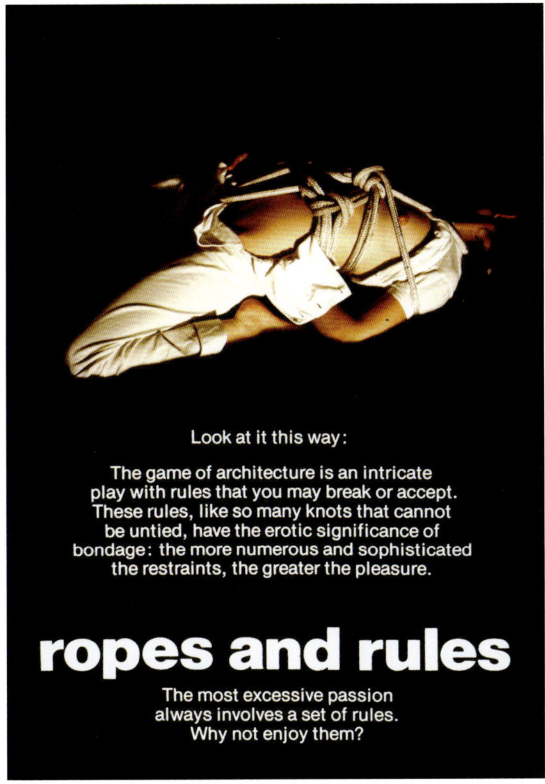

Fig. 20.20 Bernard Tschumi, Advertisements for Architecture, 1975–77.

Acknowledgments

The essays collected here took the shape they did thanks to the contributions of innumerable friends, colleagues, students, and mentors. I am especially grateful to:

Joe Day, for his unceasing enthusiasm, insightful criticism, excellent introductory text, and willingness to read anything I send him;

Graham Harman, N. Katherine Hayles, David Ruy, Tom Wiscombe, and Andrew Zago for enlightening collaborations;

Gordon Goff and Jake Anderson at Applied Research and Design Publishing for careful oversight through all phases of this book's production;

Ben Wilke for exacting graphic design and Curtis Roth for a brilliant cover;

Cynthia Davidson at *Log*, Rob Livesey and Mike Cadwell at Ohio State, Ming Fung and Eric Moss at SCI-Arc, the late Bill Menking at the *Architect's Newspaper*, Arie Graafland, Doug Jackson, Mitra Kanaani, and Jennifer Volland for inviting me to contribute to their publications;

Stan Allen, Hernán Díaz Alonso, Jacki Bloom, Beth Blostein, John Bohn, Laura Bouwman, Ewan Branda, Mark Danielewski, Tom Daniell, John Enright, David Erdman, Mark Gage, Marcelyn Gow, Margaret Griffin, Craig Hodgetts, Georgina Huljich, Dora Epstein Jones, Jason Kerwin, Jeff Kipnis, Karel Klein, Tali Krakowsky, Sylvia Lavin, Caroline Levine, Karen Lewis, Elena Manferdini, Thom Mayne, Mike Meehan, Michael Osman, José Oubrerie, Dwayne Oyler, Jason Payne, Florencia Pita, Heather Roberge, Mohamed Sharif, Bob Somol, Marcelo Spina, Katrin Terstegen, Marrikka Trotter, Constance Vale, Amit Wolf, Jenny Wu, Michael Young, Peter Zellner, and everyone mentioned elsewhere on this page for so many great conversations;

and, most of all, Yumna, Tycho, and Zarina.

Credits

We gratefully acknowledge the following sources for permission to reprint copyrighted material. All reasonable efforts have been made to trace the copyright holders of the visual materials reproduced in this book. Please report any errors to the publisher for correction in future editions.

Texts

All texts © Todd Gannon except as noted below.

"Figments of the Architectural Imagination" originally appeared in *Log* 37: *The Architectural Imagination* (Spring 2016).

"Tschumi's Roadside Attraction" originally appeared in *Bernard Tschumi: Zénith de Rouen*, ed. Todd Gannon (New York: Princeton Architectural Press, 2003), and is reprinted by permission.

"Animate Urbanism: The Metabolic Infrastructures of UN Studio" originally appeared in *UN Studio: Erasmus Bridge*, ed. Todd Gannon (New York: Princeton Architectural Press, 2004), and is reprinted by permission.

"The Shape of Things to Come" originally appeared in *Log* 2 (Spring 2004).

"Return of the Living Dead: Archigram and Architecture's Monstrous Media" originally appeared in *Log* 13/14 (Fall 2008).

"A Confederacy of Heretics" originally appeared in *A Confederacy of Heretics*, eds., Todd Gannon and Ewan Branda (Los Angeles: SCI-Arc Press and Getty Research Institute, 2013).

"Pragmatic Radicalism, Aesthetic Bliss, and Other L.A. Stories" originally appeared in *Log* 30 (Winter 2014).

"Facts and Effects: Oyler Wu's Pendulum Plane" originally appeared in *Pendulum Plane: Oyler Wu Collaborative*, ed. Todd Gannon (Los Angeles: L.A. Forum, 2009).

"Of Raspberries, Rawhide, and Rhetoric" originally appeared in *Log* 24 (Spring/Summer 2012).

"Experiment and Crime" originally appeared in Marcelo Spina and Georgina Huljich, *PATTERNS—Embedded* (Beijing: AADCU, 2010).

"Grand Gestures and Intelligent Plans" originally appeared in *Grand Hotel*, eds. Jennifer Volland and Bruce Grenville (Vancouver: Vancouver Museum of Art, 2013).

"Strange Loops" originally appeared, in a different form, as "Strange Loops: Toward an Aesthetics for the Anthropocene," in *Journal of Architectural Education* 71:2 (Oct 2017). © Association of Collegiate Schools of Architecture, Inc. Reproduced with permission of John Wiley & Sons Limited through PLSclear.

"What's Wrong with Making Federal Buildings Beautiful Again" appeared as "On Beauty, Value, and Justice in Federal Architecture in America" in *The Architect's Newspaper* (10 Feb 2020) and is reprinted courtesy of *The Architect's Newspaper.*

"Mood Swings: The Aesthetics of Ambient Emergence" originally appeared in *The Mourning After: Attending the Wake of Postmodernism,* eds. Neil Brooks and Josh Toth (Amsterdam: Rodopi, 2007) and is reprinted by permission of Brill Publishers.

"Virtual Architecture / Actual Media" originally appeared in *The SAGE Handbook of Architectural Theory,* eds. Hilde Heynen, Stephen Cairns, and Greig Crysler (London: SAGE, 2011). © Todd Gannon and N. Katherine Hayles.

"The Object Turn: A Conversation" originally appeared in *Log* 33 (Winter/Spring 2015).

"Tabloid Transparency" originally appeared as "Tabloid Transparency, or Looking through Types, Legibility, Abstraction, and the Discipline of Architecture," in *The Routledge Companion for Architecture Design and Practice: Established and Emerging Trends,* eds. Mitra Kanaani and Dak Kopek (London: Routledge, 2015), and is reprinted by permission.

"On Prophets and Professionals" originally appeared as "On Prophets and Professionals: A Response to Peter Zellner" in *The Architect's Newspaper* (21 Sept 2016) and is reprinted courtesy of *The Architect's Newspaper.*

"Mind the Gaps!" originally appeared as "Mind the Gaps! Toward a Pedagogy of Models and a Model Pedagogy" in *Log* 50 (Fall 2020).

"Five Points for Thesis" originally appeared in *Offramp* 13: *Guise* (Fall 2017).

Images

Cover and section breaks: Courtesy of Curtis Roth
1.1: The Metropolitan Museum, New York
2.1: Photo © Peter Mauss/ESTO. Courtesy of Bernard Tschumi Architects
3.1, 13.1: Photo by Martin Falbisoner
5.1: © Archigram 1964
6.1, 9.1, 10.1: Photo by Joshua White / JWPictures.com
6.2: Courtesy of Morphosis Architects
6.3: Courtesy of Craig Hodgetts and Robert Mangurian
6.4: Courtesy of Gruen Associates
6.5: Courtesy of Coy Howard
6.6: Photo by Grant Mudford
7.1, 7.2, 7.3: Photo by Brian Forrest. © The Museum of Contemporary Art, Los Angeles
7.4, 10.2, 10.3, 10.4: Image courtesy of PATTERNS
7.5: Image courtesy of Atelier Manferdini
8.1, 8.2: Image courtesy of Oyler Wu Collaborative
10.5: Photo by Gustavo Frittegotto, Courtesy of PATTERNS
11.1: Photo by Joi Ito
12.1: Photo by Plazak
14.1: Photo by Michael Erdman. Courtesy of servo
14.2: Photo by Todd Gannon
14.3, 17.1: Architekturzentrum Wien, Collection. Photo by Margherita Spiluttini
15.1: Photo by Beat Widmer. Courtesy of Diller Scofidio + Renfro
15.2: Photo by Binche
15.2: Courtesy of Diller Scofidio + Renfro
16.1: Courtesy of Tom Wiscombe Architecture
16.2: Photo by Magnus Linquist
16.3: Courtesy of Ruy Klein
17.2, 17.6, 20.15: Courtesy of Bouwman Zago
17.3: Photo by Piper Severance / Art Resource. © Jeff Koons
17.4: © Mike Kelley Foundation for the Arts. All rights reserved / Licensed by VAGA at Artists Rights Society (ARS), NY
17.5: Courtesy of Johnston Marklee
18.1: Photo by Morton Neikrug. Courtesy of SCI-Arc
19.1, 19.2: Photo courtesy of the Knowlton School
20.1: Photo by Harmanani
20.2a: © Gehry Partners
20.2b: James Stirling/Michael Wilford fonds. Canadian Centre for Architecture
20.2c, 20.3: © F.L.C. / ADAGP, Paris / Artists Rights Society (ARS), New York 2021.
20.2d: Reproduced from Karl Friedrich Schinkel, *Sammlung Architektonischer Entwürfe* (Berlin: Verlag Von Ernst & Korn, 1858): plate 38. Smithsonian Libraries.
20.2e: Reproduced from William Kent, *The Designs of Inigo Jones, Consisting of Plans and Elevations for Publick and Private Buildings* (1727). Smithsonian Libraries.

20.2f: Reproduced from *I quattro libri dell'architettura di Andrea Palladio.* (1581). The Metropolitan Museum, New York. Bequest of W. Gedney Beatty, 1941.

20.5: Photo by Sailko

20.10: Photo © Andrew Dunn

20.11, 20.14: Courtesy of Douglas Graf

20.13: Courtesy of Eisenman Architects. Drawn by Jay Johnson

20.16, 20.19: Courtesy of Stephen Turk

20.17: Courtesy of Jason Payne

20.20: Image © Bernard Tschumi

Published by Applied Research and Design Publishing, an imprint of ORO Editions.
Gordon Goff: Publisher
www.appliedresearchanddesign.com
info@appliedresearchanddesign.com

Author: Todd Gannon
Introduction: Joe Day
Book Design: Benjamin Wilke
Cover Design: Curtis Roth
Project Manager: Jake Anderson

10 9 8 7 6 5 4 3 2 1 First Edition
ISBN: 978-1-954081-97-0

Support for this project was provided by the Knowlton School, The Ohio State University.

Color Separations and Printing: ORO Group Ltd.
Printed in China.

AR+D Publishing makes a continuous effort to minimize the overall carbon footprint of its publications. As part of this goal, AR+D, in association with Global ReLeaf, arranges to plant trees to replace those used in the manufacturing of the paper produced for its books. Global ReLeaf is an international campaign run by American Forests, one of the world's oldest nonprofit conservation organizations. Global ReLeaf is American Forests' education and action program that helps individuals, organizations, agencies, and corporations improve the local and global environment by planting and caring for trees.